Achieve Your Potential Throu
Positive Psychology

Tim LeBon

Tim LeBon is a UKCP registered psychotherapist. He specialises ... CBT, positive psychology and philosophical approaches to ... to overcome depression, anxiety and other mental he... as. He combines a private practice as a therapist and ... in London with working for the NHS as a CBT therapist. He is also an experienced educator, teaching positive psychology, CBT and personal development at several London colleges and universities.

He was educated at Trinity College, Oxford where he gained a first-class degree in Philosophy, Politics and Economics and later returned to Oxford to study at the Oxford Centre for Cognitive Therapy, where he was awarded a distinction in a Diploma in CBT. He was the founding editor of *Practical Philosophy* and is the author of *Wise Therapy* (2001). He lives with his family in Surrey. His website is http://www.timlebon.com.

Teach® Yourself

Achieve Your Potential Through Positive Psychology

Tim LeBon

First published in Great Britain in 2014 by Hodder & Stoughton. An Hachette UK company.

First published in US in 2014 by The McGraw-Hill Companies, Inc.

This edition published 2014

British Library Cataloguing in Publication Data: a catalogue record for this title is available from the British Library.

Library of Congress Catalog Card Number: on file.

10 9 8 7 6 5 4 3 2 1

Paperback ISBN 978 1 444 19092 2

eBook ISBN 978 1 444 19099 1

Cover image © Andrzej Wilusz – Fotolia

Typeset by Cenveo® Publisher Services.

Printed and bound in Great Britain by CPI Group (UK) Ltd., Croydon, CR0 4YY.

Hodder & Stoughton policy is to use papers that are natural, renewable and recyclable products and made from wood grown in sustainable forests. The logging and manufacturing processes are expected to conform to the environmental regulations of the country of origin.

Hodder & Stoughton Ltd

338 Euston Road

London NW1 3BH

www.hodder.co.uk

Also available
in ebook

Acknowledgements

I would like to thank all those who have helped me with this book. Many have generously offered me advice, including Ryan Niemiec, Mike Steger, Paul Wong, Stefan Schulenberg, as well as Ian Morris and Jules Evans. I would also like to thank my students on various positive psychology courses over the years, particularly at City University and City Literary Institute, for making teaching the subject a very enjoyable experience. A particular debt is owed to all those who agreed to submit case studies. I would also like to express my gratitude to Ilona Boniwell and Nash Popovic who started me on my positive psychology journey and with whom I worked at University of East London (UEL) for a number of years.

In the cognitive behavioural therapy (CBT) world, I would like to thank all my colleagues at TalkPlus for their support and wisdom. Particular thanks go to Nigel Sage for sharing his 'Step-by-step planning tool'. In the philosophical world, I have benefited especially from my discussions with David Arnaud, Shamil Chandaria and Antonia Macaro over many years. I would like to express particular gratitude to David for his helpful feedback on several chapters.

Last but not least, I would like to express my heartfelt thanks to my family for their forbearance and tolerance during 'the year of writing the book'. I dedicate this book to my wonder-full children, Mike and Katie.

Contents

Introduction

'Psychology can play an enormously important role. We can articulate a vision of the good life that is empirically sound and, at the same time, understandable and attractive. We can show the world what actions lead to well-being, to positive individuals, to flourishing communities, and to a just society.'[1]

(Martin Seligman, 1998 Inaugural Address as President of the APA)

Positive psychology is the scientific study of well-being and how to enhance it. It began in 1998 when its founder, Martin Seligman, a well-known academic psychologist and educator became President of the American Psychological Association. Seligman remarked on the significant progress psychology had made since World War II. Psychologists now knew how to help people manage panic attacks, depression and many other mental health problems. But if 'psychology as usual'[2] had helped people move from minus ten to zero in terms of their well-being, it had produced little to get them from zero to ten. Seligman made it his mission to correct the balance. And so positive psychology was born.

Of course, many people had written about how to be happy and lead a fulfilling life before 1998. The self-help bookshelves have always been full of titles promising to change your life. What was different here was Seligman's plan for a new generation of books to cover the same topics but based on sound scientific evidence. Academic psychologists would do the research, which would then be given to the world in simple but not simplistic terms.

Key idea: What is positive psychology?

Positive psychology is the scientific study of well-being and how to enhance it. It began as a movement as recently as 1998. It covers the same topics as some self-help books, but differs in that it aims to provide a scientific understanding and be evidence based.

Positive psychology is not the same as positive thinking. Indeed, one of the worst recent excesses of the self-help industry is a prime example of what positive psychology is trying to overcome.

Case study: What positive psychology is not: *The Secret* and the law of attraction

The Secret, a 2006 self-help book by Australian TV Producer Rhonda Byrne, exemplifies the opposite of positive psychology; positive thinking based on little or no evidence. The Secret topped the *New York Times* best-seller list for a mind-boggling 146 weeks. Its recommendations are based on the 'law of attraction', which claims that positive energy from people attracts positive energy from the universe. According to the law of attraction, thinking that you will get a good job will draw the good job towards you. If you imagine beating a serious illness such as cancer, positive thinking on its own can make that happen too.

Unfortunately, the law of attraction has no scientific basis whatsoever. There are advantages to having a positive attitude, but there is no evidence that positive thinking magnetically draws good things towards you. Indeed, the evidence suggests that this may be counterproductive if it stops you taking the steps required to make good things happen. Having a positive attitude to getting a job is good in so far as it motivates you but very unhelpful if it means you decide you do not have to update your CV, enhance your skills and post job applications. Worse still, the law of attraction implies that people who are the victims of natural disaster or illness are somehow to blame in that they are not being positive enough. *The Secret* is not positive psychology. It is positive thinking without scientific evidence. Positive psychology is the evidence-based alternative to books like *The Secret*.

Remember this: Positive psychology is not the same as positive thinking

Positive psychology is positive in that is concerned with developing the positive things in life – happiness, well-being, strengths, good relationships and the like. Positive thinking will be part of its recommendations only to the extent that it turns out to be helpful.

While *The Secret*'s advice is positively bad, there are other self-help books that seem to offer much wiser advice. For example, at the age of 57 the Nobel prize-winning philosopher Bertrand Russell wrote a very good self-help book combining his life experience and philosophical learning called *The Conquest of Happiness*. It contains some wise pronouncements about both how to be happy and how to conquer unhappiness. However, even good self-help books about well-being are of limited value unless they are backed up with solid evidence. Most such books prior to positive psychology are based on the author's own experiences, which may or may not be applicable to everyone else. Take, for example, Russell's advice about having a family. Russell is very much in favour of this idea because it made him much happier. 'I have found the happiness of parenthood greater than any other that I have experienced', Russell tells his readers. However, research has repeatedly found that on average parenthood does not make people happier.[3]

David Clark, a leading clinical psychologist and researcher, compares untested theories to bedtime stories. He puts it very nicely: 'We [social scientists] think of theories as rather like bedtime stories: they may be true or they may not be. Mostly they are not, it turns out. So the first thing you have to do with a theory is test it; see if you can get any good evidence for it.'[4]

Very many plausible ideas – like Russell's belief that parenthood makes people happier – turn out not to be generally true. Consider the ten popular techniques in 'Try it now' for bringing about changes in your life. Which of these theories (adapted from Wiseman, R. *59 Seconds*) do you think turns out to be true?

Try it now: Techniques for change

Which of the following ten ideas do you think is likely to help you change an important aspect of your life (such as dieting, finding a relationship or changing career).

1 Make a step-by-step plan.
2 Motivate myself by focusing on someone whom I admire for achieving so much (e.g. a celebrity role model or great leader).
3 Tell other people about my goal.
4 Think about the bad things that will happen if I don't achieve my goal.

5 Think about the good things that will happen if I achieve my goal.
6 Try to suppress unhelpful thoughts (e.g. avoid thinking about eating unhealthy food or smoking).
7 Reward myself for making progress toward my goal.
8 Rely on willpower.
9 Record my progress (e.g. in a journal or on a chart).
10 Fantasize about how great my life will be when I achieve my goal.

Case study: What positive psychology is – Richard Wiseman's research on what really helps to bring about change in your life

Psychologist Richard Wiseman was aware of the many and varying tips in self-books about how to effect positive change. He decided to conduct some research to establish what worked and what did not. In order to do this, he asked 5,000 people who were trying to make changes (such as stopping smoking, losing weight, finding a good relationship or changing careers) what they were doing to help achieve their aim. The ten most popular answers are listed in the 'Try it now' exercise above. Wiseman later contacted the same people to see whether they had achieved their goals. Only 10 per cent had done so. He then calculated which techniques had proved to be useful. Half of the most popular techniques turned out not to help people at all.

Now it is time to look at your answers to the 'Try it now' exercise. Wiseman found that only the *odd-numbered* strategies were effective. For example, if you are trying to make a change, it is a good idea to make a step-by-step plan. However, it is a bad idea to rely on willpower alone. We will be looking further at the psychology of making successful changes in Chapter 5, Accomplishment and achievement.

Key idea: Positive psychology is not the same as self-help

Positive psychology itself produces many self-help books and at first sight it may seem difficult to distinguish them from other self-help books. The difference is that the recommendations in positive psychology books have been subject to scientific testing. This means that they have been shown to work for the majority of people.

How do you create a science of well-being?

This book is aimed to provide you with the output of positive psychology research rather than a detailed account of the research itself. It is a book primarily for the consumer of positive psychology rather than the academic psychologist. However, since the main difference between positive psychology and other self-help books is the use of the scientific method, it will be helpful to say a little bit about how positive psychologists go about their work. Feel free to skip to the next section 'Positive psychology's progress' if this is of no interest to you.

There are five steps to producing scientifically acceptable positive psychology findings:

1 Identify an area of relevance to human well-being to investigate. The chapter headings of this book give a good idea of the range of these areas – including happiness, achievement, strengths and wisdom.

2 Make the concept precise and measurable (the technical term is 'operationalizing'). For example, take the concept of 'happiness', which we will look at in the next chapter. 'Happiness' is too vague a term to lend itself to measurement or precision. Psychologists have settled for 'subjective well-being' (SWB) which, as we shall see, is both precise and measurable and roughly corresponds to what most people mean by 'happiness'.

3 Produce testable theories. For example, for happiness, psychologists produce theories about both the causes and consequences of happiness. They are then in a good position to suggest ways to boost it.

4 Test theories. There are a number of ways to test out theories. Not acceptable is the single case study, which is not really any better than the anecdotal experiences described in standard self-help books. Some better ways of testing theories include:

   a Surveys and questionnaires – psychologists might, for example, ask many people to report on their level of SWB and their age. They can then use statistical measures to see if there is generally a significant association between age and SWB.

b Experiments – for example, to test out whether happiness makes people more altruistic, psychologists have induced a good mood in one group and a neutral mood in another group and seen which group are more likely to give to a charity worker.

c Longitudinal studies – these studies follow groups of people over time. For example, having identified some people as happier when they were in their twenties, psychologists could then see how this affects other things such as their health, weight and life expectancy throughout their life.

d The 'gold standard' for testing interventions is the randomized control trial (RCT). In an RCT, psychologists take a large number of people and give some of them a proposed intervention and another group a placebo[5] control. It is then possible to see whether the suggested intervention is more effective than the placebo.

5 Disseminate information about the findings. Research findings will normally be published first in peer-reviewed journals. The highlights are then spread to the general public using less technical language in positive psychology self-help books.

Scientific research is a difficult, expensive and long-winded process. Positive psychology has been going for less than two decades. How is it doing?

Positive psychology's progress

In many ways, positive psychology has flourished. Hundreds, if not thousands, of research studies have been carried out. Many books and articles have been written and published. We now know more than we did in 1998 about well-being and how to enhance it. In 2005, an article, 'Positive Psychology Progress', was published that described how the discipline had already identified a number of simple interventions that could boost well-being over a sustained length of time. We will look at these in more detail in the next chapter and throughout the book.

The range of positive psychology goes well beyond happiness to other elements of the good life, including character strengths, achievement, purpose, relationships and psychological resilience. A movement that started out in academia has extended into the worlds of psychotherapy, coaching, business, education and even the US Army.

The aim of this book is to help you learn about the most important findings so far. As you can probably tell, I am enthusiastic about positive psychology and believe it has much to teach us about how to live well. However, positive psychology is still young – 15 years old at the time of writing. Like any teenager, it can sometimes make mistakes. The fact that articles are subject to peer reviews by other experts in the field means that these errors are minimized – however, as we shall see, this does not ensure complete accuracy. We will be on the lookout for places where positive psychologists have claimed more than is warranted. In particular, the 'Remember this' sections will guide you as to when caution needs to be exercised.

Remember this: Positive psychology is fallible

Although positive psychology has already produced many valuable ideas, sometimes it gets it wrong or expresses the ideas a little too enthusiastically. The 'Remember this' sections will alert you to this. 'Remember this' sections are also used to flag up other possible sources of confusion or misunderstanding.

Like many adolescents, positive psychology places a high value on its independence. It has attempted to distance itself from its elderly relatives 'psychology as usual' and philosophy. Although this approach has led to significant progress, the view taken in this book is that positive psychology can be strengthened by integrating ideas from both 'psychology as usual' and philosophy. To live good lives, people need not just to accentuate the positive; they also need to be able manage negative emotions well.

Key idea: Positive psychology is not just about accentuating the positive

Positive psychology is about enhancing well-being in the round, which includes overcoming difficult emotions, being resilient and being emotionally intelligent. Having a positive attitude may well be a part of this, but this is not all there is to positive psychology.

Cognitive behavioural therapy (CBT) includes traditional CBT, which aims to change thoughts and behaviours, and third-wave CBT, which aims for mindfulness and committed value-directed action. Incorporating ideas from CBT in both its traditional and third-wave forms, can help positive psychology achieve this. For this reason, the chapters on resilience, CBT and mindfulness in this book are more comprehensive than you will find in many positive psychology books.

Key idea: CBT has a significant part to play in positive psychology

Cognitive behavioural therapy is the approach with the best evidence to help with resilience and dealing with emotional difficulties. CBT includes traditional CBT and third-wave CBT. Traditional CBT, which will be described in Chapter 9, involves understanding and then changing unhelpful thoughts and behaviours. Third-wave CBT, which we will look at in Chapter 10, focuses more on being aware of difficult thoughts rather than challenging them directly (mindfulness) and on helping us be aware of what matters to us and take committed action to achieve it.

The role granted to philosophy in positive psychology has also been rather limited. Yet to help people lead the good life we have to understand just what the good life means. To enhance well-being, we first have to understand its nature. Is well-being more than just experiencing positive emotions? Is it good to be optimistic all the time? Do we need to make wise judgements in order to flourish?

In *Flourish*, Seligman tells us that he was once a student of philosophy but found the subject sterile and uninspiring. Perhaps that has unduly influenced Seligman in divorcing positive psychology from philosophy. In this book we will aim to produce a philosophically plausible version of positive psychology which, at the same time, keeps it understandable and practical. The chapters on values, meaning and wisdom will be of particular interest to those looking to integrate philosophical ideas into positive psychology.

Key idea: Ideas from philosophy are important

Positive psychology raises many philosophical questions. By addressing these questions, and incorporating philosophical ideas into positive psychology, it can be made wiser.

About this book

This book is intended to help you in a number of ways. It will:

▶ Provide you with a sound introduction to the key topics of positive psychology. You will learn about the most important theories about happiness, character strengths, relationships and the other main topics of positive psychology.

▶ Introduce many of the exercises and activities devised by positive psychologists. The 'Try this now' sections contain clear descriptions about how to do these activities. A number of case illustrations are provided to help you see how these work in practice. This book is a very practical introduction to positive psychology

▶ Incorporate ideas from 'psychology as usual' and philosophy that are very relevant to positive psychology but do not always get as much attention as they deserve.

Focus points

* Positive psychology is the scientific study of well-being and how to enhance it.
* It differs from 'psychology as usual' in that it deals with human flourishing rather than just problems.
* Positive psychology differs from traditional self-help books in that it is scientific.
* Theories need to be tested, otherwise they are no more than 'bedtime stories'.
* Positive psychology has tended to 'go it alone'. However, it is considerably strengthened if it incorporates ideas from CBT and philosophy.

Next steps

We will begin, in the next chapter, with a look at happiness and positive emotions. You will be able to take a baseline measurement of your well-being, which will allow you to see if it improves as a result of trying out ideas from positive psychology. We will also begin to look at whether happiness is a good thing or whether it is perhaps overrated.

1

Happiness and positive emotions

In this chapter you will learn:

- ► *what happiness is*
- ► *how happiness can be measured*
- ► *why happiness is important*
- ► *whether there is a desirable amount of happiness.*

Diagnostic test

1 Why do psychologists usually use the term 'subjective well-being' (SWB) rather than 'happiness'?

2 What are the three components of SWB?

3 What was the occupation of the writers of the diaries analysed by Danner?

4 What did Danner's study show?

5 Name three benefits of happiness and positive emotions.

6 What is the name of Barbara Fredrickson's theory about the positive consequences of happiness?

7 What is activity scheduling?

8 What is meant by the 'undoing effect' of positive emotions?

9 Negative emotions help us avoid danger. According to Fredrickson's theory, what is the purpose of positive emotions?

10 What is Losada and Fredrickson's positivity ratio of the desirable number of positive to negative emotions?

What is happiness?

A dictionary will give you two different meanings of happiness[6], namely:

▶ a state of well-being and contentment or

▶ a pleasurable or satisfying experience.[7]

To overcome the ambiguity of the everyday term, psychologists have invented the term 'subjective well-being' (SWB) to cover *both* meanings of happiness. SWB additionally includes a third component, the absence of negative emotions.[8]

How can happiness be measured?

Many are attracted to positive psychology by its potential to provide a scientific basis for understanding and enhancing happiness.

You can find out your own level of happiness (SWB) quite easily by taking two simple self-report questionnaires. The satisfaction with life scale (SWLS) measures your thoughts about your overall well-being. The scale of positive and negative experience (SPANE) calculates the two emotional aspects of SWB.

THE 'SATISFACTION WITH LIFE' SCALE[10]

On the next page are five statements (a–e) that you may agree or disagree with. Using the 1–7 scale, indicate your agreement with each statement by allocating it a number. Be open and honest in your responding.

Scale:

7 – Strongly agree

6 – Agree

5 – Slightly agree

4 – Neither agree nor disagree

3 – Slightly disagree

2 – Disagree

1 – Strongly disagree

Statements:

a In most ways my life is close to my ideal.

b The conditions of my life are excellent.

c I am satisfied with my life.

d So far I have got the important things I want in life.

e If I could live my life over, I would change almost nothing.

To calculate your SWLS score, simply add up your scores for the five statements. Your SWLS score will be between 5 and 35; 20–24 is average.

Scores:

31–35 Extremely satisfied

26–30 Satisfied

21–25 Slightly satisfied

20 Neutral

15–19 Slightly dissatisfied

10–14 Dissatisfied

5–9 Extremely dissatisfied

THE SCALE OF POSITIVE AND NEGATIVE EXPERIENCE (SPANE)[11]

Think about what you have been doing and experiencing during the past four weeks. Then report how often you experienced feelings that you would describe using the words listed in the box below, on a scale of 1–5.

Scale:		
1 – Very rarely or never	Good	Bad
2 – Rarely	Pleasant	Unpleasant
3 – Sometimes	Positive	Negative
4 – Often	Happy	Sad
5 – Very often or always	Joyful	Afraid
	Contented	Angry

This list gives six positive and six negative items.[12] Other positive emotions include being loving, grateful, calm, interested, hopeful, proud, amused, inspired and in awe. Additional negative feelings include being anxious, stressed, ashamed, guilty, in despair, humiliated, apathetic and bored.[13]

To calculate your SPANE score, first add up your scores for the six positive items to get a positive score between 6 and 30. Then add up your scores for the six negative items, again getting a score between 6 and 30. Your overall SPANE score is calculated by subtracting your negative score from your positive score. SPANE scores vary from +24 (very positive) to –24 (very negative).

To obtain your overall SWB score, add together your SWLS and SPANE scores.

Keep your results so you can re-take the tests when you have finished this book. This is a really good way of testing whether the ideas in this book increase your happiness.

Key idea: Subjective well-being can be measured

You can easily measure your level of SWB by taking simple self-report questionnaires. These include the satisfaction with life scale (SWLS) and the scale of positive and negative experience (SPANE).

By taking these now and then when you have completed the suggested activities this book, you can gauge whether positive psychology has improved your happiness.

Why is happiness important?

Most people want to be happy and would wish happiness upon their loved ones. However, there are some people, happiness sceptics, who doubt whether happiness really is so important, or even whether it is to be numbered among the good things in life at all. The following thought experiment helps test out whether or not happiness sceptics are right.[14]

Try it now: Is your life better if you are happy?[15]

Take a moment to imagine two versions of your life.

In the first version, you are dissatisfied with your life and have very few periods of joy and contentment. Most of the time you are angry, sad or worried. How would you feel at the prospect of living this sort of life?

The other option is that you are very satisfied with your life. You feel contented and happy most of the time. You experience negative emotions some of the time but much more often you feel positive emotions.

Which life would you choose?

Most people have a strong preference for the happy life over the miserable life. So, other things being equal, happiness would appear to be a good thing. Happiness sceptics would reply, 'of course people prefer happiness, but other things are not equal. Being happy makes you selfish and complacent'. This is where psychology research comes into its own. Psychologists can test out whether being happy has positive or negative consequences. In fact, a whole host of research studies have been carried out and come to some very interesting conclusions. With how many of the following benefits do you think happiness is associated?

▶ Better health

▶ Longer life

▶ Higher achievement

- More wealth
- Better productivity
- More pro-social behaviour

The answer is – all of them! So, completely against the armchair speculations of happiness sceptics, happiness proves to have very many positive consequences.

HAPPINESS IMPROVES HEALTH

Many studies have demonstrated the link between positive emotions and health. One memorable study was carried out by Carnevale et al. (2003). Volunteers were injected with a virus that made them susceptible to catching a cold. Those who scored lowest on a test for positive emotions were three times more likely to become ill than those who scored high on positive emotions.

One explanation as to why positive emotions improve health is that they may reduce the impact of negative emotions. Experiments have shown that positive emotions make us able to recover more quickly from stress and related harmful cardiovascular reactivity. Fredrickson (Fredrickson et al., 2000) told volunteers that they would shortly have to give a surprise presentation. Naturally enough they became stressed and their heart rates and blood pressure increased. A few moments later, they were informed that they did not have to give the presentation. The volunteers were then divided randomly into three groups. Some were shown a short film clip inducing positive emotions, others a different film inducing negative or neutral emotions. Those people shown the positive clip returned to their normal blood pressure and heart rate significantly faster than the others.

Fredrickson talks about the 'undoing effect' of positive emotions and suggests that they act like a 'reset button' to take us back to our normal state.

▶ The undoing effect of positive emotions – a list of 'reset buttons'

Doing something physical
Running
Swimming
Exercise
Tennis
Dancing
Yoga
Gardening
Going for a walk

Making a connection with those I care for
Hugging
Talking to a friend
Playing with a pet
Feeding seagulls
Charity work

Doing something to make my body feel calmer
Having a bath
Sleep
Massage
Power nap
Hitting a punch bag
Boxing
Making a cup of tea
Slow breathing
Guided imagery
Relaxation exercises
Meditation

Doing an activity that I can get involved in that takes my mind off things
Baking
Preparing a nice meal
Comedy
Watching a thriller
Listening to music
Cleaning
Singing
Photography
Buying myself something nice
Booking a short break
Puzzles
Playing an instrument
Having a makeover
Looking at photos that make me feel happy
Reading

Thinking about things differently
Accepting the situation
Reframing the situation
Counting my blessings
Writing it down in a journal
Giving myself a pep talk

The reset buttons are grouped in five categories:

▶ doing something physical

▶ making a connection with those I care for

▶ doing something to make my body feel calmer

▶ doing an activity that I can get involved in that takes my mind off things

▶ thinking about things differently.

Can you think of other activities in each category that work well for you?

Try it now: Identify and start using your 'reset buttons'

How do you best recover from negative emotions? Which of the popular 'reset buttons' listed on the left work best for you? A useful follow-up activity is to test them out. Jot down your favourite three 'reset buttons', try them out when you experience a negative emotion and then jot down how beneficial each reset button proves to be.

HAPPINESS LEADS TO LONGER LIFE

Positive emotions not only improve your health, they also make it more likely you will live longer. To demonstrate this, Danner et al. (2001) analysed the diaries of a group of young nuns[16] who had regularly recorded their feelings about their lives back in the 1930s. Each nun's diary entries were rated for positive emotions such as love, hope and interest. The researchers then tracked down the nuns to see if there was a relationship between which nuns expressed the most happiness in the 1930s and which nuns were still alive decades later. Remarkably, those nuns who recorded the most positive emotions lived on average nine years longer – more than the life expectancy gain from quitting smoking. This finding is particularly persuasive because nuns have very similar lifestyles. It is likely, therefore, that the difference in happiness caused the extra longevity, rather than variable diets, occupations or geographical locations. The finding has been replicated analysing famous psychologists (Pressman and Cohen, 2012) and elderly people in the UK (Steptoe and Wardle, 2011).

HAPPINESS LEADS TO HIGHER ACHIEVEMENT, WEALTH AND PRODUCTIVITY

Happier people tend to do better in achieving their goals both at work and in their personal lives. This is most likely connected with happier people being more curious and energetic (Leitzel, 2000), creative (Fredrickson, 2009) and more self-controlled (Fry, 1975). Happy people also tend to earn more money (Neve and Oswald, 2012).

HAPPY PEOPLE EXHIBIT MORE PRO-SOCIAL BEHAVIOUR

There is strong evidence that happier people give more to charity (Morrison et al., 2012) and are more likely to volunteer (Oishi et al., 2007). Happier people also tend to have more friends and to be better friends (Diener and Seligman, 2002). Causation probably goes both ways. Happier people are more sociable and altruistic, and being sociable and altruistic makes them happier. To demonstrate the causal nature of happiness towards altruism, experimenters have induced various mood states and found that when people are in a good mood they are both more altruistic (Carlson, Charlin and Miller, 1988) and more compassionate (Nelson, 2009).

Key idea: The benefits of happiness

Happiness is associated with a number of positive spin-offs, including:
* longer life
* better health
* higher achievement
* better productivity
* more pro-social behaviour.

The broaden-and-build theory

There are, then, many studies confirming the positive spin-offs of happiness. Happiness leads to positive consequences, which in turn lead to more happiness. Barbara Fredrickson's influential broaden-and-build theory provides one way of understanding this process.

Imagine a day when you wake up in a positive mood. You text a friend and suggest meeting up. You go out with them and, since you are feeling adventurous, agree to do something new. Maybe you decide to go ice-skating, visit an art gallery or go to the countryside. You enjoy yourself, discover something novel and meet new people. How will the day affect your mood? What effect do you think this sort of day will have on your personal resources, such as your support network, knowledge, skills and level of optimism?

Now think of another day. This time you wake up feeling grouchy. You decide you would prefer your own company. You spend the day in an unfocused way watching daytime TV, dozing and aimlessly browsing the internet. Would such a day develop your personal resources? How would it affect your mood?

The broaden-and-build theory proposes that positive emotions lead to a broadened mindset. This leads you to build personal resources such as psychological strengths, sociability and physical health. These make you more likely to have more positive experiences and leads to an ascent to positive well-being.[17]

Activity scheduling and behavioural activation

If positive emotions are so beneficial, just how should you go about trying to have more of them? Activity scheduling is an evidence-based technique that was originally developed to help people overcome depression. Studies have shown that it can also help those who are not depressed have more positive emotions and enhanced well-being.[18]

The first stage of activity scheduling is to spend a week recording information about how you spend your time. You also record how much pleasure (P) and how much sense of achievement (A) you get from each activity.

Time	Susan's activity diary (ratings out of ten)
09.00–11.00	Got up, had breakfast, watched daytime TV
	P = 3 A = 1
11.00–13.00	Went shopping, met friend for coffee
	P = 6 (shopping) P = 8 (friend) A = 3 (both)
13.00–15.00	Did my coursework – finished it!
	P = 3 A = 8

For example, Susan found that the most pleasurable time was between eleven o'clock and one o'clock. Meeting her friend turned out to be the most enjoyable activity. Finishing her coursework gave her the biggest sense of achievement, though it was not as enjoyable.

It is best practice to record what you did as close to the time as possible, otherwise it becomes difficult to remember what you did and how you felt. Each time period recorded should contain:

▶ a brief description of how you spent the time during that hour

▶ two numbers labelled P (for pleasure) and A (for achievement) out of 10.

Notice from the example that for the same activity pleasure and achievement ratings can be very different. For example, eating chocolate is likely to be high P but low A, while completing a chore is more likely to be low P and high A. a blank activity schedule is available to download at http://cbtfortherapists. blogspot.co.uk/p/activity-scheduling-template.html.

After this first stage, activity monitoring, the next stage is to then plan activities in the next week to aim for higher scores. Some useful tips are:

▶ Repeat activities with high scores for P or A.

▶ Think about related activities to those with high scores – for example, if playing one sport gives a high score, think about other sports you could try.

- Try to cut out activities with both low A and low P. If you cannot reduce them, think creatively of ways to improve your experience of them. For example, a checkout cashier might decide to experiment with smiling at customers and asking them about their day so far.

- Aim for an overall balance of high A and high P activities. It is fine to have some activities that are just high A and some that are just high P.

You can enhance this basic method by identifying and scheduling positive emotions other than enjoyment. The other positive emotions picked out by Barbara Fredrickson are interest, hope, awe, serenity, joy, inspiration, pride, amusement and love. You could record your level of each of these in your activity log.

Remember this: Take the first step towards positivity even if you don't feel like it

Positivity feeds on itself. By doing something to help you feel more positive you can start a positive ascent towards well-being. Often the hardest step is taking the first step when you are not feeling very positive. The trick is to do something positive whether or not you feel like doing it.

Some people are put off the idea of activity scheduling because it seems too simple. The truth is that it is one of the most effective and robust techniques to increase positive emotion. It does have a limitation though, in that it only rates activities that you currently engage in, so it can sometimes be useful to supplement activity scheduling by reflecting on activities that you no longer do that you found enjoyable in the past. It was this latter approach that was particularly useful for Fred, whom I treated for depression.

Case study: Fred

Fred was neither broadening nor building his life when I first met him. Fred was languishing. He got up late, pottered around the house (thereby annoying his wife) and napped in front of the television. He had lost touch with friends since being made redundant and did not see any way his life could improve. As he talked about his life I found his sense of hopelessness spreading to me.

We tried to understand his depression, and talked about how his depression might be perpetuated by his low level of activity. If he was not doing anything enjoyable, how could he expect to feel less blue? However, in Fred's case, activity monitoring merely confirmed that pretty much everything he did at the moment resulted in low levels of both enjoyment and achievement.

It was only when we started talking about what Fred had enjoyed in the past that things started to improve. Fred had a lifelong interest in rugby and used to play for a local club when he was younger. Our conversation prompted Fred to drop by his club to see if any of his old friends were still working there. It turned out that a couple of them were still around. He enjoyed talking to them and, more importantly, learned that the club needed help with one of the youth teams. Fred started to get very involved in the rugby club. He found that he enjoyed coaching the youngsters and chatting with old friends. Soon he was getting out most days and his mood lifted accordingly. He built new relationships and found himself in a positive spiral towards well-being rather than a vicious cycle of depression. Within a few weeks, his depression had lifted.

As well as explaining how positive emotions benefit us, Fredrickson's broaden-and-build theory provides an explanation as to why positive emotions have developed. Evolutionary psychologists have, for a long time, been able to explain the purpose of negative emotions. When faced with an imminent threat, your anxiety narrows your attention so you can deal with it. Negative emotions trigger fight-or-flight behaviour, which had a clear evolutionary advantage for our ancestors.[19] What, though, asks Fredrickson (2009), could be the evolutionary purpose of positive emotions? They feel nice, but what is their point? Her theory is that though positive emotions may not give us much evolutionary advantage in the short term, in the longer term they build personal resources.

Key idea: The broaden-and-build theory

Barbara Fredrickson's broaden-and-build theory ties together an explanation of how the various benefits of happiness work together to help people increase their happiness. It also provides an evolutionary explanation for positive emotions.

The 3:1 positivity ratio – a cautionary tale?

In 2005 Barbara Fredrickson and Marcial Losada informed the world of an exciting discovery. They said that in much the same way as ice turns to water above freezing point, languishing becomes flourishing if, and only if, you go above a certain tipping point of positive to negative experiences. The ratio of positive to negative experiences and emotions, calculated by Losada using complex mathematical modelling, was said to be approximately 3:1.

For a full eight years the 3:1 positivity ratio became part of the canon of positive psychology. Numerous articles advised readers to aim for at least three positive experiences for every negative one. Then, in early 2013, Brown and Sokal wrote a damning article debunking the whole idea. They argued that the mathematics on which it was based was deeply flawed. Losada, who had been responsible for the maths, has so far declined to defend his work. So Frederickson has been left in the invidious position of having to accept that the maths on which the positivity ratio was based is probably wrong. While, she says, there is no reason to doubt the broaden-and-build theory, there is no longer very much evidence for a 3:1 positivity ratio. There may be a tipping point where individuals really begin to flourish, but Losada's data does not demonstrate that it is 3:1.

Remember this: The 3:1 positivity ratio is now disputed

While older positive psychology texts may confidently proclaim that when you have more than three times as many positive as negative emotions and experiences you reach a tipping point, this claim is now in doubt.

Could too much happiness be a bad thing?

Healthy foods and exercise are good for you as long as they are not taken in excess. The same principle applies to happiness. Ed Diener, a leading happiness theorist, agrees that, 'happiness does not mean a complete absence of negative feelings'. This is not surprising when we remember that negative emotions have the purpose of protecting us from danger. Would you want your pilot to be optimistic even if strange noises were coming from the engine before you took off? Research supports the common sense view that extreme positive emotion can lead to overconfidence (Ifcher and Zarghamee, 2011).

Moreover, there is an argument for thinking that positive emotions need to be appropriate to the situation. Would joy be appropriate if someone close to you had just died? Is pride a good thing for someone who actually did very badly? In these cases, would not sadness and regret be more appropriate emotions? While Fredrickson and Losada suggested that having a positivity ratio above 11:1 was a bad thing, it seems unlikely that such a 'magic number' is particularly helpful. We need judgement to decide which emotions are appropriate to a particular situation. Historically, this quality has been called 'practical wisdom'. We will explore this important idea more fully in Chapter 11, Wisdom.

Remember this: The need for practical wisdom

Happiness feels good and in general has positive consequences. However, there are some situations where positive emotions are inappropriate and unhelpful. Practical wisdom, an understanding of a situation and what it calls for, is required.

Focus points

We have covered a lot in this chapter so it is a good time to take stock of some key points.

* Happiness is a vague concept, so is defined in psychology as subjective well-being (SWB). Using SWB allows for precise measurement and experimentation, for example about the consequences of happiness.

* As well as it being something that you would want for its own sake, happiness has a number of positive spin-offs.

* The broaden-and-build theory attempts to explain these spin-offs in an evolutionary context. It also argues for the potential for an upward spiral of happiness.

* Fredrickson and Losada proposed a 3:1 positivity ratio which formed a tipping point for flourishing, but the mathematics upon which this was based has now been challenged.

* There are some situations where positive emotions are not appropriate. We need practical wisdom to guide us as to which situations demand positive emotions and in which situations negative emotions are more appropriate.

Diagnostic test answers

1 Happiness is too vague a term for the science of positive psychology.

2 Life satisfaction, positive affect and the absence of negative affect

3 They were nuns.

4 The happiest nuns lived more than nine years longer than the least happy nuns.

5 Three from: better health, longer life expectancy, more pro-social behaviour, more productivity and achievement.

6 The broaden-and-build theory.

7 Activity scheduling is the evidence-based technique of first monitoring your activities to find out how much pleasure and achievement they produce and then scheduling activities to increase the amount of pleasure and achievement.

8 Positive emotions undo the cardiovascular after-effects of negative emotions.

9 Positive emotions make us more open and curious and so can lead us into a positive ascent of well-being where we broaden and build our personal resources.

10 Three to one.

Next steps

Having found out how happiness is measured and why it matters, the next step – in the next chapter – is to learn about how to enhance happiness. In the following chapter we will return to the question of whether happiness is the only thing that matters, looking at broader notions of well-being.

2

What makes people happier?

In this chapter you will learn:

- ▶ *what the causes of happiness are*
- ▶ *the relative importance of genetics, circumstances and voluntary activities in determining happiness*
- ▶ *how happiness varies across nations*
- ▶ *what hedonic adaptation is and how it can be overcome*
- ▶ *how positive psychology interventions can enhance happiness.*

In fact, only the odd numbers are true; the even-numbered statements are all false. How many of these answers surprise you?

Is happiness all in your genes?

To what extent do you believe your own happiness level is determined by the personality of your parents and grandparents? Psychologists have been able to answer this question using twin studies. This research compares the happiness levels of identical twins, who share 100 per cent of their genes, with fraternal twins, who share only 50 per cent. These studies show that on average about 50 per cent of personality, including the disposition to be happy, is down to genetics.

Key idea: Genetics has a strong influence on your happiness level

Twin studies suggest that about 50 per cent of the difference between happiness levels in people is down to genetics.

If, on average, 50 per cent of happiness is down to genetics, it still means that there is 50 per cent left to play with. David Lykken, one of the psychologists behind the twin studies, puts it eloquently:

> 'If we let our personal genetic steersman have his way, we shall tend to follow a course laid down for us in our DNA. But if much of what is inherited consists of behaviour tendencies that can be resisted, modified and shaped, there is a real possibility for intervention, for countermanding the genetic steersman'.[20]

One way to do this is to manage the personality traits most associated with unhappiness.

HOW TO IDENTIFY AND MANAGE KEY PERSONALITY TRAITS

Although it is unlikely that a single 'happiness gene' will be found, scientists are already speculating about how certain genes are associated with happiness. [21] In the future, it may be possible to genetically engineer people to have happier genes. At the moment, though, this is science fantasy. It might be thought that anti-depressants such as Prozac, could reliably make us happier. Unfortunately, while medication may help with depression, safe and non-addictive 'happy people pills' do not yet exist.[22]

However, while science cannot at present directly manipulate your genes or dispense you a happy pill, it can, as Lykken suggests, help you identify and manage relevant personality traits.

Psychologists have identified the 'big five' personality traits, namely: openness to experience, conscientiousness, extraversion, agreeableness and neuroticism. Of these, two are most associated with happiness: extraversion and neuroticism.

Are you an extrovert or an introvert? If you like being with other people then you are most likely an extrovert. Introverts prefer being with their own thoughts. If you are an introvert, the bad news is that genetics has dealt you a hand that means you are less likely than the average person to be happy.

The better news for introverts is that you do not have to accept that you are destined to misery. A key question is whether you are an introvert through choice or through fear. If you genuinely like being with your own thoughts and find being with others boring, then the best strategy may be to engage more in those solitary activities that make you happy. Activity scheduling could be really helpful. So could the idea that you do not have to do things with other people just because that is what most other people do. However, you may be introverted not through choice but because of social anxiety. If you would like to do things with other people but avoid it because of fear of negative judgements, then the best step may be to try to overcome social anxiety. A good guide to doing this is Gillian Butler's *Overcoming Social Anxiety and Shyness*. If you are uncertain which category you fit into – whether you are a happy or an unhappy introvert – then experimenting with acting in an extroverted way may be worthwhile. You could try reminding yourself that although you may not feel very inclined to socialize, you may become happier if you do. There is some evidence that this approach is helpful. Against their expectations, introverts found they were happier when they acted more like an extrovert (Fleeson, 2012).[23]

Neuroticism is strongly associated with unhappiness. This is hardly surprising, since the definition of neuroticism is high negative affect (i.e. negative emotions). If you scored high in the negative experience questions of the SPANE, then you may have a tendency towards neuroticism. If you are neurotic, then you can still manage your tendency to experience more negative emotions by using CBT and other evidence-based techniques, which you will find described in later chapters.

Remember this: Temperament is not destiny

While your genetic steersman pushes you towards feeling more or less happy, this does not fully determine your happiness level. While 'happy people pills' do not yet exist, you can learn to manage successfully personality traits that may predispose you to being less happy, such as introversion and neuroticism.

How important are life circumstances?

Were you surprised by some of the answers to the 'causes of happiness' diagnostic test at the beginning of this chapter? Here are some more key findings about how life circumstances, such as income, age, education, gender and attractiveness, are associated with happiness.

▶ When basic needs such as food and housing are not being met, income is strongly associated with happiness. Once basic needs are satisfied, income is only moderately associated with happiness. One study found the 100 richest Americans to be happier than less wealthy Americans, but not by very much.[24] As long as basic needs are met, relative income becomes more important than absolute income (see Layard, 2005). These facts help explain why happiness has not increased in developed countries since World War II, despite huge improvements in absolute income and lifestyle.

▶ When happiness is plotted against age it follows a U shape. People tend to be happiest in their early 20s and early 60s and least happy in their mid-40s.

▶ Objective measures of physical attractiveness and physical health are not strongly related to happiness, though whether people *think* they are attractive or healthy is.

▶ Satisfying work boosts happiness while being unemployed can significantly reduce it.

▶ Those currently married are happier than the single, but those divorced are less happy than those who never married.

▶ Children do not, on average, make people happier. However, having children may increase a sense of purpose and meaning.

Fascinating as these findings are, there are two reasons to be cautious about reading too much into them. First, they are averages, so they should be treated as a guide, in much the same way as average temperatures and rainfall are a guide about when and where to go on holiday. Even if children do not, on average, make people happier you might be one of the people (like Bertrand Russell, mentioned in the 'Introduction') who becomes much happier after having children.

The second reason for caution is that most of the data on happiness is correlational. This means that researchers measure how closely happiness and another variable, such as being married, are associated. If they are not associated at all, this would tell us something important – in this case it would tell you that being married does not make you happy. But if happiness and another variable are associated, this does not necessarily imply that one causes the other. In fact, it turns out that being married is positively correlated with happiness. However, this says nothing about the direction of causation. Does being married make you happier? Or are those who are already happy more likely to get married? Or perhaps a third factor, like being an extrovert, makes people more likely to get married and more likely to be happy.

Remember this: Storks deliver babies[25]– correlation does not necessarily prove causation

The following study provides a vivid reminder of the danger of reading too much into correlational data.

When he plotted the number of stork pairs against the number of births in 17 countries, Matthews (2000) noticed a strong degree of correlation between the two, which would be more than a 100:1 shot to happen by chance. So, does this mean that the fairy story told by parents to their inquisitive young children is true, after all? No, because two items may be associated without one causing the other. It so happens that storks live in rural areas where there are higher birth rates.

Matthews concludes his article with these cautionary words: 'While storks may not deliver babies, unthinking interpretation of correlation can certainly deliver unreliable conclusions.'

National differences in happiness

The ten most happy countries, according to the World Database of Happiness, are Costa Rica (8.5/10), Denmark, Iceland, Switzerland, Finland, Mexico, Norway, Canada, Panama and Sweden. The least happy countries are Togo (2.6/10), Tanzania, Burundi, Benin and Zimbabwe. The UK came twenty-eighth, Ireland fourteenth and the USA twenty-first.

The least happy countries offer no surprises, being examples of extreme poverty, disease, lack of political freedom or all three. Scandinavian countries fare very well in the top ten. Eric Wiener, who has written a book on the subject, believes that a sense of community, trust and equality all play a part in making people happy. Before taking your emigration plans too far, though, it should be pointed out that the differences between the happiness levels of developed, democratic nations are quite small. The UK scored 7.2 out of 10 while Switzerland, which came 24 places higher, scored 8.[26]

So why is Costa Rica top? It has a great climate, is very environmentally friendly, and people there are trusting and quick to forgive. They are also eager to please, so it is just possible that they gave themselves high scores in their SWB self-reports to please the interviewers.

Hedonic adaptation and the hedonic treadmill

If you jump into a warm bath, your body acclimatizes to the temperature with the result that after a short while it no longer feels nearly so hot. Objectively the temperature remains almost the same, but your body has adapted to it and so it feels much cooler. It turns out that a similar process occurs when your circumstances change. Lottery winners tend to be much happier for a while, but before too long they often revert to close to their happiness level before they won. On the other hand, those who have been left paralysed by an accident tend to recover to almost their previous level of happiness. This process is called hedonic adaptation. While events may have a strong impact on your mood for a while, this tends to reduce over time.

Try it now: Are you prone to hedonic adaptation?

When was the last time you got excited about buying something? Perhaps a new smartphone or some other gadget? Or maybe it was buying an item of clothing or jewellery? Or maybe a new kitchen or new car?

How did you feel just after you bought it? How about a week later? How about now?

The theory of hedonic adaptation would predict a short burst of improved mood, with happiness returning to its usual level after a while. Was this true for you?

Key idea: Hedonic adaptation may limit the effect on happiness of changes in life circumstances

Hedonic adaptation is the tendency to adapt to either positive or negative events. Research suggests that people have a surprising tendency to return to their previous levels of happiness after even major fortunes or misfortunes.

Hedonic adaptation poses a challenge for those trying to improve their happiness. Some psychologists have even labelled the struggle for happiness as a 'hedonic treadmill'.[27] We buy things, move to sunnier climes or get married in a doomed attempt to be happier. We may feel better for a while, but soon revert to our baseline.

However, while feeling cooler in a warm bath is a purely automatic process over which you have little control, you have a choice about how you react to positive events. Two ways to capitalize on positive events and reduce the effects of hedonic adaptation are to cultivate gratitude and savour the good things in life.

GRATITUDE

If we are prone to take good things for granted, we can counteract this tendency by cultivating an attitude of attending more to the good things that have happened to us. In other words, we can learn to become more grateful. Positive psychologists have developed a number of effective ways to develop gratitude.

Try it now: Cultivate gratitude

Read the two evidence-based gratitude interventions. Try both of them now, and notice which one has the most impact. If you would like to develop gratitude, practise your chosen gratitude exercise in the way suggested below.

▶ Gratitude developer 1: Three good things

Each night for one week, write down three things that went well that day.

In addition to writing three things that went well, provide a causal explanation for each thing. In particular, try to pay attention to how your behaviour caused the positive thing.[28]

When carrying out the 'Three good things' activity, it is important not to set the bar too high. The 'good thing' does not have to be that you won the Nobel Prize. For a depressed person the good thing may be that they got out of bed.

Do not forget to include how you caused the positive thing, even if this was in a very indirect way.

Two examples may help:

- ▶ I had a nice chat with my friend. I made this happen by calling her.

- ▶ The sun shone today. The good thing was that I noticed it!

▶ Gratitude developer 2: Feeling grateful

For the next two weeks, list three things for which you are grateful each day. As well as writing down the three things each day, spend time trying actually to feel grateful about those things.[29]

If you are not sure how to generate feelings of gratitude, try out the following meditation.[30]

Quieten your mind for a few moments by taking a few deep breaths and closing your eyes. Bring to mind three things in your life for which you are grateful. Spend a few moments feeling happy that you have been blessed with these pieces of good fortune. Now, for each of these good things in turn, imagine that it had not happened. Reflect for several moments on the ways in which your life would be worse. For example, if your good thing was that you are healthy, imagine what your life would be like if you were ill. When you have imagined your life without all three of the good things, take a few more deep breaths and open your eyes. Notice how you are feeling now.

If you want to discover more about gratitude interventions, read the work of psychologist Robert Emmons who has been working on the topic for decades.

While gratitude helps us appreciate good things that have already happened to us, to appreciate things that are happening right now we can learn how to savour. Savouring is focused attention on pleasant experience. The leading researcher on savouring is American psychologist Fred Bryant. His research supports the claim that savouring boosts positive emotion, life satisfaction and optimism. You can savour the past ('reminiscing'), the future ('looking forward to') and the present ('taking time to stop and smell the roses'). You can savour on your own and with others. You can savour sensual pleasures such as tasting coffee or smelling flowers, aesthetic pleasures such as in art and music, and accomplishments.

Try it now: Savouring

Next time you eat or drink, take a few moments to savour it. A cup of coffee would be ideal, but you can choose whatever food or drink you prefer.

Once you have decided on what food or drink to savour, be sure to:
* Set aside at least ten minutes to enjoy it undisturbed by interruptions.
* Before tasting, vividly imagine what it will taste like.
* Smell it and enjoy the aroma.

* Slowly take the first bite or sip and roll it around your mouth.
* Enjoy the flavours in your mouth.
* Slowly take the next bite or sip.
* Notice all the sensations.
* Continue enjoying your food or drink, paying full, concentrated attention on the sensations that arise.

Case study: Lisa's daily vacation

Lisa, a student of positive psychology, decided to try one of Bryant's exercises called the daily vacation. This involves setting aside 20 minutes each day for a week for a positive savouring experience. Lisa decided to take her 'daily vacation' during her journey to work and her lunch breaks. This is what she wrote:

'I work in Central London, but like most Londoners I take London for granted. I've noticed the difference between tourists, who seem really excited about all the sights and history of our capital city, and us Londoners, who walk past them without even noticing them. I wondered what it would be like to pretend I was a tourist in London for a week – while still working!

'On my way to work I always get the bus from Waterloo across Westminster Bridge. I decided to make this part of my daily vacation each day – one day looking left and taking in the Houses of Parliament in detail, the next day soaking up St Paul's. I even learned Wordsworth's poem "On Westminster Bridge" and recited it in my head while going over the bridge.

'On another day I visited the galleries. I like art but hadn't been to the National Gallery for years. It was amazing and I made sure to linger on my favourite pictures in the Impressionist room, especially the Renoirs. I couldn't believe how much beautiful and invaluable art was on display.

'The weather wasn't too great for most of the week, but on the day that it was sunny I went to Green Park and soaked up the sunshine. I paid attention to families enjoying themselves and for a moment had this wonderful feeling of being really glad to be alive.

'This was the cheapest vacation I have ever had, and I'd recommend others try it out.'

To discover more about the psychology of savouring, consult Bryant and Veroff's *Savoring, A New Model of Positive Experience* (2008).

Remember this: Gratitude and savouring can help reduce the effects of hedonic adaptation

Gratitude and savouring are two skills which have been shown to increase happiness and life satisfaction. One reason why they help is that they make us focus on good things and so reduce hedonic adaptation.

Can positive psychology make people lastingly happier?

Positive psychologists answer this key question with a definite 'yes'. One of the purposes of positive psychology is to provide a scientific basis for this claim. A landmark in positive psychology was an article written by Martin Seligman and colleagues in 2005, entitled, appropriately enough, 'Positive Psychology Progress'. They describe an experiment that provides strong evidence for the effectiveness of positive psychology interventions. Participants were signed up through the internet to try out one of six 'happiness exercises' for a week. In fact, one such exercise was a placebo, to provide a control against which the other exercises could be measured. The results? Two exercises – 'Three good things' (see earlier in this chapter) and 'Using signature strengths in a new way' (see Chapter 4, Strengths) – proved to have a significant and lasting effect on happiness. A striking finding was that even though participants were instructed to carry out an exercise for just one week, on average they had a significantly higher level of happiness than the control group six months later.

Key idea: Positive psychology has shown that there are things we can do to lastingly increase our happiness and well-being

A central goal of positive psychology is to develop and test ways to increase happiness and well-being. The 2005 article 'Positive

Psychology Progress' describes an important experiment Seligman and colleagues carried out, which showed that certain exercises can improve happiness enduringly.

Since 2005, psychologists have developed and tested more ways to enhance happiness. In this book you will find descriptions of many more of these empirically validated exercises (usually called 'interventions'). It is important to note that although these interventions boost happiness, this is not all they do. For example, the 'Three good things' exercise also boosts optimism; the strengths interventions can also help you achieve your goals. This is hardly surprising given what we learned in the previous chapter about the positive consequences of happiness and the broaden-and-build theory. If we do something that makes us happier, then it is likely to help other areas of life and get us moving on an upward positive spiral.

Is it possible to say how much of our happiness can be attributed to different factors?

Following the lead from most positive psychology books, this chapter has described three types of things that influence happiness. These are genetics, life circumstances and voluntary intentional activities. Some books then proceed to try to divide up the amount of happiness that can be attributed to each factor. For example, in *Authentic Happiness* Seligman introduces the 'happiness equation': $H = S + C + V$, where S stands for the set range said to be determined by genetics, C stands for life circumstances and V stands for voluntary intentional activities. In *The How of Happiness*, Sonja Lyubomirsky presents this as a happiness pie chart, which is given prominent view on the front cover in some editions. The authors then put numbers to each category, usually about 50 per cent for the genetic factor, 10 per cent for life circumstances and 40 per cent for voluntary activities. Being good psychologists these authors are very careful to state what these percentages actually mean. If you had 100 people in a room and measured the difference in their happiness levels and the difference in their objective life circumstances, only 10 per cent of the difference would be attributable to life circumstances. Unfortunately, as happiness guru Ed Diener points out, average differences across a range of people do not necessarily tell us much about what makes a difference to one individual person. For example, though life circumstances do not, on average, make very much difference to happiness, if you are in an abusive relationship this may make a very big difference to your happiness.

Remember this: Be careful how to interpret averages about happiness

The happiness pie chart is an average across many people. It does not mean that for a particular individual a change in, for example, circumstances would only make a 10 per cent difference.

Focus points

* Happiness has a significant genetic element. If you are introverted or neurotic this will tend to make you less happy, but there are things you can do to reduce the impact.

* Psychologists have found out a good deal about what is associated with happiness. Caution is needed when using this data, because correlation does not necessarily imply causation.

* Hedonic adaptation, the tendency to adjust to events, means that changes in life circumstances have less impact than you might expect.

* Gratitude and savouring exercises are two evidence-based interventions that reduce hedonic adaptation and increase happiness.

* Positive psychology has proposed and tested many other exercises aimed at increasing happiness. You will learn about many of these evidence-based ideas to boost happiness in this book.

Diagnostic test

The odd-numbered statements are all true; the even-numbered statements are all false.

✳ Next steps

In the last two chapters we have looked at the positive psychology of happiness. In the next chapter we will look at why some thinkers have argued for broader views of well-being, and how psychology can help to enhance that.

Values, well-being and flourishing

In this chapter you will learn:

▶ *why there is more to well-being than positive emotions*

▶ *about values and their relationship to well-being*

▶ *about the informed preference satisfaction theory*

▶ *about values clarification as a path to higher well-being*

▶ *about flourishing (objective list theories of well-being)*

▶ *about Seligman's authentic happiness and PERMA theories*

▶ *about Carol Ryff's theory of psychological well-being*

▶ *about philosophy-based theories of well-being.*

Diagnostic test

1 What is the name of the thought experiment that asks you to decide whether you would want to spend your life feeling perfect happiness while stuck in a virtual reality world?

2 Why does positive psychology need to have a credible theory of well-being?

3 What is the name of the philosophical theory of well-being which states that it consists in the satisfaction of informed preferences?

4 What is the name of the process by which values are clarified, reflected upon and satisfied?

5 Deci and Ryan's self-determination theory argues that intrinsic goals are to be preferred to extrinsic goals. Give an example of an intrinsic and an extrinsic goal.

6 Robert Emmons concludes that WIST goals are conducive to well-being. What does WIST stand for?

7 Name Seligman's new theory of flourishing put forward in *Flourish*.

8 What two components has Seligman added that were not present in 'authentic happiness'?

9 Name the elements of well-being in Carol Ryff's theory.

10 Name a value that is not included in any of the three theories of flourishing but which might be considered very important.

Are positive emotions all there is to well-being?

We have seen that positive emotions not only feel good, they also have positive consequences for both ourselves and others. There is a theory about well-being, called hedonism, that proposes that a balance of positive over negative emotions is all there is to living a good life. In this chapter we will investigate whether hedonism is a plausible theory of well-being and, if not, what provides a better foundation for positive psychology.

THE EXPERIENCE MACHINE

Imagine that a machine was invented that could enable you to experience as many positive emotions and as few negative emotions as you like. You could feel as much hope, joy, excitement, interest and pleasure as you want, and never have to feel boredom, sadness, guilt, shame, anxiety or anger again. Think of it as a sophisticated virtual reality machine. You simply plug yourself in to the machine and while you are plugged in your experiences feel absolutely real. You can assume that you would never realize that you were plugged in to the machine. There is no chance of it breaking down and your physical needs will be looked after fully.

Try in now: The experience machine

You are given the option of plugging into the experience machine for the rest of your life. Would you choose to live the rest of your life plugged into the machine?

What is your answer? Most people would rather not plug in for the rest of their life (though many would not mind plugging into it for a holiday!). One reason for not wanting to live attached to the experience machine is this. Even though you *experience* a very good life in the machine, you are not *living* a very good life. You feel good but you are not doing any good and you are not being the sort of person you would like to be. Many people say they do not just want to feel like they are in a loving relationship – they want to actually be in one. They do not want just to believe they have won an Olympic medal or found the cure for cancer – they want actually to have done so.

The experience machine thought experiment implies that hedonism is not a good theory of well-being. There is more to well-being in the round than just experiencing emotions. Psychologist Joseph Ciarrochi[31] puts it very well. He asks:

> 'Do we really want our life to be about having as many positive thoughts and feelings as possible? Maybe. Maybe not. Is this the kind of statement you want on your tombstone?

"Here lies ... , a man (or woman) who successfully managed to experience a 3 to 1 ratio of positive to negative thoughts."

'I think I want my tombstone to say something about me being a loving father, caring husband, and someone who sought to improve this human condition. I bet you ... have similar hopes and values.'

The role of ethical philosophy

Psychology is the science of the human mind and human behaviour. It is well equipped to investigate how well-being is associated with certain styles of thinking and behaviours. However, it is not able to determine the nature of well-being, nor to help us make judgements about the desirable trade-off between various ingredients of well-being. Those questions are the province of philosophy, and one branch of philosophy in particular, namely ethics.[32]

Some positive psychologists, including Seligman, want to keep psychology 'values neutral'. By this they mean that psychology just finds out the facts and leaves it to others to decide about right and wrong. Yet positive psychology is not neutral about values. Whenever a psychologist suggests it is a good idea to investigate more ways to make us happy, they are placing a positive value on happiness. When they suggest other areas of value – such as achievement and relationships – they are also implicitly endorsing these areas as being part of well-being. Positive psychology needs to understand what it means by well-being.

Key idea: The role for ethical philosophy in positive psychology

Positive psychology implicitly promotes ideas about what it is to flourish as a human being. This raises questions about, for example, the nature of well-being, which is the domain of philosophy rather than psychology. This book takes the view that positive psychology needs to embrace ethical philosophy rather than ignore it.

Philosophical theories about well-being

THE INFORMED PREFERENCE SATISFACTION THEORY

What does the experience-machine thought experiment show? It suggests that happiness is not the only thing that we want from life. So perhaps a better theory of well-being would state that it consists in us getting what we want. As it stands, that theory would be too simple. For example, suppose you want to eat a juicy-looking berry. Would well-being consist in eating the berry if it turned out to be deadly nightshade? Sometimes the ill effects of satisfying a desire are not so immediately apparent. Suppose taking a first shot of heroin would be blissful in the short-term but lead to a life-threatening addiction. Would fulfilling your desire for the first shot of heroin be conducive to your well-being?

A better theory of well-being is to suggest that it is about the satisfaction of your well-informed preferences. This would rule out the preferences for deadly nightshade and heroin, since if you were fully informed about the consequences of these desires you would change them. The informed preference satisfaction theory is a more subtle theory than either the simple desire satisfaction theory or hedonism. It has many strengths as a theory of well-being.

If this theory is accepted, then positive psychology could help in a number of ways. It could provide tools to help people:

▶ clarify and reflect on what is important to them in life

▶ work towards satisfying these important values.

We shall map out tools for achieving these in the next section, which draws on both values clarification and 'acceptance and commitment therapy' (ACT, pronounced as in the word 'act').

VALUES CLARIFICATION

Values clarification is a process that can help you discover which values are most important for you. Originally popular as an educational approach to moral development in the USA in the 1960s, it has also become a part of evidence-based therapies such as ACT and behavioural activation. In fact, values clarification does not just help you clarify your values, it also helps you to reflect on them and to realize them. Examples of values include:

- friendship
- love
- achievement
- success
- fame
- pleasant experiences
- positive emotions

- being a good person
- making a positive difference to the world
- wisdom
- fulfilment
- freedom.

Values are like goals in that they are desired qualities or desired outcomes. Values differ from goals in that they are more general, being about life as a whole. The satisfaction with life scale (SWLS), which we learnt about in Chapter 1, is a reasonable measure of how much you think your important values are currently being satisfied. To help you increase your life satisfaction, there are three stages: identifying, reflecting upon and then realizing your values.

Remember this: Values clarification

Values clarification means reflecting on and moving towards your values, not just clarifying them.

▶ **Step 1: Identify your values**

You could no doubt name some of your core values right now if you were asked. However, the list you would come up with would be limited by your memory and it would also be influenced by your current life priorities. A useful strategy to overcome this is to ask questions – 'values clarifiers' – which give you a broader perspective.

Values clarifier 1: Your good day

Pick one really good day from your life so far. Then write down in a few sentences the highlights of the day, and what makes you pick it out as a good day.

Examples:

▶ Suzie's good day was when she passed her driving test. She chose this day because she remembers her overwhelming sense of achievement.

▶ Naomi chose the day she gave birth to her first child. She adds that she prefers the moment when she first held her baby to the labour itself! She chose this day because of the intense love she felt for her baby.

▶ George's good day was being on a safari, seeing animals in the wild for the first time. He chose this because he loves being in contact with nature.

Values clarifier 2: A reaction you are proud of
Think of a time when you responded well to a challenge or difficulty in your life. Jot down briefly the situation and why you are proud of your reaction.

Example: Jamie was teased by his male colleagues because he was studying psychology. Rather than responding angrily, which would have escalated matters, he ignored the teasing and it soon stopped. He was pleased because he was able to exercise self-control and wisdom.

Values clarifier 3: Who do you admire?
Pick someone, real or fictional, famous or unknown, who you particularly admire. Write down their name and the qualities you admire them for.

Example: Nelson Mandela for his qualities of courage and forgiveness

Values clarifier 4: Three months to live
If you had only three (healthy) months to live, how would you spend the time? What would you do? What would you stop doing? What does this tell you about your values?

Example: Jane realizes that she would want to do two things: spend more time with her friends, and fulfil her long-cherished wish to visit Asia. She decides she would quit her job, and in the first month see all her friends – close friends on a one-to-one basis, other friends in groups. In an ideal world one or more of her friends would decide to travel with her. She would then go for a month on her travels to Asia. In the final month, she would return home and again spend time with close friends and family. She would also read her favourite books and watch her favourite films one last time.

Try it now: Identifying your most important values

First, jot down your answers to the four values clarification exercises above. Then look at the list of values below and put a cross against values that connect with your answers to the exercises. Finally, put a cross against any other values you personally think are important.

Add to the list any values important to you that are not on the list.

Acceptance	Brilliance	Curiosity
Accomplishment	Calmness	Daring
Achievement	Carefulness	Decisiveness
Adventure	Certainty	Dependability
Affection	Challenge	Determination
Altruism	Cheerfulness	Dignity
Ambition	Cleverness	Diligence
Amusement	Commitment	Discipline
Appreciation	Common sense	Discovery
Art	Compassion	Diversity
Assertiveness	Competence	Duty
Autonomy	Competition	Ecstasy
Awareness	Confidence	Education
Awe	Conformity	Efficiency
Balance	Connection	Emotional intelligence
Beauty	Conservation	Empathy
Being the best	Consistency	Encouragement
Belonging	Contentment	Endurance
Benevolence	Contribution	Energy
Bliss	Cooperation	Enjoyment
Boldness	Courage	Enthusiasm
Bravery	Creativity	Environmentalism

Excellence
Excitement
Experience
Expertise
Exploration
Extroversion
Fairness
Faith
Fame
Family
Fashion
Fidelity
Financial
independence
Fitness
Flexibility
Flow
Forgiveness
Freedom
Friendship
Fulfilling my potential
Fun
Generosity
Genuineness
Gratitude
Gregariousness
Happiness
Hard work
Harmony
Having a family
Health
Helpfulness
Helping society
Heroism
Honesty

Honour
Hopefulness
Humility
Humour
Imagination
Impartiality
Independence
Individuality
Industry
Innovation
Insightfulness
Integrity
Intellect
Intelligence
Intimate relationships
Intuition
Inventiveness
Joy
Justice
Kindness
Knowledge
Leadership
Learning
Legacy
Liberty
Liveliness
Logic
Loved (being loved)
Loving (being loving)
Loving humanity
Loyalty
Making a difference
Marriage
Mastery
Meaning

Mercy
Mindfulness
Modesty
Motivation
Nature
Non-conformity
Obedience
Open-mindedness
Optimism
Order
Originality
Passion
Patience
Patriotism
Peace
Perfection
Perceptiveness
Persistence
Personal growth
Perspective
Persuasiveness
Philanthropy
Piety
Playfulness
Pleasure
Popularity
Power
Pragmatism
Pride
Privacy
Proactivity
Prudence
Punctuality
Purpose
Rationality

Contd.

Realism	Sensuality	Tradition
Recognition	Serenity	Tranquillity
Reflection	Service	Transcendence
Relationships	Sharing	Trust
Relaxation	Significance	Truth
Reliability	Simplicity	Understanding
Religiousness	Sincerity	Usefulness
Reputation	Social intelligence	Variety
Resilience	Solitude	Vision
Respect	Spirituality	Volunteering
Responsibility	Spontaneity	Warm-heartedness
Science	Stability	Wealth
Security	Status	Winning
Self-actualization	Strength	Wisdom
Self-awareness	Structure	Wonder
Self-control	Success	Work
Self-direction	Sympathy	Zest
Self-reliance	Teamwork	
Self-respect	Thoroughness	

Step 2: Reflecting on your values

Having identified your key personal values, the next stage in values clarification is to reflect on your chosen values and to prioritize them. In practice, this means reducing the number of values to a manageable level.

While other values clarification processes recognize that reflecting on values is important, they have not integrated ideas from positive psychology into the process. In this section we will see how research findings from psychology can help you arrive at wiser values.

Intrinsic values are to be preferred to extrinsic values

Deci and Ryan's (1985) self-determination theory predicts that extrinsic goals for things like wealth, fame and looks lead to worse outcomes than intrinsic goals for things like meaningful relationships and personal growth. Research studies carried out among students support their theory. [33] Deci and Ryan also suggest that values should be owned by you. This means that you really identify with your chosen values, as opposed to choosing them because everyone else does.

WIST values are associated with meaning and purpose

Robert Emmons' work on personal strivings [34] concludes that some values have a positive association with meaning, purpose and well-being while others have a negative association. He uses the acronym WIST to help remember the positive values. WIST stands for:

W – work, including achievement and commitment

I – intimacy, including close relationships, trust and being helpful

S – spirituality, including religion and being part of a religious community

T – transcendence, being concerned with other people, the community, the future and generally the world beyond oneself.

On the other hand, values connected with power, wanting to influence, financial success, social recognition, physical attractiveness and wanting to control or dominate people are associated with negative emotions and lower life satisfaction.

Choose values that actually enhance your well-being, rather than values that reflect desires which will not improve your well-being when they are satisfied

The brain has two different systems relating to liking and wanting (Nettle, 2005). Though we often want something and like it once we have it, this is not always the case. Addictions are a classic example. Cigarette smokers want to smoke far more than they actually like the experience. Barry Schwartz (2005), writing about the paradox of choice, provides another good example of wanting something that does not actually improve well-being. We tend to want more choice, but actually too much choice wastes time and increases regret at the possibility of making the wrong choice. So having a lot of options and choice is not a wise value. When reflecting on our values, we should consider whether attaining a particular value would in actual fact improve our well-being.

Getting a wise balance between both our short- and long-term interests and our interests and the general good

Applying Robert Sternberg's (1998) balance theory of wisdom (see the 'Psychological theories of wisdom' in Chapter 11) to values, you should ask whether your list of most important values satisfies these two criteria: values that positively harm other people should be treated with suspicion and your list of values should be balanced.

Putting all this together, the following list can help you decide on your most important and wisest values.

▶ Is this an intrinsic value?

▶ Is this a WIST (work, intimacy, spiritual or transcendent) value?

▶ Do I have evidence that attaining this value increases my well-being?

▶ Is this mainly in my short-term or long-term interests, or both?

▶ How does this affect me? How does it affect other people?

Try it now: Reflecting on and choosing your top values

Having read the above ideas drawn from psychology about how to prioritize your values, ask yourself the questions in relation to each of the values you originally selected in step 1. You should end up with (about) six values that are both important to you and take into account research about how to choose values. If you end up with more than five or six values, then to keep it manageable it is good practice to combine related values.

This is illustrated in the table opposite by Sharon's reflection on her values. Sharon is a recently divorced woman who we will learn more about in the case study later in this chapter.

Example: Sharon's reflections on her top values

Value	Is this an intrinsic value?	Is this a WIST value (work, intimacy, spiritual or transcendent)?	Do I have evidence that attaining the value increases my well-being?	Is this mainly in my short-term or long-term interests or both?	How does this affect me? How does it affect other people?	Put an X here if the value is to be included in your top 6 values
Learning		Work	Yes, university	Both	Good for me, may help others	X
Autonomy			Yes, university			
Friendship	Very much me	Intimacy	Yes, university and later	Both	Good for me, may help others	X
Resilience				Both, but definitely need it now	Good for me, may help others	X
Positivity				Both, but definitely need it now	Good for me, will help others	X
Hope				Both, but definitely need it now		X
Fulfilling my potential		Work		More future	Good for me, may help others	
Happiness				Both		
Cheerfulness				Especially now	Will help others too	
Being constructive			Yes, at other difficult times	Both	Good for me, may help others	X
Daring	Very much me			Now – perhaps need to be aware of risks		X
Benevolence		Transcendent		Both	Mainly others	
Education	Very much me	Work	Yes, university	Both		X
Conservation		Transcendent			Me and others	X
Tranquillity					Mainly me, doesn't harm others	
Nature	Very much me	Transcendent			Me and others	X
Making a difference		Transcendent			Mainly others	
Relationships		Intimacy	Sometimes	Intimate relationships maybe not so much now	Mainly others	

Key idea: Positive psychology can help people reflect on their values wisely

Values clarification can be enhanced by drawing on psychological research into which values enhance well-being. This can help people reflect on their values to make them wiser.

▶ Step 3: Realizing your values

Having chosen your most important values, the final step is to put them into practice. Insight about values is good, but will not make any difference unless it changes what you do. That is why this step, where you build up your motivation to change and decide which values to focus on, is crucial.

An evidence-based strategy that can help boost motivation as well as hope, optimism and planning is the 'Best possible self' exercise. A study by Laura King (2001) suggests that doing this exercise for just four days can increase SWB significantly and that the effects lasted at least five months.

'Best possible self' exercise

Think about what you expect your life to be one, five or ten years from now. Visualize a future for yourself in which everything has turned out the way you wanted. You have tried your best, worked hard and achieved all your goals. Now describe in writing what you imagine.

It is recommended to try doing this on four days in the next week, using different areas of your life (e.g. career, relationships and recreation) and/or different timeframes on each day.

Another useful tip, adapted from acceptance and commitment therapy (ACT), is to concentrate on those values where there is the biggest shortfall at the moment between actual and potential.

Create a table similar to the one below.

Value	Actual	Potential
Love		
Friendship		
Serenity		
Trust		
Humour		
Values realization		

Give each value a rating out of 10 in terms of how much you are actually living it and how much you could potentially be living it in the next week. Add a third column headed 'Discrepancy' and calculate the difference between actual and potential for each value.

For example:

Value	Actual	Potential	Discrepancy
Love	6	7	1
Friendship	5	8	3
Serenity	7	8	1
Trust	7	7	0
Humour	6	8	2

Which value has the largest discrepancy between actual and potential? This is the value you will work on realizing next week.

Every day next week, do something you would not otherwise have done to try to satisfy your chosen value. For example, in the table above there is a discrepancy of 3 for friendship. The action plan could be to text a friend whom you would not have texted otherwise.

You will learn about another powerful way to implement your values, step-by-step planning, in Chapter 5.

Case study: Sharon's values clarification

Sharon is recently divorced, in her early 50s with no children, working as an events organizer. She joined a positive psychology class because she was interested in turning over to a new positive chapter in her life. She approached the values clarification exercises enthusiastically. The day she chose as a good day was the day she first went to university, which for her connected with the values of learning, autonomy and friendship. She was proud of her reaction to her divorce. By taking this course she was letting bygones be bygones and looking to the future. This reaction exemplified hope, positivity and being constructive. Her choice of whom she admired was the author J.K. Rowling, because she believed in herself and persisted in doing what she believed in spite of difficulties, and also did good for the world (both through enjoyment of her books and charity).

Sharon had a long original list of values. She whittled it down to 18: learning, autonomy, friendship, resilience, positivity, hope, fulfilling potential, happiness, cheerfulness, being constructive, daring, benevolence, education, conservation, tranquillity, nature, making a difference and relationships.

Sharon reduced these to ten key values using the table in step 2. She chose learning, friendship, resilience, positivity, hope, daring, conservation, nature, being constructive and education. She reduced this to six by combining similar values, so ended up with: learning and education; friendship; being constructive and resilience; positivity and hope; nature and conservation; daring.

Moving on to step 3 and realizing values, she carried out the 'Best possible self' exercise for four days, focusing on different areas of her life. This is what she wrote when thinking about how she would like her life to be in five years' time.

'I will be working in a business promoting nature and conservation. I will be using my organizational skills in my work, and will be earning a living doing something I believe in. I will also be using my love of learning; perhaps the business will involve helping people learn about conservation and nature. I imagine myself feeling enthusiastic and feeling that I am doing something really useful with my life. I am not sure where I will be located. My marriage tied me to the London area, but now I am free to work wherever I want. Thinking of the prospect of this work, I feel really motivated to taking the first step right away!'

When she did the discrepancies exercises, Sharon realized she was already being constructive with regard to learning by doing the course. However, friendship and being daring needed to be prioritized. She resolved to meet up with friends, especially those who might be interested in a daring business venture promoting nature and conservation.

Key idea: Why do values clarification?

Values clarification is part of several evidence-based therapies, including acceptance and commitment therapy. It can help people understand their values better, make their values wiser and plan how to satisfy them.

According to some philosophical theories of well-being, including the informed preference satisfaction theory, this process can help to increase well-being.

Flourishing: 'objective list' theories of well-being

The values clarification approach goes naturally with philosophical theories of well-being that begin with the individual's stated values followed by attempts, by a process of reflection, to make these personal values wiser. A second approach to well-being is to start, instead, by considering what makes life in general go well for human beings. This notion of well-being is often called 'flourishing'. Its supporters believe that just as a plant needs water and nutrients to flourish, so human beings need to live in a certain way to flourish.[35]

Like the informed preference satisfaction theory, flourishing is not just about feeling good. Its main difference from the informed preference satisfaction theory is that it argues that well-being does not depend on what an individual thinks is important in life. According to flourishing, these things are objectively important, regardless of what an individual thinks.

Key idea: What is flourishing?

Flourishing is an objective notion of well-being. Flourishing is more than just feeling good, and it is not dependent on what people happen to value. It is said to consist of the satisfaction of a number of objectively valid values and virtues.

We will consider three theories of flourishing: Seligman's original 'authentic happiness' theory, Seligman's later PERMA theory and Carol Ryff's theory of psychological well-being (PWB).

Seligman originally proposed that well-being had three parts: the pleasant life, the engaged life and the meaningful life. He later revised this by adding two more components: relationships and achievement (or accomplishment).

Key idea: PERMA

In his book *Flourish*, Seligman proposes the PERMA theory of flourishing. This supersedes his earlier 'authentic happiness' theory of flourishing. PERMA stands for:

▶ Positive emotion
▶ Engagement (or flow)
▶ Relationships
▶ Meaning and purpose
▶ Achievement and accomplishment.

In this book there is a chapter devoted to each component of PERMA (positive emotion is covered in our Chapter 1, Happiness and positive emotions), so you will have plenty of opportunity to learn about the nature of PERMA and how to attain it. PERMA is an attractive theory of well-being, but that is not to say that it is not without problems. One potential difficulty with PERMA is that it does not question an individual's own view about whether their life is positively meaningful. If someone gets PERMA from torturing animals, then, according to PERMA theory, that is acceptable. Seligman himself gives the example of Osama Bin Laden as someone who could well have had PERMA. This difficulty could be overcome if PERMA added wisdom as a requirement, since wisdom includes a notion of what is right and wrong.

Remember this: Osama Bin Laden could have had PERMA

PERMA can be reached as long as an individual has a sense of meaning or purpose and as long as they feel positive emotions. It deliberately excludes any ethical components.

Seligman's authentic happiness and PERMA are not the only psychological theories of flourishing. A third theory is Carol Ryff's theory of psychological well-being. It has six components:

► self-acceptance (positive evaluation of oneself and one's life)

► personal growth

► purpose in life

► positive relations with others

► environmental mastery (the capacity to effectively manage one's life and the surrounding environment)

► autonomy.

Psychological well-being shares with PERMA the values of 'purpose in life' and 'positive relations' but adds four new, plausible, conditions for flourishing. For example, it seems sensible to suggest that environmental mastery is an important part of flourishing, yet it is not in PERMA. This highlights a problem with flourishing; there is no one universally agreed theory about its components.

We have considered three theories; many more are possible. In fact, you could make up your own theory of flourishing by listing your own chosen list of values and virtues from the table of values and virtues listed earlier in the chapter.

Remember this: There is no agreed list of the components of flourishing

There is no universal agreement about the constituents of flourishing. In positive psychology, the three main theories overlap but also differ in important respects.

Which theory of well-being is best?

We have now looked at three types of theories of well-being: hedonism, the informed preference satisfaction theory and flourishing. Hedonism is too narrow a theory; it includes feeling good but not doing well or being good. The informed preference satisfaction theory and flourishing are both an improvement on hedonism. Seligman's presentation of PERMA makes it open to the 'Osama Bin Laden' objection. This could, however, be overcome by including wisdom as a component of flourishing.[36]

But should we accept the informed preference satisfaction theory or should we accept flourishing? In fact, it is possible that in practice the two theories may not deliver such different results. The process of values clarification, because it includes a strong element of considering which values are wise, will deliver a list of values and virtues that help the individual flourish. The big advantage of flourishing theories, from the perspective of positive psychology, is that we can then move on to define each element precisely and develop evidence-based strategies to bring more of it into our lives. This is precisely what we will do in the rest of the book. There is a chapter on each of the elements of PERMA and, because it has been argued that it is the 'missing ingredient' in PERMA, one on wisdom too.

Focus points

✶ The experience-machine thought experiment implies that hedonism is too narrow a theory of well-being.

✶ The informed preference satisfaction theory is a better theory because it can take into account wanting to do good things and be a good person as well as feeling good.

✶ Values clarification is a process by which an individual can clarify, reflect upon and plan to achieve their important values.

✶ Flourishing is a more objective theory of well-being that lists a number of qualities that are said to constitute the good life of a human being.

✶ PERMA, psychological well-being and Seligman's authentic happiness are three theories of flourishing in positive psychology.

Diagnostic test answers

1 The experience machine.

2 If it is based on an unacceptable theory of well-being it will not be accepted widely and may do harm.

3 The informed preference satisfaction theory.

4 Values clarification.

5 Intrinsic goals include meaningful relationships and personal growth.

   External goals include fame, money and physical attractiveness.

6 WIST stands for work, intimacy and spiritual and transcendent values.

7 PERMA.

8 Relationships and achievement (or accomplishment).

9 Self-acceptance, personal growth, purpose in life, positive relations with others, environmental mastery and autonomy.

10 It has been argued that wisdom is a key value, although you could also have included other values from the table of values and virtues.

Next steps

In subsequent chapters we will be looking at all the elements of PERMA. Before then we will explore the positive psychology of strengths, which forms the foundations for many of the ideas to enhance well-being and flourishing. Chapter 5 includes more ideas on how to achieve your values, including step-by-step planning.

4

Strengths

In this chapter you will learn:

▶ *how to identify your strengths*

▶ *about three strengths inventories*

▶ *about evidence that focusing on strengths is beneficial*

▶ *about objections to using strengths too naïvely*

▶ *how to use strengths wisely.*

Diagnostic test

1 Name three different strengths inventories developed by psychologists.

2 Name three benefits of identifying and developing your strengths.

3 Roughly how many people had taken the VIA online test by July 2013? Is it a) 50,000 b) 500,000 c) over a million people?

4 What precisely is the intervention based on VIA strengths which has been shown to have a lasting benefit?

5 What are the six virtues listed in the VIA strength classification?

6 Which of the inventories is most specifically designed for use in business?

7 According to Gallup, what is the difference between a talent and a strength?

8 What are the four quadrants of CAPP's Realise2 strengths model?

9 In the CAPP scheme, what is the difference between a strength and a learned behaviour?

10 Name three possible problems with using the strengths inventories too naïvely.

Why strengths?

Are you fully aware of all your good points, talents and skills? Are you regularly using your strengths in pursuit of what matters most to you? Could becoming more mindful of your strengths and using them more improve your work or personal life?

The psychologists who developed the 'positive psychology of strengths', of whom Chris Peterson, Martin Seligman, Ryan Niemiec, Alex Linley, Donald Clifton, Marcus Buckingham and Tim Rath are among the most eminent, argue that for many people the answers to the first two questions are 'No' and to the third a resounding 'Yes'.

The positive psychology of strengths aims to provide a technology for identifying and measuring strengths, as well as an evidence base for interventions designed to enable you to use your strengths fruitfully.

What are your strengths?

Alex Linley, a leading British strengths psychologist, has suggested ten questions to help you identify your strengths. You might like to consider these questions with different areas of your life, such as work, recreation and daily tasks, in mind.[37]

Try it now: What are your strengths?

1 What do you remember doing well in childhood?
2 When do you feel the most energized?
3 When do you feel most like the 'real you'?
4 What activities come naturally to you?
5 What do you usually pay attention to?
6 What do you learn quickly?
7 What do you do just because you like doing it?
8 What do you talk passionately about?
9 What do you say you love doing?
10 What never makes it to a 'to do' list (because it gets done automatically)?

Adapted from Linley, A., *Average to A+: Realizing Strengths in Yourself and Others*

These questions are a good starting point to identifying your strengths. However, positive psychology aims to go beyond the type of discussion of strengths you might have with a life coach[38] by providing classifications of strengths, enabling more precise measurement and a shared vocabulary. We will consider three of the most well-known such classifications: VIA-IS, Strengthsfinder 2.0 and Realise2.

Key idea: Strengths

In positive psychology, strengths are considered as important or more so than weaknesses. Positive psychologists have developed a number of classifications to help you identify and measure your strengths.

THE VIA STRENGTHS CHARACTER CLASSIFICATION – 'A MANUAL OF THE SANITIES'

A manual, the DSM[39], exists to help psychiatrists classify psychological ailments and plan appropriate treatment. Wouldn't it be great if a manual existed to help people identify their good qualities? Such thinking led to the creation of the 'values in action inventory of strengths' (VIA-IS), a positive version of the DSM. Its creators, Chris Peterson and Martin Seligman, recruited a large team of researchers to conduct a literature search of the most universally valued qualities. They came up with six, namely:

▶ wisdom and knowledge – qualities useful to acquire and use knowledge

▶ courage – overcoming difficulties

▶ humanity and love – interpersonal strengths

▶ justice – living well in a community

▶ temperance – to protect against excess

▶ transcendence – connecting with what is larger than us.

This list looks plausible, sharing similarities with traditional lists of virtues (such as the four cardinal virtues of Ancient Greece, namely practical wisdom, self-control, courage and justice). The virtues seemed to the VIA team to be a bit too vague and broad, so they broke them down into 24 specific character strengths. Below is the full VIA-IS classification.

The VIA Classification of Character Strengths

....

1. **Wisdom and knowledge** – cognitive strengths that entail the acquisition and use of knowledge

   - **Creativity** (originality, ingenuity): thinking of novel and productive ways to conceptualize and do things; includes artistic achievement but is not limited to it

   - **Curiosity** (interest, novelty-seeking, openness to experience): taking an interest in on-going experience for its own sake; finding subjects and topics fascinating; exploring and discovering

   - **Judgment** (open-mindedness; critical thinking): thinking things through and examining them from all sides; not jumping to conclusions; being able to change one's mind in light of evidence; weighing all evidence fairly

   - **Love of learning**: mastering new skills, topics and bodies of knowledge, whether on one's own or formally; related to the strength of curiosity but goes beyond it to describe the tendency to add systematically to what one knows

- **Perspective** (wisdom): being able to provide wise counsel to others; having ways of looking at the world that make sense to oneself/others

2. **Courage** – emotional strengths that involve the exercise of will to accomplish goals in the face of opposition, external or internal

   - **Bravery** (valour): not shrinking from threat, challenge, difficulty or pain; speaking up for what's right even if there's opposition; acting on convictions even if unpopular; includes physical bravery but is not limited to it

   - **Perseverance** (persistence, industriousness): finishing what one starts; persevering in a course of action in spite of obstacles; 'getting it out the door'; taking pleasure in completing tasks

   - **Honesty** (authenticity, integrity): speaking the truth but more broadly presenting oneself in a genuine way and acting in a sincere way; being without pretence; taking responsibility for one's feelings and actions

   - **Zest** (vitality, enthusiasm, vigour, energy): approaching life with excitement and energy; not doing things halfway or half-heartedly; living life as an adventure; feeling alive and activated

3. **Humanity** – interpersonal strengths that involve tending and befriending others

   - **Love** (capacity to love and be loved): valuing close relations with others, in particular those in which sharing and caring are reciprocated; being close to people

   - **Kindness** (generosity, nurturing, care, compassion, altruistic love, 'niceness'): doing favours and good deeds for others; helping them; taking care of them

   - **Social intelligence** (emotional intelligence, personal intelligence): being aware of the motives/feelings of others and oneself; knowing what to do to fit into different social situations; knowing what makes other people tick

4. **Justice** – civic strengths that underlie healthy community life

   - **Teamwork** (citizenship, social responsibility, loyalty): working well as a member of a group or team; being loyal to the group; doing one's share

   - **Fairness**: treating all people the same according to notions of fairness and justice; not letting feelings bias decisions about others; giving everyone a fair chance

   - **Leadership**: encouraging a group of which one is a member to get things done and at the same time maintain good relations within the group; organizing group activities and seeing that they happen.

5. **Temperance** – strengths that protect against excess

   - **Forgiveness** (mercy): forgiving those who have done wrong; accepting others' shortcomings; giving people a second chance; not being vengeful

   - **Humility** (modesty): letting one's accomplishments speak for themselves; not regarding oneself as more special than one is

   - **Prudence**: being careful about one's choices; not taking undue risks; not saying or doing things that might later be regretted

   - **Self-regulation** (self-control): regulating what one feels and does; being disciplined; controlling one's appetites and emotions

6. **Transcendence** – strengths that forge connections to the universe and provide meaning

   - **Appreciation of beauty and excellence** (awe, wonder, elevation): noticing and appreciating beauty, excellence, and/or skilled performance in various domains of life, from nature to art to mathematics to science to everyday experience

- **Gratitude**: being aware of and thankful for the good things that happen; taking time to express thanks
- **Hope** (optimism, future-mindedness, future orientation): expecting the best in the future and working to achieve it; believing that a good future is something that can be brought about
- **Humour** (playfulness): liking to laugh and tease; bringing smiles to other people; seeing the light side; making (not necessarily telling) jokes
- **Spirituality** (religiousness, faith, purpose): having coherent beliefs about the higher purpose and meaning of the universe; knowing where one fits within the larger scheme; having beliefs about the meaning of life that shape conduct and provide comfort

Try it now: Do the VIA survey and identify your top strengths

Take the 120-item inventory test for free at www.viame.org. You will be given a free report on your top 24 strengths in order. The website requires registration and offers the opportunity to pay for a detailed analysis of your strengths and recommendations.

If you do not have immediate access to a computer, read the list above and put an asterisk against those you feel apply to you most.

The online questionnaire gives you feedback about your top strengths. You are advised to look at your top strengths and ask yourself the following.

When I use this top strength, do I:

▶ feel good and energized, even excited

▶ feel motivated to use it in a variety of ways

▶ own it

▶ feel authentic?

If you can answer 'yes' to most of these questions, then you have identified a signature strength.

Key idea: Signature strengths

A signature strength is a top strength which feels like it is the real you and energizes you. VIA recommends that you identify your signature strengths and use them more in all areas of life.

Case study: Using strengths to overcome procrastination and anxiety

Jason was doing well at college until he was forced to take a business law class. He found the work difficult and put off doing assignments until the last minute. He got low grades, became increasingly anxious, procrastinated more, got still lower grades and became sufficiently anxious to need to see a therapist. Jason seemed well and truly locked into a vicious cycle of anxiety, procrastination and poor performance.

Jason's therapist conceptualized the problem as one of a lack of engagement. Jason completed the VIA strength survey and humour came out as one of his top strengths. In conversation, it was clear that two other strengths (not measured by VIA) were important to Jason, namely being playful and being competitive. The question Jason and his counsellor pondered was how he could use these strengths to make his courses more engaging.

The answer was both simple and ingenious. Jason came up with an idea to turn the boring and difficult law assignment into a fun competition. He and two friends would study for two hours independently and then set each other quizzes. They would then go out for a meal together and the winner would get a free dessert as a prize. Within a few weeks, Jason was enjoying studying. As his anxiety and procrastination diminished, his grades improved.

Source: 'Positive Psychology and Therapy' by Park, N., Peterson, C. and Brunwasser, S. in *Cognitive Behavioural Theories in Clinical Practice*, Kazantzis, N. et al. (2010)

GALLUP'S STRENGTHSFINDER 2.0 – IDENTIFYING AND APPLYING TALENTS FOR ENHANCED WORK PERFORMANCE

The Gallup organization, best known for its opinion polls, has also worked in the field of consultancy for over four decades. Back in 1998 Donald Clifton, CEO of Gallup and a pioneer of the strengths movement, led a team which analysed over 2 million interviews with professionals, looking to answer the question: 'When people in the workplace succeed, what qualities make it happen?'

Clifton identified 34 qualities which he judged to be most important, such as looking for areas of agreement ('harmony'), liking to think ('intellection') and pursuing excellence ('maximizing').

The latest version of Gallup's inventory, StrengthsFinder 2.0, includes talents themes such as 'woo' (connecting quickly with people) and 'ideation' (coming up with new ideas and concepts). You can find the complete list in Rath (2007).

These qualities are termed 'talent themes' because you need to acquire knowledge, develop skills and practise using them before they can be called strengths, which are defined as 'the ability to consistently provide near perfect performance' (Rath, 2007). Strengths, it is suggested, are built when raw talents are consolidated with an investment in skills acquisition and practice.

For example, suppose you have the 'learning' talent theme. You could develop this into a strength by reading this book, thereby acquiring knowledge about positive psychology. You would also need to think about how to apply what you have learned at work and may need to develop new skills to put it into practice, such as the skill of persuasion so your manager agrees to let you try out some of the ideas.

In Rath (2007), the author gives several 'ideas for action' for each of the 34 StrengthsFinder 2.0 talent themes.

Try it now: What talents do you have?

You do not have to be constrained by the Realise2 list – think of talents you had when you were young, which people have complimented you on or which you are proud of. The talents could be for practical skills, sporting skills or character qualities. Write these down.

Having written your list, next consider how much investment you have put into these talents. Could it be worth expending more effort on developing some more of your latent talents into strengths?

Evidence that a strengths-based approach is beneficial

There is growing evidence that identifying your strengths and using them more can enhance well-being and improve performance. Highlights from the research include the following.

▶ Using VIA signature strengths in a new way for one week was found to increase happiness and reduce depression in an internet-recruited sample of people compared with a control group. The effects lasted six months. Note, however, that the effects endured only if participants were told to use a chosen signature strength in a different and new way each day rather than if they were just told to use strengths more (Seligman, Steen, Park and Peterson, 2005).

▶ People who use their strengths more have higher levels of self-efficacy (Govindji and Linley, 2007) and self-esteem (Minhas, 2010).

▶ Using strengths can help achieve goals (Linley, Nielsen, Wood, Gillett and Biswas-Diener, 2010).

▶ Focusing on strengths improves performance at work (Corporate Leadership Council, 2002).

Key idea: Strengths identification

Identifying and using strengths has been shown to have significant and lasting benefits, including increasing happiness, reducing d depression and enhancing work performance.

However, not all studies support the view that using strengths more has a significant, lasting and distinct benefit. For example, one study found that although using two signature strengths resulted in increased happiness compared with a control group, so too did working on a signature strengths and a weakness (Rust, Diessner and Reade, 2009). This casts some doubt on the idea that working on strengths is more beneficial than working on weaknesses. Perhaps the important thing is to be doing something different, regardless of whether it is using a strength or improving a weakness. More research is needed regarding this question.

CAPP'S REALISE2 – IDENTIFYING AND USING UNREALIZED STRENGTHS
We have already come across the work of Alex Linley, founder of the Centre for Applied Positive Psychology (CAPP), when looking at identifying strengths. In Linley (2009) he poses a number of questions which he believes are raised by VIA-IS and StrengthsFinder.

1 What if your main strength is not identified by an inventory? Are the 24 VIA strengths or the 34 StrengthsFinder talent themes enough?

2 Is a strength really a strength if using it depletes you?

3 Should there be a difference in your approach between strengths that you already use a lot and strengths that you use very little?

4 What is the best policy in dealing with weaknesses?

CAPP's Realise2 inventory aims to overcome these difficulties. Realise2 lists as many as 60 strengths (overcoming objection 1) according to the three dimensions of energy, performance and use. It reclassifies strengths that deplete you as 'learned behaviours' (dealing with objection 2) and discourages their use. Furthermore, Realise2 distinguishes between realized and unrealized strengths and encourages more emphasis on realizing the unrealized strengths (dealing with objection 3). It does not euphemistically call weaknesses 'bottom strengths' as VIA does (overcoming objection 4) and provides some detailed ideas about how to deal with them. The Realise2 four-quadrant model is shown below.

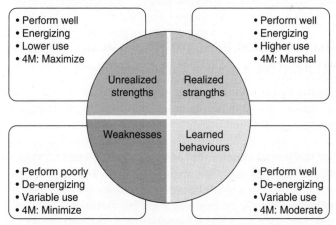

- Perform well
- Energizing
- Lower use
- 4M: Maximize

Unrealized strengths

Realized strangths

- Perform well
- Energizing
- Higher use
- 4M: Marshal

Weaknesses

Learned behaviours

- Perform poorly
- De-energizing
- Variable use
- 4M: Minimize

- Perform well
- De-energizing
- Variable use
- 4M: Moderate

The Realise2 four-quadrant model (source: www.cappeu.com)

The Realise2 four-quadrant model is also called the 4Ms model, because of the specific advice given regarding how to treat each quadrant (Linley et al, 2010) as follows:

▶ Realized strengths: *marshal* their use towards achieving your goals, use them to compensate for your weaknesses but do not overuse them.

▶ Unrealized strengths: *maximize* their use, looking for new opportunities to practise them and keep practising them.

▶ Learned behaviours: *moderate* their use, perhaps by delegation or creating 'strengths sandwiches' (a learned behaviour sandwiched by strengths).

▶ Weaknesses: *minimize* their use, for example by changing your role or by working with people who complement your weaknesses. If necessary, undertake training to improve your performance.

Having learned about Linley's objections to the naïve use of strengths which he believes are rectified in the Realise2 model, we will now look at two other objections, namely that you may not be the best judge of your own strengths and that good judgement is required to use strengths.

Are you the best judge of your strengths and weaknesses?

Positive psychologist Ilona Boniwell has cast doubt on the reliability of our own judgement regarding our strengths and weaknesses (Boniwell, 2012). She recalls how optimism came out as one of her top VIA strengths, and yet friends said that she was one of the most pessimistic people they knew. More universally, psychologists speak about a social desirability bias in self-reports, meaning that respondents tend to overstate desirable qualities and underestimate less desirable ones. To overcome such a bias and blind spots regarding our own strengths and weaknesses in general, it is an extremely good idea to enlist one or more people who know you well to verify the findings of the strengths inventories. It is suggested you try the following two activities

▶ Ask friends, colleagues or relatives to identify three strengths and also one weakness, giving evidence for each.

▶ Show them your results from your strengths inventory and ask them whether they agree.

Should you be using your strengths more *often* or more *wisely*?

Although positive psychology often cites the ancient philosopher Aristotle as an inspiration (e.g. Seligman, 2002), Aristotle's views about virtues are very different from those expressed in VIA-IS and StrengthsFinder. [40] Two key ideas for Aristotle are that practical wisdom (*phronesis*) is a foundational virtue, without which you cannot really have the other virtues, and that virtue lies in a golden mean between two excesses. We will look at each of these ideas in turn in relation to strengths.

Practical wisdom means understanding the situation we are in, what matters most and being able to find the appropriate action to achieve what matters most. Without practical wisdom, Aristotle would argue, applying 'strengths' could be rather hazardous. Imagine that you are going on holiday, and as a special treat you are invited to meet your pilot in the cockpit. He smiles warmly, shakes your hand and informs you that it is very sunny at your destination and he hopes that you and your family will have a wonderful holiday. You might guess that optimism was one of the pilot's strengths, and you would be spot on. So far he has been using his optimism appropriately, combining it with social intelligence to make you feel good about your holiday. But suppose that you hear an unusual noise coming from the engine. 'Nothing to worry about,' he reassures you. You feel a little uneasy, but that is nothing to what you feel when you see black smoke. The pilot brushes it off: 'Not sure what that is, but let's hope it's OK.' Would you want to stay on the plane? Aristotle would argue that the pilot has been using his optimism strength inappropriately; he lacked the practical wisdom to understand the situation and to do what mattered.

Connected to Aristotle's idea that practical wisdom is a requirement is his theory of the golden mean. We already know that Aristotle would not have thought that any of the strengths listed in the classifications were always strengths; it depends on the context. He further believed that either an excess or a deficiency of a quality was not a virtue but a vice.

It is important to realize that the problem is not confined to optimism. Should you use your humour strength when someone has told you some sad news? How about persistence once it is clear that the task is either too difficult or not worth the additional effort required? Even fairness can be problematic if it conflicts with total well-being (for example, a fair tax may lead to a brain-drain and reduce the total amount of income of a nation).

In short, Aristotle's theory of the mean is a very different theory from the view that strengths should be used as much as possible. Aristotle would argue that strengths have to be used wisely, and that depends on context. We will be returning to this theme in Chapter 11, Wisdom.

Remember this: Strengths should not be identified or used too naïvely

A review of Linley's objections and Aristotle's philosophy counsels against a naïve use of strengths. If we merely focus on using more of our top strength as identified by an inventory we may

* misidentify a strength (for example by relying on an inventory without getting feedback from others that it really is a strength)
* neglect weaknesses (as opposed to managing them)
* overuse a strength that does not energize us
* use a strength inappropriately (for example, an airline pilot being unwisely optimistic regarding an unusual engine noise).

Which strengths should you use?

The focus of all three inventories (VIA, StrengthsFinder 2.0 and Realise2) is essentially person-centred, in the sense that they emphasize identifying and using more of your strengths. We have just considered the possibility, based on Aristotle's view of practical wisdom, that context is at least as important, i.e. it is not just about using your strengths as much as you can, it is also about finding a good fit between your strengths and the situation. Consequently it is helpful to think about which strengths are most likely to bring about which sort of outcome.

For example, if you wanted to feel better (increase positive emotions), would you choose humour or self-regulation? What about if you were interested in achievement? There is a growing body of evidence linking specific strengths with outcomes. This is summarized in the table below.

This table needs to be interpreted carefully. An X indicates that there is evidence indicating a link between a particular strength and outcome; that does not necessarily indicate causation. The absence of an X (or the absence of a particular strength in the table) does not necessarily mean that the strength cannot be used to achieve that outcome; it just means that this particular literature search has not found empirical evidence to support this. However, it does suggest some interesting links between strengths and outcomes, and also implies that zest, hope and curiosity may be particularly important strengths.

Strength	Life satisfaction	Positive emotion	Engagement and flow	Meaning	Achievement and accomplishment
Zest	X	X	X	X	
Hope			X	X	X
Curiosity	X		X	X	
Gratitude				X	X
Love	X	X			
Persistence					
Perspective			X		
Social intelligence		X			
Fairness					
Self-regulation					X
Humour		X			
Religiousness				X	

Source: viapros.org

Remember this: Some strengths may have particular benefits

Although positive psychology tends to recommend using your signature strengths, not all strengths have the same benefits. There is good evidence that zest and hope are particularly beneficial. If these happen to be your strengths, the message from positive psychology is to use these strengths in more ways.

Which of the three inventories should you use?

Here are some comparisons between the inventories discussed.

▶ VIA is free, whereas the other two inventories have to be purchased.

▶ There is over ten years' research data supporting VIA.

▶ StrengthsFinder 2.0 is based on a huge amount of data, and there is some data to support its efficacy.

- Realise2 is relatively new and not so proven, but has a larger number of strengths and more sophisticated four-quadrant framework.

In short, all three are recommended – VIA is free, StrengthsFinder 2.0 has a business focus and Realise2 is a promising and more refined framework.

Remember this: Strengths inventories

In positive psychology there is not one but at least three well-known inventories of strengths. Each has their advantages and its probably a good idea to try all three.

Perhaps more important than the choice of inventory is the insight that you need to use an inventory wisely.

Key idea: How to use the positive psychology of strengths wisely

The argument from this chapter suggests the following points:

- Choose an inventory depending on your budget and whether it is mainly for personal or career development.
- Consider the inventory reports in the light of feedback from other people and other evidence.
- Consider which are your 'signature strengths', i.e. strengths that energize you and feel like the real you.
- Think about which strengths or potential strengths are underused, and brainstorm different ways to practise them and learn new skills or information to be able to use them.
- Consider what is important for you in life at the moment. What are your important goals for the next week? What values are most relevant? Which strengths might help you achieve them?
- Reflect on how to use your chosen strengths wisely. What is a skilful way to use each in your situation?[41]

Try it now: Using signature strengths in a new way

Work through the previous 'Key idea'. Pick one of the strengths you identified previously to use in the next week (this does not stop you using the others!).

With this one strength, your task is to use it each day in a way that you would not have done without having to do this activity. For example, if your chosen strength is love of learning, you might decide to read something on a subject that you have always wanted to find out about.

It is important that you do something extra as a result of this exercise, not something you would have done anyway.

You should also try to use the strength in a different way each day (do not do the same thing each day).

You might like to think about how you can combine using this strength with other strengths, as well as using this strength in a new way.

Focus points

✳ Identifying and using strengths has been shown to have significant and lasting benefits, including increasing happiness, reducing depression and enhancing work performance.

✳ Positive psychology considers using strengths as equally important to, if not more so than, managing weaknesses.

✳ There are a number of inventories to help you identify your strengths, including VIA-IS, StrengthsFinder 2.0 and Realise2. These recommend that you identify and use your signature strengths (VIA), develop your top talent themes into strengths (StrengthsFinder 2.0) and make more of your unrealized strengths (Realise2).

✳ There are a number of objections to the naïve use of strengths, including their misidentification, overuse and neglect of weaknesses.

✳ It is important to consider not just the identification and increased use of strengths, but also their wise use.

Diagnostic test answers

1 Values in action inventory of strengths (VIA-IS) developed by Peterson and Seligman; StrengthsFinder 2.0 developed by Gallup; Realise2 developed by CAPP.

2 The research described in this chapter suggests many benefits of using strengths, including increased happiness, less depression, better productivity and more self-efficacy.

3 c) Over a million people.

4 Using a top strength in a new and different way for a week increased happiness and reduced depression for six months. However, just using a top strength more often was not found to have such a significant and lasting benefit.

5 Wisdom and knowledge, courage, love and humanity, justice, temperance and transcendence.

6 Gallup's StrengthsFinder 2.0.

7 Talents are the raw materials that can be turned into strengths by developing skills, acquiring knowledge and practice.

8 Realized strengths, unrealized strengths, learned behaviours and weaknesses.

9 In Capp's terminology, a strength involves high performance, usage and energy. A learned behaviour is something you are good at but depletes you.

10 May misidentify a strength (for example by relying on an inventory without getting feedback from others that it really is a strength). May overuse a strength or use it inappropriately (for example an airline pilot being inappropriately optimistic regarding an unusual noise from the engine). May neglect weaknesses (as opposed to managing them). May overuse a strength that does not energize you (learned behaviours, in Realise2's terminology).

Next steps

The next chapters will look in detail at the elements of PERMA we have not yet considered: accomplishment and achievement, meaning and purpose, engagement (or flow) and relationships. We will look at wisdom, which it has been suggested is a vital component of well-being, in a later chapter.

5

Accomplishment and achievement

In this chapter you will learn:

- ► *how to become an expert*
- ► *about the importance of mindsets*
- ► *how optimism can be learned*
- ► *about a positive role for pessimism*
- ► *how to be hopeful*
- ► *about SMART goals and beyond*
- ► *how to make a step-by-step plan*
- ► *about the darker side of achievement.*

Diagnostic test

1 According to Ericsson's theory, which is more important in becoming an expert, innate talent or deliberate practice?

2 According to psychologists, on average how long does it take to become an expert?

3 What does SMART stand for in SMART goals?

4 According to Edwin Locke's goal theory, what four other criteria not included in SMART should we use when setting goals?

5 Martin Seligman's 'learned optimism' theory focuses on the 3Ps. What are the 3Ps?

6 Seligman's Met Life study showed that optimism helped which type of workers to be more effective?

7 According to Carol Dweck's theory, what are the two types of mindsets?

8 According to the psychology of hope, there are the two types of thinking that help us be more hopeful. What are they?

9 What is the name for a useful type of pessimism?

10 In using step-by-step planning, as well as looking at steps to take you towards your goal, what else should you consider?

In this chapter we will look at what psychology tells us about achievement and accomplishment.[42] This will take us on a tour of a number of important areas of positive psychology, including goals, hope, optimism and mindsets.

Is accomplishment due to nature or nurture?

Although many people assume that accomplishment is down to IQ or talent, a wave of research has attempted to demonstrate that nurture matters much more than nature.

One study (see Bloom, B. S. 1985) analysed the childhoods of 120 top performers in such diverse areas as sport, music and medicine. It concluded that outstanding success could not be attributed to IQ or other innate qualities. Three things distinguished the best performers: intense practice, good teachers and supportive parents. K. Anders Ericsson, a leading researcher on the nature of expertise, singles out deliberate practice as the most important factor. He concludes that, 'The differences between expert performers and normal adults reflect a life-long persistence of deliberate effort to improve performance.' (See Ericsson, A. et al. 2007)

Note that Ericsson states that it is deliberate practice that is crucial. Matthew Syed, a journalist and former champion table tennis player,[43] prefers the term purposeful practice. He suggests that to attain excellence you need to learn the right skills, accumulate knowledge and practise repeatedly. Syed recommends that to be a high achiever you should have a clear idea of both the standard you want to reach and what you need to do to get there. In sport, playing against slightly better players is a good idea; in the arts, learning from a mentor or role model.

Key idea: The Importance of deliberate (or purposeful) practice

A good performer becomes an excellent one through deliberate practice and good coaching. In order to attain excellence, these are more important than raw talent.

Psychologists have estimated the amount of practice required to attain expertise in any domain. Based on studies of sportspeople, scientists, writers and artists, it takes an average of ten years of deliberate practice to become an expert. Assuming about three hours a day, this translates to about ten thousand hours of deliberate practice.

Key idea: The ten-year rule

Psychologists have found that on average it takes ten years of practice to attain expertise.

Case study: The Polgar sisters

Laszlo Polgar wanted to prove that given the right nurturing anyone could be turned into a genius. In the 1960s he was just an obscure Hungarian educationalist having a hard time convincing the Communist regime that his theories were correct. He wanted them to adopt his policies; they suggested he see a psychiatrist. Polgar decided to prove his theories on his own children. First he had to recruit a wife willing to take part in such an unusual experiment. Then, when their first child, Susan, was born he had to choose a field in which he could enable her to excel. He chose chess partly because its rating system made it possible objectively to rate his child's success in a way which would be impossible for an artist, writer or even doctor.

Young Susan was delivered into a world where chess took centre stage. She was given toy chess pieces at an age when most little girls were given their first doll. Daily chess lessons with her father were made as entertaining as his skills as a teacher permitted. He made teaching his young daughter to play chess his life's work. When two sisters, Sofia and Judit, followed, they joined the family chess school. The Polgar sisters soon clocked up their ten thousand hours of deliberate practice. No one could deny that they had a skilled and enthusiastic mentor.

The result? Susan and Sofia became highly accomplished chess grandmasters. Judit Polgar, the youngest daughter, became by far the best female chess player of all time. Laszlo Polgar's experiment had succeeded beyond even his wildest expectations. Skilled mentoring and hours of deliberate practice had produced three of the best female chess players ever.

Does this research really prove that nurture is all that matters? It would be overstating the case to reach this conclusion. Remember that the research by Bloom and Ericsson proves that top performers practised more than average ones. It does not prove that an average performer could be turned into a genius by practice alone. What about the Polgar sisters though? While this is an impressive demonstration of the power of mentoring and practice, it is impossible to know how much genetic influences were at play.

Perhaps the Polgar sisters all had brains well suited to chess. Laszlo Polgar wanted to rule out this possibility by adopting a baby and making it into a chess grandmaster, but by then his wife had had enough of her husband's experiments. Marital harmony's gain was science's loss.

It would be utterly implausible to argue that genetics plays no part in expertise. Is someone who is seven feet (2.1m) tall more likely to be a successful basketball player or jockey? How about someone five feet (1.5m) tall? Yet height is mainly genetic. Could you perform well in the next Olympic 100m sprint if only you practised enough?

Martin Seligman provides a more balanced view when he suggests the following equation:

achievement = skill × effort.

Effort, it would appear, is a crucial part of expertise; skill is also important, and skill is partly learned and partly innate.

Remember this: Nurture is important, but nature matters too

Although much recent research aims to prove the dominance of nurture over nature, it is likely that accomplishment is a combination of the two. Seligman's equation acknowledges the importance of both skill and effort.

How positive psychology can help you achieve more

While learning domain-specific skills is undoubtedly important for high achievement, positive psychology offers a number of useful ideas and techniques to complement these.

GOAL THEORY

'Goals are signals that orient a person to what is valuable, meaningful and purposeful' (Robert Emmons).

The first step towards attaining your goals is to spend some time framing them appropriately. Research backs up the idea that training in goal-setting increases well-being.[44]

SMART goals, as taught on many management and personal effectiveness courses, are specific, measurable, achievable, relevant and time limited. Goal theory, developed by Edwin Locke, supports each of these criteria and adds four more. Locke's research (Lunenburg, 2011) suggests that, in addition, goals should be positive, challenging, committed to and provide feedback. We will call this improved goal criteria SMART+[45].

Remember this: Goal theory suggests adding more criteria to SMART

Locke's goal theory suggests that as well as being specific, measurable, achievable, relevant and time limited, goals should also be positive, challenging, committed to and provide feedback. In this book we are calling these SMART+ goals.

Let's look at an example of how to set SMART+ goals. Suppose you decide you want to improve your diet and eat less junk food. Clearly this is not a very SMART+ goal. We need to make it:

▶ Positive – if you are not eating junk food, what will you eat?

▶ Specific – you need to be clear about what counts as junk food and what counts as healthy food.

▶ Challenging – do not just aim to cut out crisps.

▶ Achievable – on the other hand, do not set yourself a diet of celery.

▶ Feedback needs to be available. How will you be able to tell that you have made progress towards your goal?

▶ Measurable – how will you be able to measure progress?

▶ Relevant – your goal should be relevant to you. It should not be something a peer, boss or an advertiser wants you to do that is not relevant to your view of what matters in life.

▶ Committing – you need to commit yourself to the goal. It is a goal, not an aspiration.

▶ Time limited – this means setting a specific timescale to reach the goal.

Putting all these criteria together, a SMART+ goal to replace the initial unSMART goal of cutting out junk food is:

> In the next month I will eat no junk food, by which I mean burgers, sweets and fizzy soft drinks. I will have at least five portions of fruit and vegetables a day and substitute fizzy water for fizzy soft drinks.

Try it now: Set a SMART+ goal

What area of life would you like to work on? Your goal could be related to career, relationships or lifestyle, for example. Spend five minutes setting a SMART+ goal to help you in your chosen area.

Research suggests that although setting goals appropriately is a very useful start, it is only the first step towards achieving your important goals.

The late American psychologist Rick Snyder pulled together a lot of relevant and useful evidence-based ideas in his work on the psychology of hope. There is substantial evidence of the benefits of hope (sometimes referred to as 'hope theory'). Snyder found that higher hope is associated with greater academic achievement, better health, improved athletic performance and improved coping. Other studies have found that hope predicted higher grades at law school even when optimism did not,[46] and that hope also predicted well-being better than optimism or self-efficacy.[47]

Snyder proposes that once you have set goals appropriately, you still need to develop both the 'will and the way' to achieve them. He labels these as agency and pathways thinking and provides useful tips for each, which we will bolster with ideas from other psychologists.

DEVELOPING PATHWAYS TOWARDS YOUR GOALS

Having set a SMART+ goal, the next step is to work on routes to achieving the goal. Snyder's advice is to:[48]

▶ Break up large goals into steps so they become more manageable.

▶ Consider different routes to the goal, then select the best route.

▶ Think of possible obstacles and how you would deal with them.

▶ Identify new skills you will need and learn them.

▶ Consider how your existing network of relationships can help and if you need to cultivate any new relationships.

▶ Concentrate on the first step, and do one thing at a time.

There are a number of other evidence-based tips we can add, which are considered below.

▶ Use your strengths

Develop pathways that use your strengths. For example, consider two people with the goal of a healthy diet. Suppose one of them has humour as their main strength and the other one excels at teamwork. Can you think how these people might develop somewhat different pathways to enable them to stick to their diet?

▶ Use defensive pessimism

We will later see how optimism can help when motivating yourself towards achieving your goal. However, when planning your pathways, optimism is not helpful. To realize this, ask yourself whether it is helpful to assume you know a route when you do not, or assume there will be no traffic in rush hour.

Instead, a strategy that has become known as defensive pessimism[49] is recommended when planning how to achieve your goals. This means imagining things that could go wrong and then working out how to overcome them. For example, a defensively pessimistic dieter would realize that a party invitation might lead her astray. She might either decline the invitation or to tell her friends at the party that she is on a diet so she does not get plied with unhealthy food. This dieter would also remember that she is tempted to stop on the way home at the cake shop. Being aware of this danger, she might decide to go home by a different route or pack a sandwich so she is not hungry. Defensive pessimism does not mean not believing you will achieve your goal, it means defending yourself against things that are likely to make it go wrong.

Remember this: There is a place for pessimism in positive psychology

Although we normally associate positive psychology with optimism, there is a place for a certain sort of pessimism. Defensive pessimism, where we look for obstacles to our goals and work out how to overcome them, is a useful tool. However, it is important to remember that pessimism is only good at the planning stage. When you are trying to motivate yourself, optimism is a far better mindset.

Research also indicates that making a step-by-step plan, recording progress and telling other people about your goal all help. (See Richard Wiseman's *59 Seconds*)

Clinical psychologist and author Nigel Sage has developed a very useful step-by-step diagram, which makes these ideas more vivid (see Sage, N. et al, 2008). It is very straightforward to use; simply work out the steps needed to reach your goals and the likely obstacles you might face, then begin with the first step. The neat trick is that overcoming an obstacle can then become a goal in itself. For example, continuing with the SMART+ goal relating to a more healthy diet, the steps might be:

▶ Go to the supermarket and buy fruit and fizzy water and food I can eat at home.

▶ Write down my goal and put it on the fridge where I can see it.

An obstacle might be feeling hungry on the walk home. So the dieter would set another goal of sticking to the diet on the way home. The steps to achieve this might be:

▶ Eat a sandwich at work late enough so I am not so hungry on way home.

- Change my route home to avoid walking past cake shop.
- Pack some fruit to eat on the journey home.

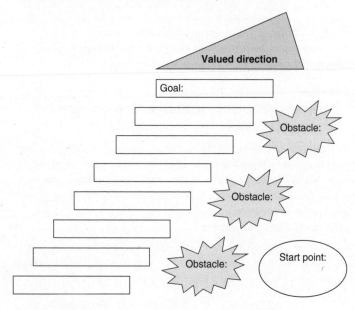

Step-by-step plan, © Nigel Sage, reproduced with kind permission

Try it now: Develop a step-by-step plan for your goal

Continue working on your SMART+ goal by filling in a step-by-step plan. Remember that this a working document – as you work your way towards your overall goal you will no doubt encounter unanticipated steps and obstacles. It is a good idea to put the plan somewhere where you can see it, such as on your fridge, and to review it regularly, e.g. every Sunday evening.

DEVELOPING MOTIVATION

Snyder emphasizes the importance of motivation, which he terms 'agency thinking'. He makes some suggestions about how to enhance agency thinking, including:

- Tell yourself it is your job to go after the goal.
- Use humour to laugh at yourself if things go wrong.

- ▶ See problems as challenges.
- ▶ Make sure you are in the right physical condition to work on your goals – look after your diet, exercise well and have enough sleep.

Motivation can be further enhanced by incorporating ideas about optimism and the growth mindset.

OPTIMISM

> 'Optimism is the faith that leads to achievement. Nothing can be done without hope and confidence.' Helen Keller[50]

Although a certain type of pessimism is useful when planning how to achieve your goals, pessimism is counterproductive when trying to motivate yourself. Pessimists are less likely to try to achieve their goals and are more prone to give up at the first sign of trouble, turning their pessimism into a self-fulfilling prophecy. Optimists, on the other hand, are more likely to attempt to achieve their goals and persist in the face of difficulties.

There is considerable evidence that optimism can be beneficial. Most famous, perhaps, is Seligman's study of insurance salesmen at Met Life in the1980s. Insurance salesmen get so many rejections that three-quarters of them quit in their first three years. The problem was so severe for Met Life that it called in Seligman for advice. Seligman suggested that as well as the normal interviews and aptitude tests, the company should give candidates optimism tests. His hunch was that optimists would do well in insurance sales, since optimists would be less affected by doors being (literally and metaphorically) slammed in their faces. Sure enough, optimists outsold pessimists by 21 per cent in their first year and by as much as 57 per cent in their second year.[51]

Optimism has also been found to be associated with success in public life. Seligman et al. have looked at US Presidential candidates and found optimism as expressed in election speeches to be a better predictor of success than opinion polls.

The title of his classic book *Learned Optimism* conveys Seligman's belief that optimism can be learned.[52] How do you respond when bad things happen to you? A pessimist will assume that things that have gone wrong ('adversities') are:

► permanent – they will last forever

► pervasive – they affect all of their life and

► personal – it is their fault.

Pessimists interpret good things as temporary, specific and accidental. An optimist will believe the opposite.[53]

It is not hard to understand why the optimistic insurance salesmen at Met Life fared better. Imagine yourself as a salesperson, faced with a 'numbers game' where most attempts to sell are going to result in failure. The likely interpretations are illustrated below. Is an optimist or a pessimist more likely to carry on and make the next call enthusiastically and confidently? [54]

Adversity: A series of failed calls trying to sell insurance

Optimist's interpretation	Pessimist's interpretation
Temporary	**Permanent**
'I wonder what it is about Monday mornings that makes selling so difficult?'	'No one is ever going to buy any insurance.'
Impersonal	**Personal**
'I was doing exactly the same thing last week and I made a lot of sales so I can't be doing anything wrong.'	'I'm a hopeless salesperson.'
Specific	**Pervasive**
'I may not be doing well at selling insurance this morning, but I was a damn good parent to my children at the weekend.'	'I'm hopeless.'

To stay motivated to achieve your goals, there are some good questions to ask yourself when things go badly:

► Am I unhelpfully applying the 3Ps, assuming that this adversity is permanent, personal and pervasive?

► If I was turned down, is it just a numbers game?

► Have I ever succeeded at anything similar to this?

▶ When I have succeeded, what strengths and talents have I used?[55]

▶ Was this setback down to a very specific problem that may not apply to my next attempt?

Try it now: Reflect on your own explanatory style
When things go wrong, how do you explain them? Do you tend to have an optimistic or pessimistic explanatory style? Think back to the last few times things have gone awry. If you err on the pessimistic side, then you might well benefit from learning to interpret failures more optimistically.

Key idea: Optimism can be learned and can help keep you motivated
How you explain events is strongly connected with motivation. Pessimists will assume that negative things are permanent, pervasive and personal and so become demotivated and give up. Optimists will challenge such negative interpretations and keep trying.

MINDSETS
Do you believe that your capacity for achievement is fixed, depending on your IQ and innate talents? Or do you think that you can learn skills and improve abilities? If you tend towards the first view, you have what psychologist Carol Dweck (2006) calls a fixed mindset. The second, more helpful mindset is the growth mindset.

People with a fixed mindset do not put so much effort into practice or trying because they do not think this is important. Why bother to practise if all that matters is IQ or talent? Equally, if a person with a fixed mindset is told they are poor at something they will not try to improve, since they interpret this criticism as meaning that they have not got the required talent. Conversely, those with a growth mindset make more effort, are more resilient and take on challenges. They would treat criticism as helpful feedback.

Thomas Edison is an excellent historical example of a growth mindset. It is said that when he was asked if he felt like a failure after 10,000 attempts to invent the lightbulb, he replied, 'I have not failed. I've just found 10,000 ways that it won't work.' [56] He is also reputed to have said, 'Genius is 1 per cent inspiration and 99 per cent perspiration', which is also very much in keeping with a growth mindset.

So how do you go about developing a growth mindset? If you have read this chapter, you have already gone some of the way. Reading about the research findings relating to the importance of nurture as opposed to nature is sometimes sufficient to alter people's belief in a fixed mindset. Reading case studies about people who have improved through hard work and good teaching is also helpful.

Betty Edwards' five-day art course provides evidence for the growth mindset. Many people would consider drawing as a prime example of an area in which you need talent in order to achieve. Some people can draw well, others cannot. Yet Edwards has developed a way to teach the skills required to draw competently which can work even for people with no discernible talent (see Edwards, 2012). You can see for yourself the remarkable differences in quality of students' self-portraits before and after taking the course by looking at the gallery on her website at http://drawright.com/gallery.htm.

To build a growth mindset, you can also ask yourself:

▶ What specific skills do I need to achieve my goal?

▶ How can I learn these skills?

▶ How much and what do I need to practise?

▶ When things go wrong, what can I learn from that experience?

Dweck also recommends looking at case studies of high achievers to find out whether it is true that they have to put in a lot of practice. You might like to think of someone you admire. Have they had to work hard and put in years of practice to attain excellence?

Key idea: Develop a growth mindset

A growth mindset is one where you take the attitude that improvement is possible, regardless of innate talent. It is acknowledged that talent plays a role, but far more emphasis is placed on the importance of learning and practice. A growth mindset encourages you to develop skills and practise and to see mistakes as learning opportunities.

The case of Mo Farah provides a good illustration of the growth mindset and many of the other ideas about achievement and accomplishment described in this chapter.

Case study: A life of accomplishment and achievement – Mo Farah

Mo Farah arrived in England from war-torn Somalia aged eight with little English but an obvious talent for running. He was lucky to find a series of wise mentors, starting with Alan Watkinson, the PE teacher who took him under his wing and later nudged him into devoting himself to athletics rather than his first love, football. Mo did well enough to win the Junior 5,000m in 2001, when he was 18. But it was not until four years later when he house-shared with top Kenyan athletes, that he realized what he would have to do to achieve his potential.

'They sleep, eat, train and rest, that's all they do.' Farah said. 'If I ever want to be as good as these athletes I've got to work harder. I don't just want to be British number one, I want to be up there with the best.'

In 2011 Mo realized he needed the right coach, Alberto Salazar, to achieve his ambitions, even though this meant being apart from his wife and step-daughter to move to the USA.

All the hard work paid off in the London Olympics of 2012 when Farah became the first UK athlete to win the 10,000m as part of the UK's 'Super Saturday'. A week later he completed the coveted long-distance double by winning the 5,000m.

Mo Farah illustrates the interplay of talent, hard work, wise mentoring and luck. That Mo had outstanding talent was apparent when he was a child, but what separated him from other young talents was dedication. As Mo Farah put it immediately after winning the 10,000m gold medal, 'It's all hard work and grafting ... It's been a long journey grafting and grafting, but anything is possible.'

Key idea: You can achieve your goals by focusing on both agency and pathways thinking

To achieve your goals you need to focus on both the 'will' and the 'way'. Optimism and having a growth mindset can help keep you motivated; planning your steps carefully and identifying possible obstacles can help you develop flexible pathways.

Remember this: Some commonly held views about motivation turn out to be unhelpful

Some popular ideas about how to increase motivation not only do not work, they can actually make you less likely to achieve your goals. One such strategy is to rely on willpower alone. Another unhelpful strategy is to visualize yourself achieving your goal. Students instructed to visualize themselves getting a high grade in an exam actually did worse than those who did not spend any time on visualization.

The research on agency and pathways thinking makes sense of these findings. If you rely on willpower alone or if you just visualize a good outcome, then you are not identifying the required steps or possible obstacles. Positive visualization may be unhelpful if it leads to complacency and reduces the need for practice, which research demonstrates is essential for high achievement.[57]

The darker side of achievement

Achievements and accomplishments are undoubtedly part of flourishing. A life with no achievement might be a pleasant life but it would not be a full life. Lying in the sun reading a detective novel by the pool sounds great for a week, but would you like this to be the sum total of your life?

However, you can have too much of a good thing. In particular, problems will arise if you value achievements above all other things in life. We looked at Laszlo Polgar approvingly, but suppose his daughters had hated chess and he had persisted in following up his dream of producing accomplished chess players? Former tennis champion Andre Agassi's entertaining and insightful autobiography *Open* tells of the problems that can be caused by having a parent who values their child's achievement above all else. Similarly we quoted Mo Farah's decision to leave his family and go to the USA as a good example of dedication. But what if Farah had failed to win any gold medals, and what if his relationship had run into trouble as a result?[58]

Achievements and accomplishments need to be acknowledged as one value among others, including the other elements of PERMA. One of the treatments for depression, activity scheduling, involves asking clients to monitor their daily activities and rate them for both pleasure and achievement. The desired outcome is a balance of relatively high pleasure and achievement. Overvaluing achievement at the expense of other values is one of the main causes of perfectionism, which is associated with stress, depression and interpersonal problems. For this reason, when raising a child, achievement needs to be seen as one important value among many.

Remember this: Achievement is just one component of PERMA

Flourishing requires a good balance of important values. We have seen that top achievements sometimes require an enormous amount of dedication and practice. It is important to ask yourself whether this amount of practice is justified.

Focus points

✻ There is a lot of evidence that focused 'deliberate' practice is the key to high accomplishment.

✻ It takes about ten years of deliberate practice to be an expert in a chosen field.

✻ Achievement = skill × effort. Although effort is crucial, innate talent clearly has a part to play. So too does mentoring and being in the right place at the right time.

✻ It is helpful to set SMART goals. Locke's goal theory adds four more criteria that goals should meet.

✻ To achieve goals, the psychology of hope informs us to consider both the 'will and the way', agency and pathways thinking. Step-by-step planning is a tool that can help you put this into practice.

Diagnostic test answers

1 Deliberate practice.

2 It takes ten years.

3 Specific, measurable, achievable, relevant and time limited.

4 Positive, committing, providing feedback and challenging.

5 Permanent, pervasive and personal.

6 Insurance salespeople.

7 The growth and fixed mindsets.

8 Agency and pathways thinking – the will and the way.

9 Defensive pessimism.

10 You consider obstacles that may prevent you reaching your goal.

Next steps

In the next chapter we will be looking at meaning and purpose, another element in Seligman's PERMA account of well-being. Thinking about the big picture of your life will help you decide which goals are most relevant to you. At the same time, ideas from the current chapter will be helpful when you come to plan more meaning and purpose in your life.

6

Meaning and purpose

In this chapter you will learn:

- ▶ *how Viktor Frankl laid the foundations for the positive psychology of meaning and purpose*
- ▶ *how meaning and purpose in life can be measured*
- ▶ *about the benefits of meaning and purpose*
- ▶ *how to enhance meaning and purpose in your life*
- ▶ *about the positive psychology of kindness.*

Diagnostic test

1 Who wrote *Man's Search for Meaning*?

2 What is the name of the therapeutic approach associated with *Man's Search for Meaning*?

3 What does Frankl think is the meaning of life?

4 What are the three routes to meaning suggested by Frankl?

5 Name three positive outcomes associated with a life of meaning and purpose.

6 Michael Steger separates out the search for meaning and the presence of meaning. Does he think both the search and presence are equally desirable?

7 Paul Wong argues for the importance of a 'meaning mindset'. What is meant by this term?

8 Name four ways to increase meaning and purpose.

9 In a study of a peer counselling scheme for MS sufferers, who benefitted most, the people giving or receiving the counselling?

10 Which proved more effective, doing acts of kindness on a single day or spreading them out over a week?

The pioneering work of Viktor Frankl

The most important work to date on the psychology of meaning and purpose was carried out well before the birth of positive psychology. Austrian psychiatrist Viktor Frankl (1905–97) wrote more than 30 books, founded a new type of psychotherapy ('logotherapy' – therapy through meaning) and contributed to psychiatry for over half a century. Frankl's most popular work, *Man's Search for Meaning*, written in 1946, has sold over 10 million copies. It is both a personal memoir of his horrific experiences in Auschwitz and other concentration camps and an exposition of his theories about what can give life meaning, even in the most unpromising of situations.

FRANKL'S KEY IDEAS

▶ We all have a 'will to meaning'. Frankl (1946) invented the term 'Sunday neurosis' to describe the 'depression which afflicts people who become aware of the lack of content in their lives when the rush of the busy week is over and the void within themselves becomes manifest.' As well as depression, Frankl found that a lack of meaning was associated with problems of addiction and suicide.

▶ There is meaning to be found in every life. However, it would be a mistake to look for one universal meaning of life. Frankl likens the request for one meaning of life to asking a grandmaster for a best move that applies to all possible positions in a game of chess.

▶ The potential meaning in your life depends on your life circumstance, talents and opportunities. The trick is to detect the areas of overlap between these and to focus your energies there.

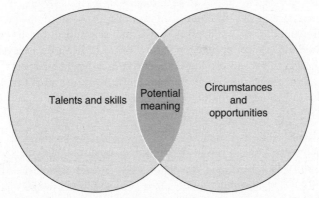

Meaning can be found in the overlap of one's talents and opportunities.

Frankl states that there are three routes to meaning: through creations, experiences and the attitude you take. Perhaps the most obvious avenue to a meaningful life is through things you do to make a difference to the world. Having a child, doing an act of charity and creating a work of art are all things you can do to add significance and purpose to your life.

Frankl (1965) also argued that experiences can be meaningful. He wrote, 'Let us ask a mountain-climber who has beheld the alpine sunset and is so moved by the splendour of nature that he feels cold shudders running down his spine – let us ask him whether after such an experience his life can ever again seem wholly meaningless'. Falling in love and religious experiences can also give people a sense of being part of something bigger than themselves and even, on occasions, a sense of awe.

The final route to meaning is through one's attitude. Frankl (1946) argued that even in apparently hopeless situations we still have the freedom to find meaning through meaningful attitudes. An elderly, depressed doctor who could not overcome the loss of his wife came to the famous psychiatrist for help. Frankl asked him, 'What would have happened, Doctor, if you had died first, and your wife would have had to survive you?' 'Oh,' replied the patient, 'for her this would have been terrible; how she would have suffered!' Frankl continued, 'You see, Doctor, such a suffering has been spared her; and it is you who have spared her this suffering; but now, you have to pay for it by surviving her and mourning her.' The man said no word, but shook Frankl's hand and calmly left his office. Existential psychotherapist Irvin Yalom gives another example of how the right attitude can give meaning to a seemingly hopeless situation. A depressed dying patient decided she could be a 'pioneer of dying' for all of her friends, showing them the right way to die.[59]

Frankl himself provides a good example of a meaningful life, illustrating each of these three ways of achieving meaning. He left the world a better place; he created a therapy, books, a child and helped numerous patients. A student summarized it thus: 'The meaning of your life was to help other people find meaning'. Frankl was engaged in activities where he found meaning, such as mountaineering, lecturing and being a psychiatrist. Finally, when put to the ultimate test in the concentration camps, his attitude turned the most horrendous circumstances around. As he said in *Man's Search for Meaning*, 'One could make a victory of these experiences, turning life into an inner triumph, or one could ignore the challenges and simply vegetate.'

Key idea: Viktor Frankl's major contribution to the psychology of meaning

Frankl towers above other psychologists writing about meaning in the 20th century. His ideas can provide a spur to many practical strategies, such as looking for the overlap between one's talents and opportunities and looking for meaning in deeds, experiences and the attitude one takes to difficulties.

Try it now: How Viktor Frankl can help your life become more meaningful

How meaningful has your life been so far? Using Frankl's three areas of meaning, what positive difference have you made, what meaningful experiences have you had, and what attitudes have you shown to turn adversity around?

If you find your answer disappointing, can you use the Venn diagram on page 99 to make your future more meaningful? Given your current work, community and family circumstances, what strengths, talents or skills can you use to make a positive difference in the world?

Frankl was a psychiatrist who based his ideas on his own personal and clinical experience. Positive psychology attempts to put theories and strategies on a firmer scientific foundation. The next section summarizes how we can use recent findings to update Frankl's ideas.

Measuring meaning and purpose

How meaningful is your life? The above exercise is a good start to answering this question, but psychologists have created a number of questionnaires to measure meaningfulness more precisely. One such measure is the 'meaning in life questionnaire' developed by Michael Steger and his colleagues.

The following five items in the questionnaire relate to the presence of meaning in life. Answer these questions on a scale of

1–7, where 1 indicates that it is absolutely untrue and 7 means it is absolutely true.

1 I understand my life's meaning.

2 My life has a clear sense of purpose.

3 I have a good sense of what makes my life meaningful.

4 I have discovered a satisfying life purpose.

5 My life has no clear purpose.

Question 5 is reverse-scored, so subtract your answer from 8 for this question (for example, a score of 2 becomes a score of 6). Then add up all your scores. For example, if your scores are 3, 4, 2, 5 and 2 then your score would be 3 + 4 + 2 + 5 + 6 = 20.

You can take this test on the Authentic Happiness website – a score above 24 indicates that you think your life is reasonably full of meaning and purpose.

The benefits of meaning and purpose

Coming from a psychiatric background, Frankl emphasized the problems arising from an absence of meaning. These have been vindicated by recent research. For example, meaninglessness proved the best predictor of suicides in the US Army. As we saw in Chapter 3 on flourishing, there are strong arguments for thinking that pleasure and enjoyment alone are not all there is to well-being. If you chose not to live in the hypothetical experience machine, one of the reasons you may have given was that you wanted your life to make a difference, you wanted to leave a legacy; you did not want to be just a consumer on planet earth, you wanted to be a producer as well. There is a strong argument for including meaning and purpose as part of well-being. Martin Seligman has recognized this by including them in PERMA, as does Carol Ryff in her theory of psychological well-being.

In addition to being part of well-being, meaning and purpose have been found to be associated with a number of positive outcomes, including:

▶ subjective well-being

▶ health

▶ longevity

▶ reduced stress

▶ resilience.

Note that meaning and purpose are associated with these positive outcomes, rather than necessarily causing them. Nevertheless, it is fair to assume that meaning and purpose are desirable for both their own sake and their consequences.

Key idea: The benefits of meaning and purpose

Meaning and purpose are part of well-being and are also associated with a number of other benefits, including health and resilience.

Is the search for meaning a good idea?

The following five questions relate to the search for meaning in life. Answer these questions on a scale of 1–7, where an answer of 1 indicates that it is absolutely untrue and 7 means it is absolutely true.

1 I am looking for something that makes my life feel meaningful.

2 I am always looking to find my life's purpose.

3 I am always searching for something that makes my life feel significant.

4 I am seeking a purpose or mission for my life.

5 I am searching for meaning in my life.

Now add up your five scores. If your total is more than 24, then you have a higher than average score for searching for meaning.[60] The twist here is that while everyone agrees that the presence of meaning is a good thing, there is much debate over whether the search for meaning is beneficial.

The existentialist psychiatrist and author Irvin Yalom is a strong critic of searching directly for meaning.

> 'The search for meaning, much like the search for pleasure, must be conducted obliquely. Meaning ensues from meaningful activity: the more we deliberately pursue it, the less likely are we to find it; the rational questions one can pose about meaning will always outlast the answers. ... meaningfulness is a by-product of engagement and commitment, engagement ... causes these questions not to matter.'[61]

Michael Steger and his colleagues have carried out research to determine whether searching for meaning is beneficial or not. They found that for many people a high score for searching for meaning was associated with lower scores on various items of Ryff's psychological well-being, such as mastery, relatedness and self-acceptance. Searching for meaning was also associated with increased anxiety, especially when people had relatively little presence of meaning. At first sight this presents a puzzle. Wouldn't you expect people who are searching for meaning to be more likely to find it? Part of the problem is that the people searching for meaning will include those searching for one meaning, which, as Frankl said, is as futile as looking for the one best move in chess. Others will be trying to answer unhelpful questions about why their life has so far lacked meaning – they may be prone to overthinking and rumination. Yalom is right when he says that committed action and engagement is much more helpful than thinking for a long time about the meaning of life.

What is less clear is whether Frankl actually argues for searching for meaning in this sense. He urges people to detect meaning, but that is not the same as searching for it. It is the difference between noticing past and present opportunities for meaning and looking for some fictional Holy Grail that will give your life a meaning it currently lacks. Paul Wong, a leading figure in the positive psychology of meaning and purpose, has constructed a scale called the Life Orientation Scale, which measures what he thinks is a more helpful attitude than the search for meaning, namely the 'meaning mindset'.

The Life Orientation Scale (LOS)

Indicate how much you agree or disagree with each of the following statements by scoring each item 1–5, where 1 means strongly disagree and 5 means strongly agree.

1 I can find something meaningful or significant in everyday events.

2 There is a reason for everything that happens to me.

3 There is no ultimate meaning and purpose in life.

4 There is no point in searching for meaning in life.

5 No matter how painful the situation, life is still worth living.

6 The meaning of life is to 'eat, drink and be happy'.

7 What really matters to me is to pursue a higher purpose or calling regardless of personal cost.

8 I would rather be a happy pig than a sad saint.

9 I am willing to sacrifice personal interests for the greater good.

10 Personal happiness and success are more important to me than achieving inner goodness and moral excellence.

© Paul T. P. Wong, PhD, reproduced with kind permission

Items 3, 4, 6, 8 and 10 are reverse-scored, so subtract your scores for these items from 6 (for example, a score of 1 becomes a score of 5 for these items). Add up your total score; the higher your total the greater your meaning mindset. An average score above 3 (i.e. total score above 30) will reflect endorsement of a meaning mindset.

If you have a meaning mindset, you will prioritize meaning and purpose over pleasure, look for some positive meaning when bad things happen, and be proactive in creating meaning. This captures Frankl's intentions better than the 'search for meaning', which overlaps with a ruminative style and trying to answer unanswerable questions about the meaning of life.

Is it true that 'What doesn't kill you makes you stronger'?

This saying, popularized in a modern pop song, originated in philosopher Friedrich Nietzsche's *Twilight of the Idols*. In recent years there has been interest in post-traumatic growth (PTG), whereby some people get stronger after trauma. For example, some people appreciate life more, understand their strengths better and have closer and more meaningful relationships. Stephen Joseph, author of *What Doesn't Kill Us: The New Psychology of Posttraumatic Growth* proposes a THRIVE model for PTG which includes many ideas from positive psychology, including hope, gratitude, resilience, cultivating a growth mindset and expressive writing. Joseph quotes Frankl at length, advocating looking towards a positive future and taking responsibility for choosing our reactions to our difficulties.

Having a limited life expectancy can motivate people to reassess their life priorities and, in the words of Irvin Yalom, 'trivialize the trivia in life'. This can sometimes make a person's last few months very meaningful. A striking example is Randy Pausch, a previously obscure 47-year-old academic dying from pancreatic cancer, whose inspirational 'Last Lecture' proved an internet sensation in 2007. At the time of writing you can view this at http://www.youtube.com/watch?v=ji5_MqicxSo

Try it now: Post-traumatic growth without the trauma

Close your eyes and meditate for a few minutes about how you would feel if you received news that you only had one year to live. What emotions come up for you? What would you do with that year? What legacy would you want to leave behind? What activities would you want to do – what is on your 'before-you-die bucket list'? What attitude would you want to have towards your dying and death?

Spend a full ten minutes imagining that this is the reality, and keep noticing your feelings and motivation. Then open your eyes and write down how you answered the above questions.

Now answer a different question – how many of these things would increase the meaning of your life now, even if you are in perfectly good health? Would you like to set the goal of making such changes? If so, you can use the material in the previous chapter on achievement (such as step-by-step planning) to help you.

Remember this: Whatever doesn't kill you doesn't always make you stronger

Research on post-traumatic growth is still in its infancy. What has been shown is that post-traumatic growth is a possibility. It should not, however, be concluded that those who do not grow through trauma are somehow to blame for not growing as a result.

The four ingredients of a meaningful life – WIST

While the Beatles informed us that all you need is love (intimacy), and Sigmund Freud, according to Erikson (1963), said that love and work are all that matters, modern researchers[62] suggest four ingredients of a meaningful life, adding spirituality and transcendence. Robert Emmons suggests the WIST acronym to help you remember these 'big four' components of meaning. We considered this briefly in Chapter 3; now we will explore it more fully.

Key idea: WIST

Robert Emmons' WIST framework is useful to help us think about the most important areas of meaning.

WIST stands for work, intimacy, spirituality and transcendence.

MEANINGFUL WORK

Fully meaningful work gives you a sense of achievement, feels engaging and makes a positive difference to the world. For a few, this comes naturally. Perhaps they followed their passion when they were young, happened to be good at what engaged them, and were lucky enough to have a passion that made a positive difference to the world and from which they could make a living. The film critic Roger Ebert exemplifies such a life very well.

Case study: Roger Ebert – a meaningful life

When film critic Robert Ebert died in 2013, President Barack Obama remarked, 'Roger was the movies'. Ebert had co-hosted top American TV film review show *At the Movies* for many years. In the age of the internet, his influence became worldwide when his *Chicago Sun-Times* review featured as the top review on internet film site imdb.com.

Ebert had his own views on meaningful lives. He concluded that, 'if, at the end of it all, according to our abilities, we have done something to make others a little happier, and something to make ourselves a little happier, that is about the best we can do.'

Judged by these criteria, Ebert certainly lived a meaningful life. He loved his work, and was very good at it. He won a Pulitzer Prize, the first film critic to do so. When Ebert died, many readers blogged their gratitude. 'I would turn to Roger when deciding whether to watch a film or, having seen it, when trying to gain a deeper understanding of it' was a typical appreciation. Maybe you can't count helping people make wise choices about which film to see as being on a par with finding the cure for a disease. But then again if we improve many lives by just a small amount, maybe that is all those of us who are not saints or geniuses can hope to do.

Unlike many critics, Ebert did not take cheap shots at bad films. He was a kind reviewer, looking for good things to say even about bad movies. Ebert said the sum total of his political beliefs was kindness. So it's fair to say that he improved the lives of film-makers as well as film-watchers.

As for legacy, his reviews are safely stored in imdb.com for future film-watchers to consult. Ebert did not believe in God, but was comforted by Richard Dawkins' theory of memes – ideas, beliefs and behaviours that we spread. 'After a lifetime of writing, teaching, broadcasting and happily torturing people with my jokes, I will leave behind more memes than many.'

Ebert developed cancer in 2002, which resulted four years later in his losing his voice, the ability to eat in the normal way and the lower part of his jaw. Undeterred, he continued his reviewing, using modern technology to produce a new voice and even appearing on *Oprah*. He carried on writing reviews until almost the end. His attitude to his cancer was realistic yet courageous and positive.

I chose Roger Ebert as an example of a meaningful life, rather than more obvious choices such as Viktor Frankl or Nelson Mandela, because he illustrates so well how a kind man with talent and passion can make a positive difference to many lives.

As one obituary writer put it, 'By any measure, Roger Ebert was a legend.'

For most people, meaningful work does not come so easily. The case study of Ken (below) illustrates how changing careers might be necessary in order to create more meaningful work.

Case study: Ken's change to a more meaningful career

At the age of 45 Ken was becoming increasingly dissatisfied with his IT job working for a large company in the City of London. He was being pushed into management when he much preferred hands-on programming work and was uncomfortable with the company's narrow profit motive. A six-month sabbatical travelling around Europe in a campervan in 1999 with his wife and two young daughters helped Ken re-evaluate what was important and showed him he could do something different from being on the corporate treadmill.

Ken applied for voluntary redundancy, but since his work was highly valued this was initially turned down. Persistent badgering resulted in his being granted a generous redundancy package in 2002.

Ken had been doing furniture-making courses and loved working with his hands, so his initial idea was to become a furniture maker. He used the redundancy money to take some courses with a world-renowned furniture maker. However, the market for handmade furniture turned out to be very small, so he ended up making shelves and kitchens for people in his local area – not quite what he had envisaged.

Reassessing his original decision to quit his IT job, Ken realized that he didn't have a problem with IT, just the use that was being made of his skills. He decided to make use of his considerable IT experience but work in a more 'socially responsible' area. After a spell doing volunteer IT work, he started looking for a job in 'IT for social good'. He got a job with OneWorld UK in February 2003.

The transition wasn't all plain sailing. But passion and the realization that this was what he really wanted to do propelled him forward. It wasn't just altruism that motivated him, it was also a quest to do something purposeful with his life and, he reflected honestly, to gain recognition. Ken's strengths of persistence and determination were crucial at times, for example when he was initially refused voluntary redundancy. His financial prudence and ability to plan flexibly proved helpful when the furniture-making plan didn't work out. Ken also recognizes that a supportive wife and some lucky breaks – like the OneWorld job coming up at the right time – were important.

Ten years on, Ken describes his job as 'wonderful'. Being part of a small company, he can now do lots of hands-on technical work. There has been plenty of opportunity to work on projects for social good, such as election monitoring and helping to improve health and agriculture in developing countries. It's a much more meaningful career than his work in corporate IT had become.

Remember this: Meaningful work may require a career change

For some, like Roger Ebert, meaningful work may come at an early age. For others, it may be that their early choice of career no longer provides meaning (if it ever did). For these, thinking about what might be a more meaningful career and then proactively seeking it out is advisable. This is not necessarily easy, so using your strengths and step-by-step planning may be important.

MEANINGFUL RELATIONSHIPS

Frankl says that the experience of love is one of the great sources of meaning. In a moving passage from *Man's Search for Meaning*, Frankl describes how it brought him a moment of bliss in the most unpromising of circumstances. Even as the icy wind froze him and his blistered feet marched on to the sound of the insults of the guards, the image of his wife, her smile and an imaginary conversation with her changed everything. 'Real or not, her look was then more luminous than the sun which was beginning to rise ... I understood how a man who has nothing left in this world may still know bliss, be it only for a brief moment, in the contemplation of his beloved.'

Try it now: Meditating on a loved one

Close your eyes and picture someone with whom you have experienced love (this could be romantic love, or love for your child, parent or close friend). Focus on their smile and all their positive qualities. Have an imaginary conversation with them. Ask them whatever you would like to ask them, and watch their reply in your mind's eye. Keep the conversation going as long as you like.

Can you find anything of the inner bliss that Frankl found?

Chapter 8, Relationships, will provide many more strategies for creating and maintaining meaningful relationships.

RELIGION AND SPIRITUALITY

There is clear evidence that for many people religion and spirituality increases their sense of meaning and well-being. Belief in the afterlife and in God's purpose can give your life a sense of eternal meaning. Going to a place of worship can increase your sense of community and provides a regular reminder of your values. For some who do not believe in God, Buddhism provides a framework for developing spiritual practices like meditation. An intriguing question is whether it is possible or desirable for atheists who do not wish to be Buddhists to develop a type of spirituality.[63]

TRANSCENDENCE AND SERVICE

There is much evidence that transcending one's own narrow interests helps create a meaningful life and provides other benefits. Transcendence can take many forms. Having children is one common route. We noted earlier the 'parenthood paradox' that many couples want to have children even though it does not increase their happiness. Baumeister (1991) suggested that this may be because having children increases parents' meaning and purpose. Richard Dawkins introduced the notion of memes – ideas and works of art we introduce into the world. By creating memes, our impact can transcend the limits of our lifetime. And we can experience moments of awe, such as when first seeing the Grand Canyon or seeing a new-born baby smile.

But the best-researched way to increase meaning through transcendence is by way of kindness. The Bible informed us that, 'It is better to give than to receive' and now there is evidence that backs up this claim. Women with multiple sclerosis who volunteered to give peer support to other sufferers benefitted seven times as much, over a three-year period, as those they were helping.[64] Lyubomirsky et al. (2005) have demonstrated experimentally that acts of kindness increase SWB. Students who were instructed to perform five acts of kindness in one single day a week for six weeks experienced increased SWB. Lyubomirsky found that the benefit was sensitive to when people did their acts of kindness. While the group told to perform the kindnesses in a single day in the week benefitted, another group instructed to spread them out over the week did not. Perhaps performing all the acts of kindness in a day magnifies the effect, or perhaps doing them every day becomes boring.

Try it now: Random acts of kindness

Spend a few moments brainstorming acts of kindness that you might carry out. Choose one specific day next week to be your kindness day. On that day, perform five acts of kindness – they may or may not turn out to be the ones that you planned.

Possible acts of kindness include:

* Let someone go ahead in a queue.
* Give money to the homeless.
* Give up your seat on a bus or train.
* Pay for the person next to you in a coffee shop.
* Give someone a compliment.
* Cook a meal for your flatmate/someone you live with.
* Phone someone who will be pleased to hear from you.
* Hold open doors for people in need.
* Teach someone something from this book.
* Say hello and smile at people.
* Share your umbrella.
* Be patient.
* Take cake to work.
* Give blood.
* Tell a friend about a time you have appreciated their friendship.

You can choose whether the acts of kindness all benefit the same person and whether they are made aware of them. Be sure not to do anything that places you or others in danger.

It is a good idea to see your kindness day as an open-ended opportunity to be kind. It is better to look out for opportunities to be kind than to pre-determine all your kind actions.

Key idea: Kindness

The positive psychology of kindness provides evidence-based ways to increase meaning, purpose and well-being. Doing five random acts of kindness in one day has been shown to be more beneficial (to the person doing the acts of kindness) than spreading them out over time.

Step-by-step planning to increase meaning and purpose

We first encountered the idea of WIST in Chapter 3. You can draw on your own list of WIST values to decide on your 'valued direction' in the step-by-step plan introduced in Chapter 5. Such valued directions might include meaningful work, close intimate relationships, a richer spiritual life, being kind and leaving the world a better place. You can then set SMART+ goals related to each area, and take the first step towards achieving them. As we saw in the 'Ken' case study, it is also a good idea to use your strengths.

Focus points

✳ Viktor Frankl's work on meaning and purpose still provides the best starting point for thinking about meaning and purpose in life. Among Frankl's most useful ideas is the Venn diagram indicating that meaning comes in the overlap between your talents and skills and the circumstances in which you find yourself. Frankl's three routes to meaning – experiences, creations and attitudes – is also a useful framework.

✳ Several measures are available to quantify meaning. The 'meaning in life questionnaire' measures overall meaning; the 'meaning mindset' measures the attitude that predisposes one to find meaning.

✳ Meaning and purpose are part of well-being and are also associated with a number of other benefits, including health and resilience. After trauma, there is the potential for post-traumatic growth, whereby the trauma can be a trigger for personal growth.

✳ The WIST framework is useful to help explore potential areas of meaning. WIST stands for work, intimacy, spirituality and transcendence.

✳ The positive psychology of kindness provides evidence-based ways to increase meaning, purpose and well-being. Doing five random acts of kindness in one day has been shown to be beneficial.

Diagnostic test answers

1 Viktor Frankl.

2 Logotherapy.

3 He does not think there is one meaning of life.

4 Creations, experiences and attitude.

5 Three from: better health, longevity, reduced stress, resilience and increased SWB.

6 No, presence of meaning is good; search for meaning can be counterproductive.

7 It means prioritizing meaning and purpose over other values and looking out for meaning and purpose in your life. It is not the same as looking for one Holy Grail of meaning or ruminating about why there is not enough meaning in your life.

8 You could have based this around the WIST framework – through work, intimacy, spirituality and transcendence. You could also have mentioned acts of kindness.

9 The givers benefitted seven times more.

10 Doing acts of kindness on a single day was more effective.

Next steps

In this chapter we have looked at overall meaning in life. In the next chapter we will look at another component of PERMA, engagement or flow. This is a kind of moment-to-moment meaning, a sense of being so absorbed in whatever you are doing that you lose track of time and everything else.

7

Flow

In this chapter you will learn:

- ▶ *what positive psychologists mean by the term 'flow'*
- ▶ *why flow is thought to be a key part of flourishing*
- ▶ *the eight most important characteristics of flow*
- ▶ *which areas of life provide the greatest sources of flow*
- ▶ *how to enable more flow in your life and the lives of others*
- ▶ *about the potential dangers and limitations of flow.*

Diagnostic test

1 Define what is meant in positive psychology by the term 'flow'.

2 What is the name of the psychologist most associated with flow?

3 List the eight most important characteristics of flow experiences.

4 List five activities where many people find flow.

5 In general, do people find flow more at work or during leisure pursuits?

6 Give three tips on how to increase flow experiences.

7 List three things that are likely to stop flow occurring.

8 What have you learned about your own experience of flow and how to enhance it?

9 Name three reasons why psychologists think flow is a good thing.

10 Identify two potential dangers of flow.

What is flow and why is it important?

Have you ever felt so absorbed in what you were doing that you lost track of time and did not notice what was happening around you? Did you enjoy the experience? If you can answer 'yes' to both these questions then you have probably experienced flow (or engagement), the second element of Seligman's PERMA theory of well-being.

When athletes speak of 'being in the zone' they are referring to flow. It is this combination of enjoyment and high performance that makes the study of flow so important.

Key idea: What is flow?

Flow is the enjoyable and performance-enhancing experience of being totally absorbed in what you are doing.

Flow has been around as long as humanity, but it did not come to the attention of psychologists until the late 1960s. While researching creativity in artists, the American Hungarian psychologist Mihaly ('Mike') Csikszentmihalyi (pronounced Me-high Chick-sent-me-high) made what turned out to be the most important discovery of his life. Asked how they felt when working at their best, a number of artists described similar experiences. They spoke of being totally immersed in their work, with little attention to spare for anything else. They were so concentrated on what they were doing that they did not even notice fatigue or hunger.[65] When Csikszentmihalyi interviewed other people who undertook activities for their own sake – such as chess players, dancers, rock climbers and basketball players – he found that they described the same phenomenon. Many said it felt like being effortlessly moved forward by the flow of a river. It was for this reason that Csikszentmihalyi chose the term 'flow' to describe this state of optimal experience.

Remember this: Flow is not to be confused with 'going with the flow'

Flow in positive psychology has nothing to do with 'going with the flow'. You are more likely to find flow by following the calling of your own passions and interests than by being conformist.

The eight most important characteristics of flow

In the early 1970s Csikszentmihalyi became Professor of Psychology at Chicago University and since then he and his colleagues have conducted many more experiments on flow. To study flow more scientifically they developed the Experience Sampling Method. Subjects were instructed to wear electronic pagers and were bleeped at random times in the day. They recorded data about both their activity (who they were with, what they were doing, how skilled they were at the activity) and about their inner experience (whether they felt bored, anxious or absorbed). One of the main findings to come from this research is that whatever its source, be it painting, conversation, chess or dancing, flow typically has the following eight characteristics.[66]

1. A CHALLENGING ACTIVITY WELL MATCHED TO YOUR LEVEL OF SKILL

You are undertaking an activity that presents the right degree of challenge. If you are an average skier, you are unlikely to get into flow skiing down a beginners' slope, since it will not be sufficiently challenging. However, should you accidentally ski on to a hazardous, mogul-ridden black run, you are equally unlikely to find flow, because then the challenge will be too high. Only when the challenge is well matched with your skill level is flow likely to result.

The point is best summarized by three equations:

Too low a challenge = boredom

Too high a challenge = anxiety

Challenge just right = flow

2. HAVING CLEAR GOALS AND IMMEDIATE FEEDBACK

You know what you are trying to do and whether you are succeeding. Clear goals allow the brain to know what it needs to focus on; immediate feedback gives it a sense of moving in the right direction. This is one of the reasons why games and competitions are such good sources of flow. A golfer knows what he or she is aiming for, and finds out soon enough whether the shot is a good one.

3. COMPLETE CONCENTRATION ON THE TASK

You are totally concentrated on the task. Your mind does not wander. The more you get into the task, the deeper your concentration gets. A chess player focuses totally on the game; a mother plays with her child single-mindedly.

4. A FEELING OF ONENESS WITH THE ACTIVITY

You do not feel separate from the task. When a singer finds flow, they do not feel like they are performing. Action and awareness are merged.

5. A LOSS OF SELF-CONSCIOUSNESS AND A FEELING OF CALMNESS AND SERENITY

Your mind is so engaged in what you are doing that there is no room left for any other mental processes. Consequently you will not feel self-conscious, worry or dwell on the past. This explains why flow is often accompanied by a sense of calmness and serenity.

6. TIME DOES NOT PASS IN THE USUAL WAY
In flow you will often experience a distorted sense of time. When friends are engrossed in a conversation, they may speak of time 'flying by'.

7. A FEELING OF BEING IN CONTROL
Even though it is challenging, you feel up to the task. The flow carries you forward seemingly without effort. A player of computer games senses they know what to do next. The gambler in flow thinks they have figured out the winner of the next race.

8. INTRINSIC MOTIVATION
You sense that what you are doing is worth it for its own sake, not just for an end product like money or status. An academic who finds flow in their work willingly accepts less pay than they would get in another field. The experience of flow makes the activity self-justifying.

Key idea: Flow is linked with intrinsic motivation

An intrinsically motivating activity is one in which people are willing to engage for no reward other than the interest and enjoyment that accompanies it. Deci and Ryan's self-determination theory (1985) argues that intrinsic motivation is superior to extrinsic motivation. It is associated with more persistence, better performance and improved well-being in general. Since flow activities are intrinsically motivated, they too enjoy these benefits.

Case study: The characteristics of flow at work

Linda, a clinical physiologist working in the NHS in the UK, describes her experience of flow like this:

'Although I do experience flow in leisure activities (for example, walking, jewellery making and needlecraft), the thing that strikes me most is how much I experience flow at work. When I am with a patient I experience pretty much all Csikszentmihalyi's important characteristics of flow.

'Total focus and concentration is pretty much required with every patient. Each patient is a challenge which tests my skills, sometimes almost to the limit. Occasionally the challenge seems to exceed my skills, and I begin to feel a little anxiety as I begin to lose control somewhat of the situation when I cannot persuade either the patient or the equipment to cooperate sufficiently but have no choice but to continue and sort it out. The opposite can happen with a simple case. In this case my skills exceed the challenge leading to boredom, though I often use this opportunity to chat to the patient and enjoy the social interaction more than the technical or diagnostic challenge.

'There is a presupposed clarity of goals in each patient that I test, namely to produce sufficient data to aid in diagnosis or to monitor a treatment regimen.

'I usually have a sense of control over what I am doing, I am pretty skilled with the equipment, interpretation of data and patient interaction, although again anxiety can result with patients who are rude, aggressive or distressed, although handling a difficult situation can be rewarding also.

'I generally become a different person when I am testing a patient, losing awareness of myself and of time. Other technicians often have to call me to remind me it is time to go home.

'The only concept I have a problem with in the work context is that the activities are extrinsically rewarding. Generally I see it as my duty to be diligent, and flow is a by-product of this.'

Try it now: Watch Martin Luther King in full flow

Watch Martin Luther King's 'I have a Dream' speech (e.g. on YouTube at http://www.youtube.com/watch?v=jqOfuZzgIP4).

At which point in the speech do you think he gets into flow? How many of the eight characteristics of flow do you think he exhibits?

The sources of flow

Csikszentmihalyi's early findings have been validated both by his own further studies and by independent researchers, across a wide range of activities, classes, genders, ages and cultures. Among the sources of flow studied are sport (Jackson and Csikszentmihalyi, 1999), art and science (Csikszentmihalyi, 1996), writing (Perry, 2001) and aesthetic experience (Csikszentmihalyi and Robinson, 1990).

There is no one activity that is productive of flow for all individuals. Finding flow depends on your subjective experience of challenge and interest. However, there is one very significant general finding which may come as a surprise.

Key idea: Flow occurs more at work than in leisure

Flow occurs more often at work than in leisure. One study showed that flow occurred on average 54 per cent of the time spent at work but only 18 per cent of the time doing leisure (Csikszentmihalyi, 1990, p.158).

Why is work a better source of flow than leisure? This may partly be due to the fact that many people settle for very passive leisure activities. The most striking example of a passive leisure pursuit is television. TV is a very poor source of flow but the most popular leisure pursuit in many countries (Sobel, 1995). The moral is to make your leisure activities more active and more challenging – and quite possibly to go on a TV diet!

How to increase flow

There are basically two routes to increasing flow:

1 Discover where you have found flow in the past and present, and prioritize these activities.

2 Create flow in activities that have not yet produced flow.

We will look at each route in turn.

Try it now: Discover where you have already found flow

Spend five minutes reflecting on where you have found most flow in your life. Go all the way back to your childhood. Did you find flow in games or activities when you were a child? How about as a teenager? When on holiday? At work? At weekends? Think about hobbies and games that you used to enjoy. To help you, here is a list of some of the activities where people have reported being in flow:

* Sports
* Hobbies
* Conversation
* Work
* Leisure pursuits
* Games
* Physical activities
* Yoga
* Sex
* Housework
* Music
* Playing jazz
* Team sports
* Reading

Record your personal past sources of flow.

Now choose one activity that you have not done recently that you would like to do again and are able to do in the next week. Commit to doing this activity and, if you find you enjoy it, make it part of your life again.

Remember this: Do not ask yourself whether you are in flow

Do not stop to think about whether you are in flow during an activity or you will break the spell. The philosopher John Stuart Mill remarked, 'Ask yourself whether you are happy, and you cease to be so'. This statement may be more true of flow than happiness. The trick is to immerse yourself in an activity, and only once it has finished to think about whether you experienced flow.

Try it now: Discover your present sources of flow

For a week, record in a table like the one below what you did and whether you got flow from each activity (refer to the eight characteristics of flow on pages 120–121 if you are uncertain whether you found flow).

Morning – Afternoon

	Before 09.00	09.00–11.00	11.00–13.00	13.00–15.00
Monday				
Activity				
Flow?				
Tuesday				
Activity				
Flow?				
Sun				

Afternoon–Evening

	15.00–17.00	17.00–19.00	19.00–21.00	After 21.00
Monday				
Activity				
Flow?				
Tuesday				
Activity				
Flow?				

For example here is part of the flow log of Jim, who works as a computer programmer.

Monday	Before 09.00	09.00–11.00	11.00–15.00
Activity	Shower, breakfast	Weekly team meeting	Started work doing programming
Flow?	Not really, on auto-pilot, not much of a challenge	No, just sat there, bored	Yes, definitely got into flow so much so that I didn't take lunch until 1500!

Here is part of what Jim wrote for the weekend.

Sunday	Before 09.00	09.00–11.00	11.00–13.00
Activity	Sleep, shower, breakfast	Read Sunday newspapers, watched TV	Playing golf
Flow?	No	Partly – got really into reading an article about holidays. I watched football highlights which actually wasn't very flow-full at all.	Definitely, though not all the time. I experienced anxiety at the start – too many people watching – but by the time we got to the fourth hole and I got my swing right I really got into the game.

Like Jim has done, it is recommended that you include a brief note on why flow happened or did not happen.

Take a few moments to take stock of what you have learned from your flow log.

The next step, in week 2, is to prioritize flow activities. For example, Jim noticed that he got more flow doing programming than in meetings. This observation confirmed his hunch that he should turn down a flattering offer to become more involved in managerial work. At the weekend he noticed that some activities (reading newspaper articles, playing golf) led to flow while others (watching TV, browsing the internet) did not. He consequently decided next weekend to have a TV diet and to play golf instead.

Decide which activities you are going to prioritize over the next week.

So the first way to increase flow is to prioritize activities that have already led to flow. The second route is to make other activities more full of flow.

The eight characteristics of flow split into two groups – some, like a feeling of oneness and a distorted sense of time, are a consequence of flow, while others are also a cause of flow. By manipulating the second group, you can increase your chances of experiencing flow in any activity. The following five tips will help to influence these second, more controllable, characteristics of flow.

FIVE TIPS TO HELP YOU GET MORE FLOW

▶ **Make sure the challenge is set at an appropriate level.**

The bar should be set neither too high nor too low.

▶ **Make sure that you have clear goals.**

Having SMART+ goals can help flow.

▶ **Automatically get clear feedback as to whether you are achieving your goals.**

Set up the activity so you automatically find out how you are doing, in the way that a golf player senses that their golf swing is just right.

▶ **Concentrate fully on the task.**

Do one thing at a time, and set your mind to doing it. The ability to concentrate may be helped by meditation and yoga.

▶ **Choose a working environment where there are no distractions.**

Many prefer a tranquil, silent place. Others prefer more idiosyncratic settings to help achieve concentration. For example, the writer Stephen King does his best work when listening to heavy metal music.

Case study: Using flow tips to help studying

Meera used to really enjoy her subject, but since starting on her PhD programme was having immense difficulties working on her thesis. Every time she tried to write, she soon found herself browsing the internet or comfort eating. Meera recognized that she used to achieve flow through studying – which was probably one of the reasons she got a first-class degree! The question she pondered with her life coach was – 'What is stopping me getting into flow now I am studying for a PhD?'

Meera was asked to write a paragraph for her PhD in her coach's presence, and froze, saying things like, 'This isn't original enough' and, 'This isn't at all well written'. She was clearly experiencing anxiety rather than flow (recall the three flow equations, page 120).

Meera looked with her coach at the five tips for creating flow and decided that two were particularly relevant. Clearly the bar was set too high (tip 1). At first, Meera was despondent – did this mean that she was not up to doing a PhD? But when Meera thought about what she was trying to do, she realized that she was actually trying to do two things at once. She was trying both to do original research and to write excellent prose. Consequently she could not concentrate fully on either task (tip 4).

She resolved to concentrate on style and content separately. Meera decided to do a first draft where she did not bother at all with style or grammar; she would just get her ideas down. Only when doing the final draft would she concentrate on style and then she would be concerned only with style. A week later, Meera reported back saying that for the first time in months she had got some useful work done. She was still unsure whether it was of a high enough standard, but at least she now had some work to show her supervisor.

Key idea: You can use the flow tips to help you achieve flow

While flow is partly about prioritizing the right activities, you can also increase your chances of finding flow by making sure you have a clear goal and feedback, that the challenge is set at the right level and that you are in a distraction-free environment where you can concentrate.

Microflow

Csikszentmihalyi has proposed the idea that it may be possible to turn mundane, boring tasks into activities where you experience a certain amount of flow. He calls this 'microflow'. For example, humming a tune or doodling may produce microflow. You could try it out now for yourself, to see if you can learn some of the key ideas from this chapter and experience microflow at the same time.

Try it now: See if you can find flow learning about flow

Create a mnemonic[67] to help you remember the eight major characteristics of flow.

  C Challenging activity

  G Goals and feedback

  C Concentration

  O Oneness with the activity

  S Self-consciousness disappears

  T Time is distorted

  S Sense of control

  I Intrinsic motivation

For example, you might try to create two words out of the letters CGCOSTSI.

Set aside four minutes for the task.

Hint: You may find it easier if you write the letters down. If you cannot find a good mnemonic with these letters, feel free to alter them (for example, changing the first C for Challenging into an A for Activity).

Now set aside a further four minutes to try to remember the eight characteristics of flow using the mnemonic.

Were you able to create a mnemonic?[68] Could you remember the eight characteristics? Did you experience flow or microflow during this activity?

The benefits of flow

The main benefits of flow are that it is enjoyable, is associated with optimal performance and increases motivation. Consequently, there are strong reasons to think that it is part of flourishing. There is also some evidence that identifying and enhancing flow can help with psychological problems.

FLOW IS ENJOYABLE

Flow activities are fun. The tennis player who is totally immersed in the game and feels a sense of improvement and accomplishment enjoys playing. Enjoyment is not the same as pleasure – the tennis player may feel little pleasure but still enjoy the game.

Remember this: Flow is not the same as pleasure

Flow is associated with being so absorbed in a task that you do not usually feel anything. This is why positive emotions and engagement (flow) are separate components of PERMA.

FLOW ENHANCES PERFORMANCE

Since flow is associated with peak performance, it is not surprising that the business world has shown some interest in it (Csikszentmihalyi, 2004). One striking example is a struggling Scandinavian transport company called Green Cargo. It decided to see if facilitating flow at work for its employees could help. It sent them on training courses about flow and gave them Csikszentmihalyi's book to read. Crucially, they followed this up by setting up extended regular monthly one-to-one meetings between workers and their managers. This enabled the workers to set clear goals in performance contracts and to get feedback from their managers. After two years, Green Cargo turned in a profit for the first time in decades. Microsoft and Ericsson have also applied ideas about flow.

FLOW AND MOTIVATION

Flow enhances motivation. Since flow activities are intrinsically motivating, people want to keep doing them. They need neither external rewards nor self-control to continue – they just want to continue the task until it is finished for its own sake.

Flow and psychotherapy

In his third-wave CBT for depression, which focuses on the disabling effect of rumination (dwelling on things), British psychotherapist Ed Watkins includes identifying and scheduling flow activities as part of the treatment. The Milan Group, which after Chicago is the major research group on flow, has also used flow as part of treatment for a variety of psychiatric problems including schizophrenia and agoraphobia. Csikszentmihalyi cites the case of a Dutch schizophrenic. Using the 'experience sampling method', it was found that she was happiest when cutting her nails. Psychiatrists helped her get a job as a manicurist and she was able to leave hospital. It should be stressed that the use of flow in psychotherapy is based mainly on individual clinical experience and further work is required to show whether it is more effective than other treatments.

Limitations and dangers of flow

▶ **Is flow really all there is to a good and meaningful life?**

Proponents of flow make some pretty extravagant claims, such as, 'A good life is one that is characterized by complete absorption in what one does.' (Nakamura and Csikszentmihalyi, 2009).

This extreme position is not very plausible. Remember that Seligman's PERMA theory has four other elements of flourishing. Would you choose a life of flow if it lacked pleasure, good relationships, meaning and accomplishment? Still, we have seen that flow has substantial benefits, so perhaps all we need to do is recognize that flow is not the only ingredient of flourishing.

▶ Can flow be addictive?

Csikszentmihalyi admits that flow has a dark side, including its addictive properties. Designers of computer games use ideas about flow to make their games as enjoyable as possible. The series of levels in computer games ensures players are able to experience an appropriate level of challenge. One of the attractions of gambling is the flow that gamblers experience. Since flow is so enjoyable, there is a danger that people will return again and again to flow activities, regardless of how engaging in them interferes with other aspects of their life.

▶ What is the relationship of flow to the other components of flourishing?

Flow is positively associated with two elements of flourishing: engagement and performance. However, there can sometimes be a tension between flow activities and other elements of flourishing. The man who spends inordinate hours playing computer games may damage his intimate relationships and find little overall meaning in life. The teenager listening to their iPod when crossing the road may endanger their life. More research is required about the relationship of flow to the other four elements of PERMA.

Remember this: Find a balance between flow and other parts of flourishing

It is important to strike a balance between flow activities and other elements of well-being. This can be achieved in two ways:

▶ Organize flow activities so they interfere less with other priorities (e.g. by reading the novel on the daily commute rather than when your partner wants quality time together).

▶ Turn the activities associated with other elements of flourishing into flow (e.g. by developing joint flow activities with your partner).

Focus points

❋ Flow has been proposed as part of flourishing, for example in Seligman's PERMA theory.

❋ Flow means enjoyable absorption in an activity.

❋ There are eight main characteristics of flow activities.

❋ There are a number of ways to increase flow experiences.

❋ Flow is associated with increased enjoyment, performance and motivation.

Diagnostic test answers

1 Flow is the enjoyable and performance-enhancing experience of being totally absorbed in what you are doing.

2 Mihaly Csikszentmihalyi.

3 A challenging activity well matched to your level of skill.
Having clear goals and immediate feedback.
Complete concentration on the task.
A feeling of oneness with the activity.
A loss of self-consciousness and a feeling of calmness and serenity.
Time does not pass in the usual way.
A feeling of being in control.
Intrinsic motivation.

4 Activities include mountaineering, chess, dancing, painting, surgery and skiing, playing team sports and playing jazz, but this list is not exhaustive.

5 Generally people find more flow at work than during leisure pursuits.

6 Find out where you currently experience flow and schedule more of those activities.

Make activities flow-full by changing aspects of them using the five tips to get more flow in the 'How to increase flow' section of this chapter.

7 Your answer might include any of the following:

❋ Anything that reduces concentration, for example, doing several things at once.

- ✻ The task being too easy, in which case boredom rather than flow is likely to arise.
- ✻ Focusing too much on attempting to find flow – you need to be focusing on the task itself.
- ✻ Not getting clear and immediate feedback.
- ✻ The task being too difficult, in which case anxiety is more likely to arise than flow.

8 Your answers to the 'Try it now' activities will help you here.

9 Flow is enjoyable.
Flow enhances performance.
Flow enhances motivation.

10 Flow activities can be addictive.
Flow activities may interfere with other priorities in life.

Next steps

In this chapter we have expanded on the second component of PERMA. The next chapter will explore how positive psychology can help us understand and enhance positive relationships.

Relationships

In this chapter you will learn:

▶ *about psychological theories regarding the ingredients of successful romantic relationships*

▶ *evidence-based strategies to improve relationships, including intimate relationships, work relationships and friendships*

▶ *how positive psychology's toolkit can enhance relationships.*

Diagnostic test

1 What are three elements of Robert Sternberg's 'triangular theory of love'?

2 What is the name given for the ideal combination of these elements?

3 What does research say about the importance of 'love at first sight'?

4 According to Gottman, what are the 'four horsemen of the apocalypse' which are most damaging to relationships?

5 Gottman and Silver have identified seven research-based ideas for making marriages work. Name three of them.

6 What is the ratio of positive to negative interactions in good relationships during conflict, found by John Gottman?

7 Name three positive psychology techniques that can help with relationships.

8 What are the four types of responding to good news identified by Shelly Gable?

9 Which is the best one?

10 Which is the least helpful one?

What are the ingredients of a successful intimate relationship?

What do you think are the ingredients of a successful intimate relationship? Is it, as Hollywood would have it, love at first sight? Or are common interests and friendship more important? Or is it, in the end, commitment to the relationship that matters most?

Psychologist Robert Sternberg has proposed an answer to this question that has become known as the triangular theory of love (1998). This theory suggests that there are three ingredients in flourishing loving relationships, namely:

▶ Passion – sexual interest and desire are perhaps the most obvious elements of romantic love. It is what distinguishes it from a Platonic relationship. Passion is what Juliet and

Romeo felt for each other. It is the 'thunderbolt' anticipated by the Hugh Grant character in the British rom-com *Four Weddings and a Funeral.*

▶ Intimacy – sharing thoughts and feelings in a friendship is Sternberg's second ingredient of successful intimate relationships. Why does the viewer want the two main characters in *When Harry Met Sally* to get together, if not because we feel their strong friendship would make for a deeper romantic relationship?

▶ Commitment – deciding to be with your partner and stay with them is crucial. Lack of commitment is the failing of the 'commitment phobics' encountered all too often by the heroine of *Bridget Jones's Diary.*

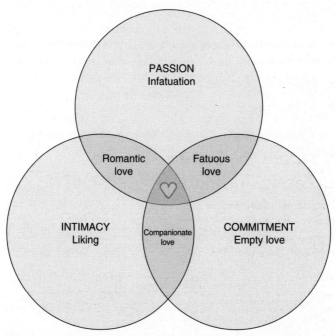

♡ = Consummate love: presence of passion, intimacy and commitment

Sternberg's triangular theory of love

The triangular theory has been vindicated by analysing the words that couples use about what is important to them in relationships (Aron and Westbay, 1996). Many of the words important to couples turn out to be about passion, intimacy or commitment.

The theory has a number of important implications. Obviously you should aim to have relationships with all three ingredients. You can also use it to diagnose what is missing in failing relationships. Sternberg has identified seven types of relationship.

► Infatuation is when there is only passion in a relationship. While many relationships might start like this, there will be problems if the relationship does not develop. Generally infatuation does not last very long (see below). Even if it did, the relationship would not satisfy your needs for friendship and commitment.

► Fatuous love means passion and commitment without emotional intimacy. A couple who commit to each other after a whirlwind romance might exhibit fatuous love. If friendship does not develop, problems are likely to arise. They might be the sort of couple who complain that, 'we can't live with each other but we can't live without each other'.

► Romantic love is, perhaps surprisingly, not the ideal. It is the name for intimacy and passion with no commitment. A holiday romance might be a positive case of romantic love.

► Liking is emotional intimacy without either commitment or passion. The relationship is more like a friendship than a romantic relationship.

► Companionate love combines liking with commitment but without passion. An elderly happily married couple may well experience companionate love.

► Empty love means commitment with no passion or friendship. An unhappy couple staying together just for the children would share empty love.

► Consummate love is the term Sternberg reserves for the ideal, the combination of intimacy, passion and commitment.

Try it now: Which sort of relationship are you in?

If you currently in an intimate relationship, you might like to identify which sort of relationship you are in. What about past relationships? Does Sternberg's theory shed any light on why the relationships did not succeed?

Sternberg's theory does not advise giving up on your relationship if it is not consummate love. Once you have learned what the missing ingredients are you can work on improving the relationship. Neither should you rest on your laurels if you rate your current relationship as being one of consummate love. Good relationships need to be worked at.

There is a natural rhythm to romantic relationships. A typical trajectory would look like this:

1 Infatuation in the early stages.

2 Romantic love as you get to know each other.

3 Consummate love when there is reciprocal commitment.

4 As you get older, the relationship may move on to a more companionate love (which is not to say that passion is impossible in older relationships!).

This may help you to understand changes in a relationship. You should not expect the same degree of passion to persist in a relationship over a long time, or for friendship to arise immediately.

Has psychology provided an answer to the Hugh Grant character's 'thunderbolt' question? Do you need to feel love at first sight to have a successful relationship? Psychologists call the thunderbolt 'limerence' and would advise the Hugh Grant character not to wait for it. John Gottman, whose extensive empirical research on relationships we will review shortly, has found that few couples experience the 'thunderbolt'. Those that have felt it do not tend to have better or worse relationships in the long run – though it is pleasant to go through at the time.[69] In his book *The Happiness Hypothesis*,

Jonathan Haidt is more outspoken in arguing against the *Four Weddings and a Funeral* view of love. He argues that passionate love is like heroin – addictive, short lasting and dangerous. In his view, the search for the 'high' and expectation that it will continue mitigates against the possibility of more enduring successful intimate relationships. In short, the thunderbolt is at best a nice to have, at worst a dangerous expectation.

There is one more very useful insight to be gained from Sternberg's theory. Not everyone needs consummate love at every stage of their life. A relationship may work well if both parties both want the same combination of passion, intimacy and commitment – for example, a couple shares infatuation in a holiday romance or romantic love before they are ready to 'settle down'. Real problems can arise when they want different things. The novel and film *The Graduate* illustrates this point very well.

Case study: Mrs Robinson and Benjamin Braddock

As well as being very funny, *The Graduate* is a good illustration of how not to find the right relationship. And this goes beyond the very obvious, 'Don't sleep with your father's business partner's wife'. Looking through the lens of Sternberg's theory helps us understand the predicaments of the two main protagonists. Ben, the young and inexperienced graduate of the title, is seduced by Mrs Robinson, the glamorous, middle-aged wife of his father's business partner. At first there is little emotional intimacy or commitment on either side – their affair is an infatuation. This isn't a problem and the couple meet regularly for mutual entertainment. After a while, however, their attitudes change. Ben craves more intimacy. But whenever he tries to initiate a friendly conversation with his lover she shuts him up. While she doesn't want intimacy, Mrs Robinson demands commitment. She is furious when Ben decides to keep to a long-standing arrangement to go on a date with her daughter, Elaine. Ben is after romantic love while Mrs Robinson wants fatuous love. It is this mismatch of relationship intentions that causes all the problems.

Key idea: Sternberg's triangular theory of love

The triangular theory of love suggests that a good intimate relationship consists of three elements, namely passion, commitment and intimacy. Not all need be present to the same degree in all stages of a relationship. The different combinations of elements lead to seven different sorts of relationship. Consummate love is the ideal. Real problems are most likely to occur when the two sides want different elements from the relationship.

Empirically validated findings on how to improve relationships

While the triangular theory of love provides a theoretical understanding with some practical implications, psychologist John Gottman and his colleagues have been carrying out empirical research about intimate relationships for over 30 years. Gottman claims a 90 per cent success rate in predicting whether a couple will get divorced from observing how they interact with each other. He has found four particularly damaging behaviours which he labels the 'four horsemen of the apocalypse'. So, what should you do if you want your relationship to fail?

▶ Criticize your partner as much as you can. Do it as harshly as you can. 'What is wrong with you?' said in a contemptuous tone would be a good stock phrase.

▶ Whenever you are being criticized, do not accept any responsibility. Be as defensive as possible. Ignore what your partner says and point out all their faults.

▶ Be contemptuous of your partner. Sarcasm, mockery and eye-rolling are all good things to try.

▶ Ignore conflict. Go to the pub or garden shed at the smallest sign of trouble. This strategy, called 'stonewalling', is a favourite horseman for men.

When presented in this way it is obvious that the 'four horsemen of the apocalypse' are destructive. Gottman's research is valuable because it suggests that these are the most unhelpful ways of communicating – worse than getting angry, which according to Gottman is perfectly normal and not necessarily so damaging as long as it is quickly repaired and does not turn into belligerence.

Key idea: Gottman's four horsemen of doomed relationships

Gottman's research shows that above all others, four attitudes predict divorce. These are criticism, contempt, defensiveness and stonewalling. Anger is not so problematic, as long as it is quickly repaired.

So what positive principles make intimate relationships flourish? In his book *The Seven Principles for Making Marriage Work* (co-written with Nan Silver), Gottman proposes seven research-based principles with tips about how to put them into practice.

1. ENHANCE YOUR LOVE MAPS

Learn what is important to your partner. The best way to do this is quite simple: ask them! Ask your partner how their day went. Ask them what's on their mind. Ask them about their hopes and dreams. A good follow-up is a 'caring day'.

Try it now: Caring days

Therapist Richard Stuart has developed the idea of a 'caring day' to help enhance relationships (Stuart, 1980).

You and your partner begin by writing down an agreed number of things you would like your partner to do in the next couple of weeks – between five and ten is a good number. These should be specific, positive and easy to do (such as 'make me a cup of tea in the morning' or 'massage my shoulders when I get home'). Avoid controversial activities, or things that have come up in arguments. You should also focus on positive things you want your partner to do rather than things you do not want them to do. The focus should be much more on small caring behaviours that are meaningful to you rather than on material gifts.

You then put the list up in a prominent place, such as on the fridge. You both agree to do one (or more) thing each day for a set number of days. What gets done is recorded on a sheet. You can decide between you how you want to use the caring days. For example, a day could be designated as a joint caring day, or one person's caring day.

As an example, Carol writes the following on her list for her personal caring day: 'massage my shoulders when I get home', 'ask about my day', 'phone me during the day', 'make me a cup of tea in the morning', 'hug me when I get home', 'look at me when you talk to me', 'hold my hand when we watch TV together' and 'share something amusing with me about your day'. She and her partner Jon agree that he will do three things on her caring list the next day, and she will reciprocate the following day. They decide to continue this for the week and at the weekend have a joint sharing day.

✳ What would you put on the list?
✳ What do you think your partner would ask for?
✳ Why not try it out and see how it works for you?

2. NURTURE YOUR FONDNESS AND ADMIRATION

Research suggests that flourishing couples are able to appreciate their partner's good points. They tend to see their partner's weaknesses as endearing foibles. For example, if your partner is forgetful, much better to say, 'dear old you, always forgetting something!' in a soft tone of voice than, 'why can't you ever remember anything!' contemptuously. If they make a mistake that is not characteristic, be sure to recognize that the problem is situational and temporary rather than a permanent trait. For example, if they react angrily because they are under a lot of pressure, remind yourself that they are saying this because they are really stressed out. Better still, do something to help them cope with the stress.

Focusing on their strengths and positive qualities can also be a good way to help you feel more appreciative. It is important that appreciation and fondness be expressed as well as felt. They can be communicated physically, for instance with a hug, and in words by genuine compliments. By nurturing your fondness and admiration you are keeping the 'horsemen' of criticism and contempt at bay.

3. TURN TOWARDS EACH OTHER INSTEAD OF AWAY

This means prioritizing time with each other. You should respond positively when your partner wants your attention, even when you do not feel like giving it. This does not mean that you cannot spend time on your own or with friends. In the first stages of a relationship, when passion is high, prioritizing the relationship often comes naturally. Later on, it might require being proactive to keep the passion going (like going on a 'date' with your partner) or doing things to build the friendship element (such as developing joint interests and joint friendships).

4. LET YOUR PARTNER INFLUENCE YOU

Good relationships involve working as a team and making joint decisions. It does not require always doing exactly what your partner wants. It does, however, mean being aware of what they want and taking it into account. This advice is a good antidote to the horsemen of defensiveness and stonewalling.

5. SOLVE YOUR SOLVABLE PROBLEMS

Some problems can be solved if couples take the right attitude. Gottman suggests a soft, gentle start-up to tackling these problems, defusing tension by taking time-outs, practising slow breathing or relaxation. You should aim for compromise rather than 'winning'. In fact, in the context of the relationship, 'winning' may actually be losing. Gottman's ideas can be usefully supplemented by considering Stephen Covey's ideas about looking for a synergistic 'win–win solution' (*The 7 Habits of Highly Effective People*, 1989).

Covey identifies four stages of seeking win-win agreements:

1 See the problem from the other person's viewpoint.

2 Identify the key issues and concerns.

3 Determine the results that would constitute a fully acceptable solution.

4 Identify new options to achieve these results.

Synergistic solutions are not compromises. For example, suppose that you want the window open and your partner wants the window shut. A compromise would be to have the window half open. But let's apply Covey's four stages to the problem. First you see the problem from the other person's viewpoint – you ask them why they want the window closed. Suppose they say that it is because they do not like the draft. Next you identify all the key issues. It is important to recognise the underlying issues – your partner's concern is not really having the window open or shut – it is the draft or coolness. You want the window open because you want the room to be more ventilated. Now you can see that the compromise solution would not make either of you happy – you would still want more ventilation, and they would still feel a draft! So what you want (stage 3) is an option that gives you the ventilation and avoids a draft for them. Stage 4 – the creative phase – is to try to think of options. Perhaps you can leave a door open and have a window open in an adjacent room to achieve the same result.

6. OVERCOME GRIDLOCK

Some problems just do not have a good compromise. Disagreements about career, where to live, religion and children's education may come into this category. If, after searching for a win-win solution or a compromise this proves impossible, Gottman's suggestion is to have a dialogue, acknowledging your partner's dream even if you cannot find a way to fulfil both your dreams.

7. CREATE SHARED MEANING

Rituals like watching a TV programme together or taking it in turns to make each other breakfast in bed may be really important. Gottman speaks of creating a shared culture that expresses joint values and gives a shared purpose.

Key idea: Gottman's seven principles for making marriage work

Gottman and colleagues have discovered seven principles which their research says are most important to help relationships flourish. The seven principles are:

1 Enhance your love maps.
2 Nurture your fondness and admiration.
3 Turn towards each other instead of away.
4 Let your partner influence you.
5 Solve your solvable problems.
6 Overcome gridlock.
7 Create shared meaning.

There is one other often-quoted piece of research associated with Gottman. While the research is sound, sometimes the interpretation is misleading.

Remember this: Be cautious of 'magic numbers' in psychology

If you do an internet search of the term 'Gottman ratio' you will get thousands of hits and see articles with titles such as 'John Gottman's Magic 5 to 1 Ratio'. They imply that you need five positive interactions for every negative to have a stable relationship. However, there are several reasons to be cautious about this idea. First, the experiments actually showed that stable relationships exhibited the 5:1 ratio when couples were asked to talk about a problematic issue. During more normal interaction, in good relationships the ratio was nearer 20:1. Second, correlation does not imply causation. It may be that the positive statements are a result of the relationship being in a good state rather than vice versa. Finally, it is unlikely that there are any magic number ratios in psychology that apply to all situations. The effect of what we do depends a lot on meaning and context. A hug could be perceived as negative if your partner suspects that you are after something. An angry outburst could be positive if it is taken to mean that you really do care.

Of course, this does not mean that you should not attempt to increase the positivity in your relationship. But you are advised to be a little sceptical if the complexities of relationships are reduced to a magic number.

How positive psychology can bolster Gottman's principles

Many of positive psychology's ideas about how to improve an individual's well-being can be easily adapted to help with relationships. Here are some ideas:

▶ Learn where your partner gets flow.

▶ Express gratitude to your partner.

▶ Find joint flow activities.

▶ Learn about your partner's values.

▶ Tell your partner about your values.

▶ Learn about their strengths.

▶ Show appreciation of their top strengths.

▶ Help them use their top strengths and help them manage their weaknesses.

▶ Tell your partner about three good things each day, and ask them to tell you their three good things.

▶ Share your answers to the 'Best possible self' activity (see Chapter 3).

▶ Use the step-by-step approach (see Chapter 5) to help plan joint goals.

▶ Use the step-by-step approach to help them plan their own goals.

Remember this: There are a lot of good ideas in positive psychology!

In this book each idea from positive psychology is introduced in a particular chapter, but remember that many of the ideas have multiple applications. For example, step-by-step planning can be used to achieve goals in every domain, so is probably relevant to every chapter. When you encounter a technique or idea, think creatively about how you can use it.

Active and constructive responding

Psychologist Shelly Gable's theory of 'active and constructive responding'[70] is intended to help with relationships in general, including romantic relationships. Her research suggests that an important relationship-builder or relationship-breaker is how you react when someone tells you about some good news.

Suppose someone told you that they had been praised by their boss or successfully completed a challenging task. How do you think you would respond? Would you:

▶ say things which diminish their achievement and find potential pitfalls ('rain on their parade')

▶ fail to acknowledge what they have said at all, for example by changing the subject

▶ acknowledge their success, but in a very muted way, for example by saying in a neutral tone, 'that's great' and then moving on

▶ respond very positively to their success, showing your excitement and celebrating their success.

These four ways of responding are ranked in order of desirability. The final possibility, active and constructive responding, is the recommended approach.

Here is an example illustrating the four ways that your partner might respond to you getting a new job. Which would you prefer?

Active and constructive	Passive and constructive
(Beaming)	(In neutral tone)
That's fantastic! Talk me through how you felt when you found out. How shall we celebrate?	Well done.

Passive and destructive	Active and destructive
(In neutral tone)	(Contemptuously)
What else did you do today?	They must be really desperate!

Remember this: Use active and constructive responding wisely

Responding to good news actively and constructively is a good piece of advice, but as with many tips from positive psychology, some judgement is needed as to how to apply it wisely. One risk is that it can come over as patronizing or false if you overdo the praise or excitement. This will obviously depend on your personality and what people are used to. However, rather than saying 'active and constructive responding just isn't me', it is better to adapt it to your personality. For example, instead of gushing you can ask people questions that encourage them to talk about their good news and thereby savour their positive emotions.

Another valid concern is this: what if it is not good news? What if a friend tells you excitedly that they are re-entering an abusive relationship? Here a 'stroke sandwich', where you start and end with positive statements, would be a good idea. For example:

1 Start by empathizing – 'You look very happy'.
2 Then express your feelings of uncertainty, perhaps by saying that you are going to play devil's advocate.
3 Finish by saying something positive which does not give the message that you agree with the decision. 'I'm really glad that you've shared this with me.'

Friendships and positive work relationships

Many of the positive psychology ideas above can also be applied to work relationships and friendships. Lyubomirsky (*The How of Happiness*, 2007) gives the following additional advice:

▶ Prioritize relationships – make time for other people.

▶ Show an interest in friends and encourage them.

▶ Communicate effectively – make eye contact, acknowledge, self-disclose.

▶ Be supportive and loyal.

▶ Hug each other. Studies show that hugging has positive physical and emotional benefits.

Case study: Tom

Years ago I worked with someone who was in most ways a nice guy, except for one very annoying and enduring foible. Everyone in the office liked their tea and coffee, but we were on the fourth floor and the kitchen was on the ground floor. It had become part of our culture to do 'rounds' of tea and coffee for each other, one person perhaps taking 15 minutes out of their work to get a round of drinks each day. Tom liked his tea as much as the next person and was a very willing beneficiary of system. But Tom was a free rider. In months he had never got a round.

This all changed one day when the technical whizz-kid in our team devised an online system of recording tea rounds. Every time you made a tea round, you got a point for each tea you made. You lost a point for every tea that was made for you. Obviously after a day or two, Tom was bottom of the league table. However, once this was brought to Tom's attention, a dramatic change took place. Whereas before it had seemed as if Tom knew the location of neither the kitchen nor the tea tray, now they were seldom parted. Tom made two or three rounds every day and leapt to the top of the tea-makers' table. What do you think Tom's strength was? You guessed it, competitiveness. The moral? If you want to change someone's behaviour, think about how you can harness their strengths to achieve it.

Try it now: Using positive psychology to enhance relationships

* Choose a relationship you would like to improve this week (romantic, family or work).
* Pick one idea from this chapter to try out this week.
* Write down your plan about what to do, and then record how it goes.
* This is a good opportunity to practise doing step-by-step planning (see Chapter 5).

Diagnostic test answers

1 Passion, intimacy and commitment.

2 The combination of all three is called consummate love.

3 The research suggests love at first sight is a 'nice to have'. Generally the feeling of love at first sight does not last more than a few months and it does not predict either a lasting or successful relationship.

4 Criticism, contempt, defensiveness and stonewalling

5 The seven principles are:

a Enhance your love maps.
b Nurture your fondness and admiration.
c Turn towards each other instead of away.
d Let your partner influence you.
e Solve your solvable problems.
f Overcome gridlock.
g Express gratitude to your partner.

6 5:1

7 Three from:

a Learn where your partner gets flow; find joint flow.

b Learn about their values and help them attain them; pursue joint values.

c Learn about their strengths; play to their strengths.

d Do the 'Three good things' activity each day with your partner.

e Ask your partner about their best possible self.

f Use a step-by-step approach to achieve goals.

8 Active constructive, active destructive, passive constructive and passive destructive

9 Active constructive

10 Passive destructive

Next steps

Well-being is not just about happiness and PERMA; it also means being able to deal with emotional difficulties and problems in life. In the next chapter we will look at evidence-based ways to help you deal with life's adversities.

9

Managing difficulties: resilience and CBT

In this chapter you will learn:

- ▶ *about resilience and why it is important*
- ▶ *how what you have already learned can improve your resilience*
- ▶ *about CBT (cognitive behavioural therapy)*
- ▶ *about problem solving*
- ▶ *relaxation techniques.*

Diagnostic test

1 In positive psychology, what is meant by the term 'resilience'?

2 Why is resilience important?

3 Name five negative emotions which CBT may be able to help manage.

4 Name three ways in which positive psychology can help with resilience.

5 What is a thinking trap?

6 Name three thinking traps.

7 A woman has just been to an interview where she did not answer all the questions correctly. She has four negative automatic thoughts:

   a 'I will not get the job.'
   b 'I completely fouled up that interview.'
   c 'I ought to be able to answer every question correctly.'
   d 'If I don't get this job, that will be terrible.'

   Match each thought with a thinking trap that best fits it. For example, if you think a) is an example of an 'unhelpful should', answer a) iv.

   Hint: each thinking trap corresponds best with one of the thoughts above.

   i   Extreme thinking
   ii Catastrophising
   iii Jumping to conclusions
   iv Unhelpful shoulds (and other personal rules).

8 What is a behavioural experiment?

9 Name the seven steps of problem solving.

10 Name three relaxation techniques.

Resilience

Resilience has been defined as the ability to bounce back from adversity. We will be using the term 'resilience' in the broad sense of being able skilfully to manage life problems and negative emotions skilfully.

Situations where resilience is called for ('adversities') include dealing with difficult people, experiencing a loss such as redundancy or a relationship break-up, being burgled or mugged and being in a stressful job. In addition, we all have our own personal 'signature' vulnerabilities. Do you know what yours are?

Try it now: Identify your personal emotional vulnerabilities

We all have our own unique personal emotional vulnerabilities. It is very helpful to be able to identify these so you are better able to manage them. The first step is to identify the negative emotions and experiences you are most prone to feel. Choose the ones from the list below that affect you most frequently.

Negative emotions and experiences

Abandoned	Broken	Guilty	Moody	Sad
Afraid	Depressed	Hating	Mortified	Scared
Angry	Down	Hopeless	Negative	Self-hating
Anxious	Embarrassed	Humiliated	Overwhelmed	Self-pitying
Ashamed	Empty	Hurt	Panicky	Shocked
Awful	Envious	Isolated	Paralysed	Stressed
Bad	Feeling blue	Jealous	Paranoid	Trapped
Bitter	Feeling lost	Lonely	Resentful	Unpleasant
Bored	Fed up	Low	Rejected	Useless

Add any other negative emotions and experiences that are not in the list above but affect you a lot. Next, think about what circumstances usually trigger the emotions you have chosen. Write down these trigger situations.

Typical triggers of your negative emotions

Other people (Who?)

Work (What sort of situations?)

Time spent on my own (Where?)

Having too much to do (What and where?)

Losses (Which ones?)

Changes (Which ones?)

Any other triggers not listed above (What are they?)

You will notice that you have been invited to elaborate on the things that trigger emotional difficulties. For example, rather than just choosing 'other people', it would be helpful if you could say which people tend to trigger negative emotions. You will find this information very useful when you come to work on developing resilience later in this chapter.

WHY IS RESILIENCE IMPORTANT?

Why have a chapter on resilience and managing difficulties in a book on positive psychology? There are at least three good reasons why achieving the positive requires skilful handling of the negative:

▶ By definition, your SWB is reduced when you experience negative emotions. It follows that if you want to have high SWB you need be able to manage negative emotions well.

▶ Negative emotions do not just feel bad, they also adversely affect health, relationships and effectiveness. So even in the unlikely event that you do not mind experiencing negative emotions, they are still likely to cause problems.

▶ There is a lot of evidence that negative emotions are stronger than positive ones. We notice the negative more and they have a greater impact (hence the idea of a 3:1 positivity ratio). Consequently, to get a good balance of positive and negative emotions a two-pronged attack is advisable. Do what you can to increase positive emotions and at the same time manage negative emotions skilfully.

Key idea: The meaning and importance of resilience

Resilience means the ability to bounce back from adversities or, more broadly, to handle difficult situations and emotions skilfully. It is important because negative emotions reduce SWB, have a negative impact on relationships, effectiveness and health and are stronger than positive emotions.

Try it now: How helpful are your behaviours when you have a setback?

Think of situations where you are experiencing negative emotions – the list of triggers and negative emotions and your response to the first 'Try it now' in this chapter will be very helpful here. Now reflect on how you tend to respond to them. Below is a list of 20 possible responses. Answer how often you do these as follows:

4 Always or nearly always
3 Most of the time
2 About half the time
1 Usually not
0 Never or hardly ever

Be sure to rate yourself on what you actually do rather than what you think you ought to do.

1   Think a lot about all the other things that have gone wrong in my life
2   Have a drink or take other substances that make me feel better for a while, even though they do more harm than good in the long run
3   Go to the gym or find another way to do some exercise
4   Notice my thoughts without necessarily getting lost in them
5   Try to work out how I'll handle all the possible consequences
6   Share my troubles with someone I trust
7   Find a way to calm myself down, such as a breathing or relaxation exercise
8   Avoid the problem
9   Shut myself away from everyone
10 Work out how to solve the problem and then take the first step
11 Think of how I've successfully dealt with problems in the past
12 Have something to eat
13 Remind myself of my past successes

HOW POSITIVE PSYCHOLOGY CAN HELP YOU TO BE MORE RESILIENT

Some of the strategies you have learned to increase SWB and flourishing can also help you be more resilient. Here is a summary of the most helpful.

▶ Do the 'Three good things' exercise (see Chapter 2). This will enable you to feel more optimistic and hopeful.

▶ Develop a more optimistic explanatory style. Consider the possibility that adversities might be impermanent, temporary and impersonal (as opposed to the 3Ps).

▶ Do the 'Best possible self' exercise (see Chapter 3) to increase your optimism and sense of purpose.

▶ Develop a growth mindset. This will help you see setbacks as learning opportunities.

▶ Use your strengths more. Manage your weaknesses.

▶ Use step-by-step planning (see Chapter 5) to achieve your goals more consistently.

▶ Identify likely obstacles to your goals and work out ways to overcome them in advance (i.e. use defensive pessimism).

This strategy makes it less likely that you will become frustrated when you meet with obstacles.

▶ Set SMART+ goals to help move in your valued direction. In particular, make sure that very large goals are broken down into achievable 'baby steps'.

▶ If one goal is blocked, think flexibly and creatively about other ways to achieve the goal. If a valued direction is blocked, put more effort into other valued directions.

▶ Try to understand the meaning of setbacks. Perhaps they are telling you something important and ultimately positive.

▶ Be open to the possibility that even traumas can be an opportunity for personal growth. Nolen-Hoeksema (2000) found that optimistic bereaved people cope better, for example by treating bereavement as a wake-up call to reprioritize their lives.

▶ Be more grateful. This can help you put setbacks into perspective.

▶ Experience positive emotions so they can 'undo' negative emotions. Identify your own personal 'reset buttons' and use them to respond to adversities constructively.

Case study: Helen Keller

Despite being blind and deaf from the age of 19 months, Helen Keller grew up to become a famous activist and writer. She campaigned for the rights of women and those with disabilities and wrote 12 books, the most famous of which is her autobiography *The Story of My Life*. Keller was one of Gallup's most widely admired people of the 20th century.

On the grand scale of setbacks, going blind and deaf comes pretty high. What enabled Helen Keller to overcome her disabilities? Undoubtedly luck and circumstances played a part. She was particularly fortunate to be taught and mentored by Anne Sullivan, her companion for many years. But it's equally true that Keller exemplified many of the qualities that positive psychology advocates to promote resilience.

Keller was undoubtedly an optimist – she even wrote a book on the subject. In it she said: 'Optimism is the faith that leads to achievement. Nothing can be done without hope and confidence.' Keller urged her readers to 'Be of good cheer. Do not think of today's failures, but of the success that may come tomorrow.'

Keller combined optimism with gratitude. She put it most eloquently when she wrote: 'When one door of happiness closes, another opens, but often we look so long at the closed door that we do not see the one that has been opened for us.' Keller was able to appreciate the good things in her life, such as her friendships. She chose not to dwell on the injustice of her disabilities. As Keller put it, 'Walking with a friend in the dark is better than walking alone in the light.'

Keller definitely had a growth mindset and demonstrated both grit and perseverance. She believed that 'we can do anything we want if we stick to it long enough'. In another passage she advised, 'You have set yourself a difficult task but will succeed if you persevere; and you will find a joy in overcoming obstacles.'

Helen Keller realized that life presents us with plenty of difficulties and setbacks, but that with optimism, gratitude and perseverance we can still cope and live a meaningful, fulfilling life. From her own experience she had learned that that, 'All the world is full of suffering. It is also full of overcoming.'

Cognitive behavioural therapy (CBT)

CBT is an evidence-based therapy that can help with a range of emotional difficulties including depression, anxiety and anger-management problems. Its origins lie in the Stoic philosopher Epictetus's saying, 'People are affected not by things but by their interpretation of them.' Albert Ellis developed his version of CBT, called Rational Emotive Behaviour Therapy, in the 1950s but it is the version developed by Aaron T. Beck a decade later that has proved the most enduring.

USING A FIVE-PART MODEL TO UNDERSTAND YOUR DIFFICULTIES

The first step in managing your emotional difficulties better, according to CBT, is to understand them better. A five-part model[71] is useful to break down a problem into a number of inter-related components.

Consider how a five-areas assessment can help Freya become more resilient. Freya is a student in her final year at college. She

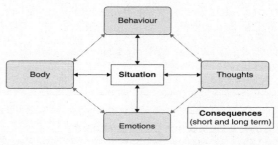

The five areas of CBT

has a final-year dissertation to write but is finding it difficult to complete. This is making her feel very worried and stressed. Freya assesses the situation using the five-part model as follows.

Situation: I need to finish my dissertation but I just don't seem to be able to do it.

Emotions: stressed, upset, anxious and worried.

Thoughts: a number of these, the ones that make me most emotional or seem most unhelpful are:

'It won't be good enough' (this goes through my mind whenever I sit down to write something).

'I'll do it later' (this helps me to rationalize postponing work).

'I'll never finish it on time' (this pops into my mind quite often and makes me very anxious and worried).

Body: I start to feel tense when I sit down to write. I sometimes get a headache thinking about the idea of writing.

Behaviour: I'm the queen of displacement activities! Whenever it's time to write, suddenly the washing up or vacuuming becomes attractive. Going on Facebook is also something I tend to do rather too often. The intention is to cheer myself up, but I often find that I get caught up in people's activities and an hour has suddenly been wasted. I'm avoiding sitting down and getting on with the dissertation.

Consequences: in the short term I feel a bit better when I don't have to sit down and write. But it's making me stressed and anxious. If I don't start to change things I'll fail my degree, which will have serious long-term consequences.

We will return to see how CBT can help Freya's case of stress, worry and procrastination later in this chapter. Now it is your turn to see if you can assess your problems in the same way.

Try it now: Assess your problems using the five-part model

If you can detect a pattern to your negative emotions, then you are in with a much better chance of changing them.

In order to achieve this, complete your own assessment.

1 Think of a recent occasion, fresh in your memory, when you reacted in an unhelpful way or felt a negative emotion disproportionate to the situation. You might like to choose an emotion or trigger situation from the first 'Try it now' exercise in this chapter. Jot down the situation, very briefly.

2 Next, write down what your emotions were. Emotion words are usually one word, such as down, upset, sad, angry or frustrated. There is a list of negative emotions in the first 'Try it now' exercise in this chapter.

3 Remember the thoughts or images that popped into your mind when you felt these emotions. What were you telling yourself that made you upset? A good tip is to imagine yourself in a cartoon with a thought bubble coming out of your head. What words would be in your thought bubble? Sometimes it is not words that pop into our minds when we are emotional but images or a series of images like in a movie. If that is the case, record the images that you saw at the time. It is not always the thoughts that you were aware of that led to the emotion but the meaning you automatically gave to the situation. So it is also a good idea to ask, 'What meaning did this event have for me that made me feel this way?'

4 Jot down your thoughts and images and what they meant to you.

5 Recall what happened in your body. Perhaps you were tired, tearful, hot or tense? Did you experience any other physical symptoms? Write down your physical reaction.

6 What did you do? What did you say? What did you avoid doing? Write these down.

7 What were the consequences? What were the immediate effects on yourself and others? What about the longer-term repercussions? Make notes, including both good and bad things.

Spend a few moments on the above activity; we will come back to it later. If you are not sure what to write for each category, have another look at the example of Freya.

Once you understand the problem better, you are in a good position to improve things. CBT focuses particularly on two areas to change: how you think about the situation and what you do.[72]

HOW YOU THINK AFFECTS HOW YOU FEEL AND WHAT YOU DO

Have a look at the picture below. First of all imagine that you think that dogs are cuddly and lovable. Jot down what emotions you would feel on seeing this dog and what you would be most likely to do when you saw it.[73]

Now imagine that you think that dogs are fierce and dangerous. What emotions would you feel and what would you do in this case?

Most people who believe dogs are cuddly and lovable come up with emotions like happy, calm and pleased. They say they would smile and go and stroke the dog. On the other hand, people who think dogs are fierce and dangerous tend to say they would feel scared and anxious and avoid the dog. This illustrates a key principle of CBT: how you think affects how you feel and what you do.

The good news is that by becoming more aware of your thoughts and beliefs you can change the way you feel. You can choose how you respond to events rather than merely reacting automatically to them.

IS MANAGING ADVERSITIES AS EASY AS ABC?

If you learn your ABCs, then you have a better chance of dealing with adversities. ABC stands for:

A –Adversity[74] – this is the setback causing the problem.

B – Belief – this is the thoughts you have about the problem. Aaron T. (Tim) Beck called them 'negative automatic thoughts' (NATs) to convey the idea that we are not always aware of them. As we have already seen, NATs can sometimes be images as well as words.

C – Consequences – these are both what you feel and what you do – the emotional and behavioural consequences.

Applying the ABC to our example, the adversity is seeing the dog, the belief is that dogs are fierce and dangerous, and the consequences are that the person feels fear and avoids the dog.

Many people, before they learn about CBT, assume that an AC model is true. A dog phobic might say something like, 'I had to run away because the dog was dangerous'. Adding the 'B' in the middle can be very empowering. The event is an adversity because of your beliefs. By becoming more aware of your beliefs, and challenging the unrealistic and unhelpful ones, you can feel better and enforce more helpful behaviours.

Remember this: The ABC model

While many people think that adverse events lead directly to negative consequences (the AC model), CBT proposes that how we think affects how we feel (the ABC model). The beliefs we have about the events influence both how we feel and how we respond.

Thinking traps

How can you tell whether a thought is unrealistic or unhelpful? Psychologists have identified thinking styles or 'traps' that often lead to problems. A thinking trap is a logical error in thinking that can lead to negative emotions and unhelpful behaviours. The table below describes four of the most common thinking traps.

Thinking traps

Thinking trap	Meaning	Example
1 Jumping to conclusions	Assuming that bad things have happened or will happen, without enough evidence. There are two types of jumping to conclusions:	
	i) Mind-reading – thinking you know what people are thinking when you don't	'She thinks I'm stupid.'
	ii) Fortune-telling – thinking you know what is going to happen when you don't	'They are going to turn me down.'
2 Extreme thinking	Thinking in an all-or-nothing way or overgeneralizing:	
	All-or-nothing thinking	'It's all your (or my) fault.'
	Overgeneralization	'I never have any self-control.'
3 Catastrophising	Overestimating how bad things will be if a feared event were to happen. This often involves underestimating your ability to cope with adversity or how other people may help you out.	'It's a disaster!' 'I'll be ruined!'
4 Unhelpful personal rules	Saying that things should or must happen when there is no real basis for this and it isn't very helpful to make this demand from the universe.	'I must do it perfectly.' 'People should always be nice to me.'

Many of the thoughts that cause emotional upsets turn out to be the result of one of these thinking traps. You will find an exercise on thinking traps in the diagnostic questions at the start of the chapter. Now would be a good time to attempt to answer that question if you have not done so already. Later in this chapter you will get an opportunity to identify your own thinking traps. Note that not every thought that causes an emotional upset is unrealistic. CBT can help you manage these realistic negative thoughts too, as we will see in 'What to do about realistic negative thoughts'.

FREYA'S THINKING TRAPS

Remember Freya, the student who used the five-part model to help her understand her procrastination better? Having identified her thoughts and learned about thinking traps, she can now see if she has been caught out by any thinking traps.

'It won't be good enough' – this is jumping to conclusions. Freya has no evidence that her work is not good enough. In fact, she has got very good grades in her previous assignments.

'I'll do it later' – this is an example of an unhelpful personal rule. She does not do it later, and so postponing it is causing the problem.

'I'll never finish it on time' – you might say that this is jumping to conclusions. On the other hand, the way things are going it might well become true. This is an example of a thought that may well be realistic unless Freya does something to solve the problem.

How to overcome thinking traps

Thinking trap	How to dispel the thinking trap	Example
1 Jumping to conclusions	What is the evidence for my negative thought? What is another possibility? What are the odds?	'There is a possibility that she thinks I am stupid but I have no evidence for this view and it's just as likely that she thinks positively about me.'
2 Extreme thinking	What is a more balanced perspective? Is it true that this is always the case? How much responsibility can I fairly place on me or others? What would a sympathetic friend say?	'I'm 30 per cent to blame, but it was hard to foresee the bad traffic so I'll put 70 per cent down to bad luck.'
3 Catastrophising	What is the worst that can actually happen? How could I deal with that? What or who might help out? Have I dealt with similar before?	'I'd rather that didn't happen but if it did I'd cope.'
4 Unhelpful personal rules	What rule in the universe says this must happen? Does it help me to have this rule?	'Perfection isn't attainable; I'll do my best.'

Key idea: Thinking traps

CBT identifies a number of thinking traps that can lead to emotional and behavioural difficulties. Four of the most common are: jumping to conclusions, extreme thinking, catastrophising and unhelpful personal rules.

What to do about realistic negative thoughts

Sometimes negative thoughts are realistic. Freya's thinking that she is not going to get her dissertation finished unless she changes something is probably spot on. When dealing with realistic negative thoughts it is helpful first to delve deeper and ask if there are any meanings she is giving to the event which are unrealistic or unhelpful. Suppose Freya thinks that not completing her dissertation would mean she was a complete failure as a person. In that case the extreme thinking and catastrophising in the meaning she gave to the thought, rather than the initial thought, could be challenged. For example, a more realistic meaning of her not completing her dissertation would be, 'It might mean I fail my degree but that would not make me a complete failure as a person.'

That still leaves the problem of what to do with the realistic negative thoughts. After all, although she would not be a complete failure as a person if she did not complete her dissertation, she still does not want that to happen. Freya probably won't pass her degree unless she changes her study regime. With realistic negative thoughts, the best approach is to ask yourself whether there is anything you can do about the situation or not. If you cannot, the best approach is to accept the situation. If you can do something about it, then problem solving, planning and taking action are the best response. We will look at problem solving in more depth later in the chapter. The approach to realistic negative thoughts is well captured by the Serenity Prayer[75]:

> Grant me the serenity to accept the things I cannot change
>
> Courage to change the things I can
>
> And wisdom to know the difference.

Remember this: Sometimes negative thoughts are realistic

When negative thoughts are realistic, the first step is to look at the meanings given to these thoughts, because these might be unrealistic even if the original thoughts are realistic.

In dealing with realistic negative thoughts, the Serenity Prayer is a very helpful idea. When you can change a situation, problem solving is a useful tool.

Let's now see how Freya can overcome both her thinking traps and her realistic negative thoughts.

'It won't be good enough' – this is jumping to conclusions. A more realistic thing for her to tell herself is, 'I've done well in my earlier assignments. There is no reason to think it won't be good enough.'

'I'll do it later' – this is an unhelpful personal rule. A more helpful rule would be, 'I'll work at a certain time each day whether I feel like it or not. I'll go somewhere where there are no distractions.'

'I'll never finish it on time' – this is an example of a realistic negative thought (unless Freya does something about the problem!). Freya decides she can do something about it: she will change her unhelpful personal rule and set aside enough time to finish her dissertation.

Try it now: Overcoming your own thinking traps

It's now time to start helping you work on the problematic issue you assessed earlier using the five-part model. Write down each of your troubling thoughts and see if you can identify your own thinking traps. Think of an alternative thought for each. If you cannot put the thought down to a thinking trap, is there anything you can do that is helpful, or should you just accept the situation?

Changing your behaviour

How you think also affects what you do. For example, when Freya thinks, 'It won't be good enough', this sets her up for being undecided about when to write (she procrastinates) and probably not writing at all (she avoids). Once you have overcome your thinking traps, you will be much more likely to take effective action.

Sometimes, however, thinking through a problem is not enough to convince you that your original thought is unrealistic or that the alternative thought is more realistic. In these situations, you need to test your beliefs. You can do this by carrying out a behavioural experiment.

> **Remember this:** Sometimes thinking about a problem is not sufficient
>
> Although thinking through issues using thinking traps is helpful, sometimes 'the proof of the pudding is in the eating'. Behavioural experiments, which are planned activities based on experimentation or observation to test out beliefs, are a very useful tool to test which beliefs are really true and which are not.

Freya, for example, may only be partially convinced that what she has written so far is good enough. It would be a good idea for her to test out her belief. She realizes that the only way to do this is to show what she has done to her supervisor. Naturally Freya feels anxious about the prospect of doing this, but realizes that even if her supervisor says that her work is not good enough, she will get useful feedback about how to improve it. Here are some useful tips for carrying out an effective behavioural experiment.

HOW TO DESIGN A GOOD BEHAVIOURAL EXPERIMENT

1 Decide what belief you are testing. This can be either a positive belief ('if I hand my essay in it will be a good learning experience') or negative belief ('if I am criticized I won't be able to cope').

2 Be clear about what you are going to do (this includes describing exactly what you are going to do, when you are going to do it, and how you are going to do it).

3 Think about potential obstacles to carrying out the experiment and how you will overcome them.

4 Think of the experiment as a 'no lose' activity. Even if it does not work out as you would have liked, you will still have learned something important.

5 After the experiment, review what happened and what you learned. In particular, review how much you now believe the beliefs being tested.

6 Think about whether more steps are required. These could be devising an action plan to solve the problem or another behavioural experiment to further test out beliefs.

FREYA'S BEHAVIOURAL EXPERIMENT

Freya decides she needs to check out whether her dissertation draft really is up to standard. She decides to schedule a long overdue meeting with her supervisor. She considers likely obstacles. One is that the supervisor, being a nice person, might not be honest. Freya decides to assertively ask for absolutely honest feedback. When she shows her work to her supervisor, she finds out that while the general standard is quite good, there are some weaknesses she needs to address. As a result of her experiment, Freya is much clearer about the steps she needs to take. She no longer believes that her work won't be good enough.

Key idea: Behavioural experiments

Behavioural experiments are planned activities based on experimentation or observation to test out either negative or positive beliefs. They should be designed to be 'no lose' – either you achieve something you hoped to, or you learn something useful.

Problem solving

Once your thinking is more realistic, the next step required is often pretty clear. Such was the case with Freya, who immediately realized she needed to meet up with her supervisor. On other occasions, the solution may not be so obvious. In these instances another CBT skill, practical problem solving, becomes useful.

In fact, one evidence-based approach to helping with psychological difficulties, problem-solving therapy, uses only problem solving to help people overcome their difficulties. This has been shown to decrease depression and increase optimism, hope, self-esteem and emotional well-being.

In problem-solving therapy, the first step is to reflect on your attitude to difficulties.[76] Can you be a bit like an ostrich, with your head in the sand hoping the problem will go away? Or do you tend to be impulsive, acting first and regretting it later? A third unhelpful way of dealing with problems is to procrastinate. Are you the sort of person who sways between one course of action and another, never actually implementing action until it is too late? Having identified and resolved to change any unhelpful attitudes to problems, the next step is to learn how to do practical problem solving instead.

A SEVEN-STEP PROCEDURE TO HELP WITH PRACTICAL PROBLEM SOLVING

▶ **1. Choose a problem to work on**

If you notice you are spending a lot of time worrying about a practical problem then that is a good clue that you might benefit from problem solving. You need to choose a problem that is at least partly under your control (if not, then the best approach is to accept the difficulty, as advised in the Serenity Prayer).

▶ **2. Think about the outcome you would like to achieve**

At this stage you think about what you need from a good solution. What matters to you here?

▶ **3. Brainstorm possible solutions**

The next stage is to brainstorm possible solutions. Start with ideas you have already considered. Then think about their deficiencies and how you might overcome them. Focused brainstorming, where you think about how to achieve the outcomes you wrote down in step 2, can be helpful.

▶ **4. Pick the option that best satisfies what matters**

Next, you evaluate your options developed in step 3 in terms of what mattered, which you wrote down in step 2. Sometimes one option will be a clear winner. On other occasions you might decide to try out one first, or to combine features of different options to create a new option.

▶ 5. Plan and schedule the best option

Decide on the first step required to carry out your chosen option and schedule it. With complex problems, step-by-step planning may be useful at this stage.

▶ 6. Carry out the plan

Be alert to negative thinking or procrastination at this stage. If this happens, challenge it.

▶ 7. Review the plan

Review to what extent the plan has achieved what you needed, and go through the process again if necessary. You may need go back to step 1 and create a new plan. Even if this is the case, take stock of what you have learned. On other occasions you may have achieved your desired result and can then congratulate yourself and take on board any learning points for the future (such as the need to tackle problems as early as possible).

FREYA'S PRACTICAL PROBLEM SOLVING

Having spoken to her supervisor, Freya is less worried about her dissertation not being good enough. She has successfully overcome one psychological barrier to her getting down to work. But Freya is still finding it difficult to find a good place to do her writing. When she tries to work at home, she finds the internet and her flatmates too distracting. The college library is a possibility, but that involves an hour and a half of travel she would rather avoid. She decides to try practical problem solving.

▶ 1. Choose a problem to work on

Freya's problem is to find somewhere she can work on her dissertation effectively.

▶ 2. Think about the outcome you would like to achieve

Freya needs to find somewhere she can work, which means it will have limited distractions, it needs to be easy to get to and she needs to be able to use a computer and read there.

▶ 3. Brainstorm possible solutions

Freya comes up with three possibilities:

▶ Work at home, disconnect the internet and ask flatmates not to interrupt her.

▶ Work in the college library.

▶ Work in a coffee shop nearby.

▶ 4. Pick the option that best satisfies what matters

Home and the college library have drawbacks, so she decides to try out the coffee shop idea.

▶ 5. Plan and schedule the best option

Freya decides on that very day to have a quick look round her local coffee shops. She identifies four shops within 15 minutes' walk. She decides to try each of them.

▶ 6. Carry out the plan

Freya enjoys carrying out the plan. One shop is a bit too busy, another one doesn't have very comfortable chairs. That leaves two which are usually quiet and comfortable. She resolves to try working in one of these.

▶ 7. Review the plan

After a week Freya has done more writing than in the previous two months! One of the coffee shops has become her favourite, because she prefers the coffee there. She enjoys writing in these comfortable surroundings and finds herself looking forward to her walk to the coffee shop each day.

Key idea: Problem solving

Problem solving is a useful strategy for dealing with situations where there are realistic negative thoughts. It is helpful first to look at your attitude and cultivate a proactive attitude to problem solving. A seven-step procedure can be practised to gain the skills to effectively solve problems.

Behavioural strategies are also very important in many of the CBT treatment plans for specific problems. For example, facing your fears is key to the successful treatment of phobias (the technical name for this is exposure). Overcoming low mood is helped by increasing your level of activity (using behavioural activation and activity scheduling as described in Chapter 1).

The body and resilience

HOW TO FEEL MORE RELAXED

Being able to calm your body is a very useful resilience skill. You may already have favourite ways to relax and may even have identified them in your 'reset buttons'. In addition there are well tried and tested methods you can learn relatively quickly to help you reduce stress. Three of the most effective methods are:

▶ controlled calm soothing breathing

▶ guided imagery, including safe-place imagery

▶ progressive muscle relaxation.

Recordings and scripts can be downloaded for free from the author's website (http://www.timlebon.com/relax.html).

Try it now: Discover your most effective relaxation technique

A good way to develop your ability to relax is to spend a week learning and trying each of the relaxation techniques. It can help to make or download a recording to learn them. Spend some time learning a method, then over a period of time monitor how effective it is for you in managing your stress. You can design your own behavioural experiments, recording your mood before and after you have carried out a relaxation exercise.

Other ways to help you be more resilient

Relaxation techniques are a good way to calm the body. In addition there are other ways of attending to the body to help you be more resilient. These include good diet, exercise and sleep.

DIET

Most of us are aware of the need for a balanced diet. We know about the dangers of too much alcohol, non-prescription drugs, caffeine and sugar. Alcohol is a depressant and while it knocks us out it actually leads to worse quality sleep. Fast foods, crisps and fizzy drinks have unhealthy sugar, fat and salt levels. Some of these make us feel better for a few minutes but then cause a crash a few hours later. Scientific advice about which foods are desirable does tend to change. Omega-3, various vitamins and minerals such as zinc may be beneficial. A balanced diet of natural rather than processed foods is to be preferred. Many of the problems arise with foods and other substances that are feel-good in the short term but do us harm in the long run.

EXERCISE

Most people do not get enough exercise. It is recommended that adults exercise for 30 minutes per day.

SLEEP

A persistent lack of sleep can lead to problems. Tips include:

▶ Avoid caffeine close to bedtime.

▶ Exercise, but not too close to bedtime.

▶ Avoid daytime naps.

▶ Avoid worrying at bedtime.

▶ Avoid catastrophic thinking about not getting enough sleep. We can survive quite well after one night's lack of sleep, for instance, recall the last time you had to get up very early to go on holiday.

For more advice on sleep, see Sage et al. (2008) or http://www. anxietybc.com/sites/default/files/SleepHygiene.pdf.

Remember this: The need for practice

If you engage in a course of CBT with a therapist, a key part of the work is learning skills at home – 'homework' or 'home practice'. The same principle applies when learning these skills from a book such as this. It is like learning to play the guitar or to do yoga. The more you practise, the more progress you will make. It would be a good idea to set aside 15 minutes a day for putting into practice the ideas from this book.

Real-time resilience

Having practised the skills for a few weeks, most people find that they start to be able to put them into practice when they are feeling upset. Often the first step is to do a little relaxation to calm yourself down, then notice and adjust your thinking, then do some on the spot problem solving and taking appropriate action. The diagram below summarizes how to carry out real-time resilience.

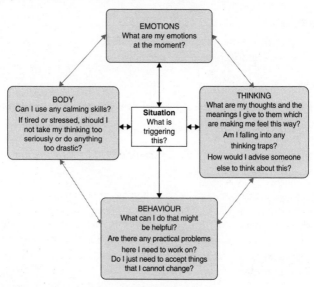

Real-time resilience using the five-part model

You can also use the thoughts and behaviours log, a comprehensive way of integrating many of the CBT ideas in this chapter. Appendix A explains how to fill in the log. The following case study illustrates how Sarah, who had been using CBT for a few months, used it to help her with a tricky situation when leaving for a holiday.

Case study: How a thoughts and behaviours log saved Sarah's holiday

Sarah has been doing CBT for a few weeks and encounters the following situation where she really needs it. This is how she uses a thoughts and behaviours log.

Step 1: Describing the situation

James and Sarah are sitting in a noisy and overcrowded airport lounge having missed their plane by ten minutes. Sarah notices a chatter of negative thoughts inside her head and feels upset.

Step 2: Noticing thoughts and images

1 'Our holiday is going to be ruined.'

2 'It's all James's fault! I told him we should have gone the other route to the airport.'

3 An image of them being stuck in the horrible lounge for another six hours, arguing about whose fault it was...

Step 3: Noticing emotions and feelings associated with the thoughts

1 'Our holiday is going to be ruined.' → anxiety 70 per cent

2 'It's all James's fault! I told him we should have gone the other route to the airport.' → anger 75 per cent

3 An image of them being stuck in the horrible lounge for another six hours, arguing about whose fault it was... → despair 80 per cent

Step 4 Noticing impulses to act and their probable consequences

    a Noticing impulses to act in certain ways
       Sarah realizes that she feels like blaming James. She also feels
       like going over in her head all the things that led to this state of
       affairs (ruminating).

    b Thinking about the consequences of these possible actions
       While in the short term blaming James will make her feel a bit
       better, it may well jeopardize the whole holiday. Ruminating
       hardly ever does any good and just brings us down more.

Step 5 Thinking traps

1 'Our holiday is going to be ruined.' – catastrophising (it isn't a great start, but it doesn't mean it's ruined).

2 'It's all James's fault! I told him we should have gone the other route to the airport.' – jumping to conclusions (the other route may have been worse) and extreme thinking (it probably wasn't all James's fault). Possibly also an unhelpful personal rule (people should do what I tell them!).

3 An image of them being stuck in the horrible lounge for another six hours, arguing about whose fault it was... – jumping to conclusions (this need not happen and indeed is partly under their control).

Step 6: More realistic and constructive thoughts and images

1 Initial thought: 'Our holiday is going to be ruined.'

  Thinking trap: catastrophising

  More realistic and constructive thought: 'This isn't a great start, but we can still have a good holiday.'

2 Initial thought: 'It's all James's fault! I told him we should have gone the other route to the airport.'

  Thinking trap: jumping to conclusions and extreme thinking

  More realistic and constructive thought: 'I can't blame James too much; my route might have been worse and the traffic was much worse than usual. Maybe I took too long to get ready too.'

3 Initial image: An image of them being stuck in the horrible lounge for another six hours, arguing about whose fault it was...

Thinking trap: jumping to conclusions

More constructive image: An image of them seeing the funny side of it while having a drink in the bar, having done some shopping first to help chill out.

Step 7: Action plan

'Instead of blaming James – which would lead to a row – and dwelling on what's gone wrong I will suggest to James that we chill out by going shopping separately and then meeting up for a meal in the airport restaurant in an hour's time. We can then take a bit more time to plan our holiday, perhaps having bought a guidebook in the bookshop.'

Step 8: Results – new emotions

'I now feel very little anger or anxiety and no despair at all. Instead, I accept what happened – that's life! – and hope that the holiday will still be good.

'So, anxiety (70 per cent), anger (75 per cent) and despair (80 per cent) have been replaced by acceptance (80 per cent), hope (70 per cent), reduced anxiety (10 per cent), very little anger (5 per cent) and no despair (0 per cent).'

Problem-specific CBT

The 'generic' form of CBT described above can be very useful to help you be more resilient. In addition, a lot of research has been carried out to find out which sort of thinking patterns and behaviours typically cause particular problems. In the UK the type of CBT currently recommended by the National Institute for Health and Care Excellence (NICE) guidelines is 'disorder-' or 'problem-' specific. While you may not be suffering from a mental health disorder, most of us have problems with low mood, worry and anger from time to time.[77] We could all benefit at these times by learning and using some of the ideas from problem-specific CBT.

ANGER MANAGEMENT

Anger is among the hardest moods to control. Anger builds on anger, the interplay of, in Daniel Goleman's words, the 'amygdala-driven surges of catecholamines and the reasoning neocortex spiralling all too easily towards fury.' You are particularly susceptible to anger when stressed, as your threshold is lowered. When you are stressed or tired is not the best time to get into a controversial discussion! Though it is impossible to prevent anger altogether, the table below gives some tips about how to limit its intensity, duration and impact.

How to cope with anger

Do	Do not
Become an expert at noticing your first signs of anger. For many people this will be either angry thinking or physiological signs (such as an adrenalin rush).	Don't pick an argument after a hard day's work or poor sleep.
Remind yourself of the disadvantages of anger. What is usually the outcome of your anger?	Don't express anger without thinking about the consequences.
Calm yourself down, perhaps by using controlled breathing or progressive muscle relaxation. If nothing else, at least take a few deep breaths.	Don't give vent to anger, hoping that catharsis will reduce it.
Become aware of the unhelpful personal rules driving the anger. These are most likely 'shoulds', demanding that other people or you behave in a certain way.	
Only confront the person who has angered you when you have calmed down, and then do so constructively. Assertive behaviour is to be preferred to either aggression or submission.	Don't work yourself up into righteous indignation by going over and over what someone else has done wrong.
Get enough sleep and use relaxation methods, as the more tired and stressed you are, the more irritable you are likely to be.	
Try to see the situation from the other person's point of view. What would a defence advocate for the other person say?	
Get some physical distance between you and the person you are angry with.	

COPING WITH WORRY

Worry is not the same as anxiety. Worry is repetitive thinking about things in an unhelpful way. If such thinking is helpful, it is not worry, it is problem solving. At its most severe, worry turns into generalized anxiety disorder (GAD), for which CBT with a therapist is recommended. For milder forms, the following list of dos and don'ts may be sufficient.

Coping intelligently with worry

Do	Do not
Ask yourself whether worry is helpful. Distinguish worrying – which is repetitive and often circular thinking about a problem – from practical problem solving.	Don't repress worries completely – they can be useful messages to take action (such as worrying about an exam being a message to revise). There is also evidence that repressing worries doesn't work – the worries come back to you. Try not thinking of a pink elephant for two minutes!
Use the worry tree (see below).	If you are a worrier it usually isn't a good idea to tackle each worrying thought and find an alternative. The problem is that worries can multiply like Medusa's snakes, and you become smothered by them. Far better to nip the whole overthinking process in the bud by using the worry tree.
Use worry time to postpone worrying until a set time each day (see below).	Don't let the worrying thoughts spiral out of control without noticing them. Don't be like a dog chewing on a bone.
Be tolerant of some uncertainty in life. Cross each bridge when you come to it.	Don't search for certainty – the world rarely provides it.
If you are feeling stressed, use relaxation techniques.	Don't continue worrying or you will get more stressed and more prone to worry.

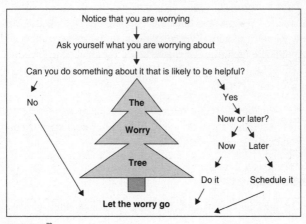

The worry tree[78]

In order to let go of the worry, you can experiment with a number of possibilities:

- ▶ Remind yourself that worry is not helping.

- ▶ Do something that takes up your attention – a flow activity might work well, such as doing a crossword or chatting to a friend.

- ▶ Postpone your worrying until your worry time (see below).

- ▶ See your worrisome thoughts as being like trains at a busy station that you do not want to catch. Just let them rush past.

- ▶ Tune out and do not pay so much attention to the thoughts – in the same way that you would tune out irritating adverts on a local radio station.

- ▶ Consider rational, balanced alternative viewpoints.

- ▶ Be mindful of your thoughts. Watch your thoughts without getting caught up in them. (See Chapter 10 for more details on how to practise mindfulness.)

What is less helpful is to try to suppress the worry. Try, right now, not to think of a pink elephant for two minutes. What happened? Most people find that the attempt to stop thinking about something actually makes them think about it more. That is why all the techniques involve being mindful of the worries or turning your attention to something else rather than trying to suppress the worry.

Rebecca decides to spend ten minutes each day reviewing her worries and using the worry tree to help her deal with them. On the first day she notices these worries:

> 'There is a new member of staff joining and I might not get on with her.'

> 'I might get cancer and then how would my family manage?'

> 'My children might get abducted while they are walking home.'

> 'My car tax is due and I might forget to renew it.'

Rebecca realizes that she has spent much of the day worrying – even when she was meant to be doing something else, like cooking, driving or working. She is acutely aware that the worrying is not helping. Before seeing how Rebecca evaluated these worries, you might like to spend a moment reflecting on these four worries. Which, if any, do you think she can do something helpful about?

This is what Rebecca concluded:

'There is a new member of staff joining and I might not get on with her.'

> 'There is not a lot I can do about that now. Let's cross that bridge when we come to it.'

'I might get cancer and then how would my family manage?'

> 'Again, this is a hypothetical worry – best to let that worry go.'

'My children might get abducted while they are walking home.'

> 'I've done all I can about this – warned them of stranger danger and told them to walk home together. Having done all I can, I need to let that worry go.'

'My car tax is due and I might forget to renew it.'

> 'This is a worry I can do something helpful about. I will go online to renew it as soon as I get home. Having decided what to do about it, I can let the worry go.'

▶ Worry time

Worry time is a good technique to help you get some control over your worrying. Decide on a specific time to worry each day. During that time you are allowed to do as much worrying as you like, though you do not have to worry then if you do not want to. You can choose the length of this worry time, though most people choose 10 or 15 minutes. Do not choose a time too close to bedtime or when you need to concentrate on something else (e.g. driving).

At all other times of the day you must postpone worrying until your worry time. Say to yourself, 'I am not going to worry now because it is not my worry time'. Then, at worry time you can decide whether or not you want to worry about it.

For example, Rebecca decides to make 6p.m. her worry time. At other times, she notices her 'what ifs' where problem solving is not possible, but manages to tell herself, 'it's not my worry time'. When 6p.m. comes along, most days she realizes that she has better things to do with her time than worry and gets on with something much more satisfying and enjoyable.

COPING WITH LOW MOOD AND DEPRESSION

While depressed people do see things in a negative way, behavioural changes are usually needed first to bring about change.

Coping with low mood

Do	Do not
Do an activity schedule to find out what gives you more pleasure and achievement. Schedule more pleasurable and satisfying things.	Do not isolate yourself.
Think of what you used to enjoy, and try these activities out again to see if they improve your mood.	Do not dwell on things. This is called rumination. If you spend a lot of time going over things that have gone wrong, ask yourself whether this is helping. You can use the worry tree and worry time for ruminations as well as worries.
Look out for thinking traps since being depressed predisposes you to negative thinking. Challenge unhelpful thoughts.	Do not be guided by your mood rather than your targets.
Do not expect to feel like doing these things; like someone on a diet, you need to go against your feelings. Act according to your goals not your motivation.	Do not believe all your negative thoughts.
Use the 'Nike principle' – just do it! Motivation often comes after action, not before it.	
Socialize.	
Help others.	
Exercise.	
Try some of the positive psychology interventions, for example: three good things, random acts of kindness, step-by-step planning towards a goal, activity scheduling.	

The example of Fred in Chapter 1 gives a good example of how these ideas can help overcome even chronic and quite severe low mood.

Focus points

❋ Resilience means the ability to bounce back from adversities, or more broadly to handle difficult situations and emotions skilfully. Some positive psychology strategies can help you be more resilient, but there is more evidence to support the use of CBT.

❋ The first step in CBT is understanding the problem. Using a five-part model is a good way to do this. The second step in CBT is to identify your thoughts, thinking traps and alternative thougths and behaviours, for example, using a thoughts and behaviours log.

❋ Problem solving is a useful strategy for dealing with situations where there are realistic negative thoughts.

❋ Behavioural experiments are planned activities based on experimentation or observation to test out either negative or positive beliefs.

❋ Problem-specific CBT provides more specific and evidence-based help about how to deal with problems such as worry, anger and low mood.

Diagnostic test answers

1   Resilience means the ability to bounce back from adversities or, more broadly, to handle difficult situations and emotions skilfully.

2   Resilience is important because negative emotions reduce SWB, have a negative impact on relationships, effectiveness and health and are stronger than positive emotions.

3   The negative emotions that CBT can help manage include anxiety, depression, anger, guilt, sadness, being worried and feeling hopeless.

4   There are many ways that positive psychology can help you be more resilient, including doing the 'three good things' exercise, using your strengths more and step-by-step planning. For a summary of ideas, see 'How positive psychology can help you to be more resilient' in Chapter 9.

5   A thinking trap is a logical error in thinking that can lead to negative emotions and unhelpful behaviours.

6 The thinking traps you learnt about are jumping to conclusions, extreme thinking, catastrophising and unhelpful personal rules.

7 The statements matched with the thinking traps as follows:

   a 'I will not get the job.' iii) Jumping to conclusions
   b 'I completely fouled up that interview.' i) Extreme thinking
   c 'I ought to be able to answer every question correctly.' iv) Unhelpful shoulds (and other personal rules)
   d 'If I don't get this job, that will be terrible.' ii) Catastrophising.

8 Behavioural experiments are planned activities based on experimentation or observation to test out either negative or positive beliefs.

9 The seven steps of problem-solving are:

   a Choose a problem to work on.
   b Think about what outcome you would like to achieve.
   c Brainstorm possible solutions.
   d Pick the option that best satisfies what matters.
   e Plan and schedule the best option.
   f Carry out the plan.
   g Review to what extent the plan has achieved what you needed, and go through the process again if necessary.

10 Controlled calm breathing
   Guided imagery
   Progressive muscle relaxation

Next steps

When it comes to ways to help you be more resilient, CBT is supported by most evidence, but there are two areas of research that are producing promising results: neuroscience and meditation. In the next chapter we will look at how these can help you not only become more resilient but also bring more intelligence to your emotions.

10

Emotional intelligence, meditation and mindfulness

In this chapter you will learn:

▶ *about emotional intelligence and why it is important*

▶ *about Daniel Goleman's five abilities of emotional intelligence and how to master them*

▶ *how neuroscience can inform us about mindfulness, meditation and compassion.*

Diagnostic test

1 Name the five abilities identified by Goleman as being emotionally intelligent.

2 Is emotional intelligence more about:

  a being free of emotions
  b expanding our emotions
  c bringing intelligence to our emotions?

3 What did the school children in Walter Mischel's classic test exhibit self-control over?

  a lollipops
  b marshmallows
  c ice cream
  d chocolate bars

4 Why might we have evolved to feel and act quickly in response to negative emotions?

5 Name five skills you have already learned that can help you be more emotionally intelligent.

6 What is mindfulness?

7 What is the difference between mindfulness and savouring?

8 What are the six core processes of ACT?

9 Name three benefits of meditation.

10 Name two types of meditation.

What is emotional intelligence?

What do you think is the right balance between reason and emotion? Should you go with your gut feeling, like Dr McCoy ('Bones') in the original *Star Trek*? Or should you be a model of logical reasoning like the half-Vulcan Mr Spock? The essence of emotional intelligence, as popularized by psychologist and writer Daniel Goleman is his 1996 book *Emotional Intelligence: Why it can matter more than IQ*, is that neither Spock nor McCoy provide the best role model. Instead, you should aim to be like Captain Kirk, who listened to both of his trusted advisors, but was ruled by neither. Emotional intelligence means bringing intelligence to your emotions.

Why is emotional intelligence important?

There is considerable evidence that emotional intelligence helps with social relationships, work performance and mental and physical health (Grewal and Salovey, 2006). Goleman claims that a high EQ (emotional intelligence quotient) contributes more to success in life than a high IQ.

A vivid illustration of the importance of emotional intelligence is the marshmallow test developed by Walter Mischel in the 1960s. Imagine yourself as a four-year-old faced with the following choice. In front of you is a tempting marshmallow, which you are at liberty to eat right now. But if you wait a few minutes for a teacher to return from an errand you can have two marshmallows. Do you exercise emotional intelligence and refrain from eating the marshmallow, or do you grab it? How children fared in this simple test proved to have remarkable predictive power not just about future levels of self-control but much more broadly about academic performance.[79]

How to become more emotionally intelligent

To become more emotionally intelligent, Goleman suggests that we develop five abilities.[80] These are:

1   Being aware of your emotions – you understand yourself well. For example, if asked to take on a new role at work, you will have insight as to whether you can do the job, whether you want to do the job and what further skills you might need. You will also have a good moment-to-moment awareness of your emotions so you are able to manage them and are informed by them.

2   Managing difficult emotions – you will be not be totally free from worry, anxiety, low mood and anger, you are after

all human, but you will be able to manage these difficult emotions effectively. They will not prevent you from achieving important things in your life.

3 Using emotions to motivate yourself – you will feel motivated to do important things in life, and even when your motivation is diminished you will exercise self-control.

4 Recognizing emotions in others – you will be understanding and empathic of other people.

5 Managing emotions in others – you will have the social skills to motivate people and calm them down.

Key idea: Goleman's five abilities of emotional intelligence

Daniel Goleman has proposed the following five domains of emotional intelligence:

1 Being aware of your emotions.
2 Managing difficult emotions
3 Using emotions to motivate yourself
4 Recognizing emotions in others
5 Managing emotions in others

Positive psychology has many techniques that can help with these abilities. In this chapter we will look additionally at mindfulness and meditation, which can help with emotional intelligence and also offer a range of other benefits.

Try it now: Emotional intelligence

Match each of these from the book so far with an emotional intelligence ability above (1–5).

a CBT
b Active and constructive responding
c Knowing someone's strengths
d Increasing your flow experiences
e Motivating someone else by facilitating their flow experiences

f   Understanding someone else's strengths and weaknesses and using this knowledge to improve their performance

g   Step-by-step planning

h   Optimism

i   Using Gottman's tips on relationships, such as trying to find compromise

j   Using calming and relaxation methods[81]

Remember this: Positive psychology can help with emotional intelligence

There are many ideas in positive psychology that can help you become more emotionally intelligent.

Case study: Mike Brearley – emotional intelligence wins matches

The England v Australia Test Match at Headingley in 1981 was one of the greatest games of cricket of all time. Captain Mike Brearley's handling of key players is also an excellent illustration of how interpersonal emotional intelligence brings success.

In 1981 Brearley was recalled to the captaincy because his successor, Ian Botham, was failing badly both as a player and as a leader. His first game back, at Headingley, did not start well. In fact, England were in such a dreadful position that at one stage bookmakers offered 500–1 against an England victory.

Botham had scored no runs at all in the first innings. Brearley understood that Botham's problems were more in his head than in his batting technique. Botham, a naturally gifted attacking batsman, had become far too defensive in his approach. In the second innings, despite England's perilous position, Brearley told Botham to 'go for it, enjoy yourself'. Botham scored a swashbuckling 149 not out.

Still, Australia needed only 130 to win, not a big total considering that they had made 401 in the first innings. England's fastest bowler, Bob Willis, had also been well below his usual form in the first innings. Brearley again diagnosed his problem to be mainly psychological. Willis had been bowling a lot of no-balls and so was bowling within himself to make sure he didn't overstep the bowling mark. Unfortunately this also meant that his bowling was much less hostile and wasn't very effective. Brearley told him just to run up and bowl fast. Willis took eight wickets and England won the match.

Brearley understood how his players' thinking was interfering with their performance. He realized that by taking responsibility himself for their mistakes, their shackles would be off and they would attack. But Brearley's leadership style wasn't always about encouragement. He made it his business to learn his players' temperaments so he could understand whether they were the sort of person who responded best to goading or encouragement. Rodney Hogg, an Australian opponent, summed it up nicely when he commented that Brearley 'had a degree in people'.

Mike Brearley was picked by England primarily for his ability to motivate his team and captain it supremely well. A real-life Captain Kirk, if you like. When he retired from cricket, Brearley went on to write a classic book, *The Art of Captaincy*, and to be a psychoanalyst. I expect he is a very good one.

Our evolved brains

While we would prefer to be the emotionally intelligent Captain Kirk rather than the overemotional McCoy or the emotionless Spock, evolution has made this difficult for us. Imagine two primitive human beings, both potentially your ancestors, walking home through the forest many thousands of years ago. Both hear a noise. It is probably just a harmless deer, but it could be a deadly tiger. One of them has a good think about the most likely cause of the noise, decides that it is most likely a deer and continues his stroll. The other instinctively runs away without even thinking about it. Which of the two primitive humans is most likely to survive? Remember that although it's probably a deer, one time in a hundred it is a tiger.

Our brains have evolved to help us cope with prehistoric dangers. When we sense danger we will go into the fight, flight or freeze response rather than think through things carefully. But though these responses made a lot of sense in a world of sabre-tooth tigers, they are not always so intelligent in the 21st century. In Goleman's words, 'we too often confront post-modern dilemmas with an emotional repertoire tailored to the urgencies of the Pleistocene'.

It seems that we literally have two brains – an 'old' brain that deals with instinctive behaviour and the processing of emotions and a 'new brain' that engages in reasoning and planning. Usually information is processed by both parts of the brain, but in some cases – which Goleman calls 'emotional hijackings' – the old emotional brain takes over and acts before the logical brain has a chance to process the information. This can obviously get us into trouble and make us do and feel many emotionally unintelligent things – rage, lust and panic being just three possibilities.

Yet it would be a mistake to think that we need to suppress the emotional brain and become like Mr Spock. Neurologist Antonio Damasio's research has found that when patients have the link between the old and new brain damaged they exhibit extremely poor decision-making skills (Damasio, 2005). The old brain contains a storehouse of emotional reactions. People without access to this are rather like a driver without a map or satnav. They can spot alternative routes, but they have no idea how to evaluate them. The old brain can sometimes cause emotional dumbness, as with overhasty actions and emotional hijackings, but Damasio's research suggests that it is also required for emotional wisdom. We need to train, listen to and evaluate the old brain rather than suppress it.

Goleman's writings are confirmed by the ideas of other writers. Nobel Prize winning psychologist Daniel Kahneman, author of *Thinking Fast and Slow*, identifies two types of thinking. What he calls System 1 is fast, emotional and subconscious. System 2 is relatively slow, logical and conscious. Kahneman argues that System 1 extends to fast decision making, such as when you decide what to buy, as well as to emotional reactions. System 1 works quickly but crudely and is prey to many fallacies and irrational biases. For example, it is System 1 that makes you take much more notice of a vivid anecdote about, say, your brother-in-law's bad experience with his Volvo, than a thousand positive reliable consumer reports. System 2, on the other hand, vastly overrates its own importance. Kahneman compares System 2 to a supporting actor who thinks they are the star performer. Jonathan Haidt compares the plight of the human being to being a rider on an elephant. We are not in control, we can advise the elephant, but if the elephant really wants to go one way, we've little chance of persuading it.

Key idea: Our two brains

Our brains are designed to deal with prehistoric emergencies more than modern melodramas. The 'new brain', which is the logical part, is sometimes overridden by the 'old brain', which reacts quickly using crude pattern matching. We are often not fully aware of the workings of the old brain and may invent stories about why we do things.

An intriguing possibility, which is being backed up in an increasing quantity of research, is that an ancient practice can help us become more emotionally intelligent, especially with respect to training our brains so that old and new brains can work together. The ancient practice is meditation, the secular version being mindfulness.

What is mindfulness?

Have you ever had the experience of not being able to remember where you put your front door keys? You are standing in your kitchen, so you must have used your keys to get in. But they are not in your pocket, or on the desk where you usually put them. You try to remember the last few minutes since opening the front door. You can't, because you were on autopilot.

Being on autopilot is the opposite of mindfulness. When we are on autopilot we pay little attention to what is going on around us or within us. We are ruled by instinctive reactions, Kahneman's System 1 'fast' thinking. We all live on autopilot at times. While sometimes it is useful, it makes us less able to rise above unhelpful habitual responses such as worrying, comfort eating or behaving in an angry manner. Mindfulness provides the antidote. Mindfulness leads to greater awareness of our thoughts, impulses and feelings. It enables us to respond wisely rather than react automatically.

Try it now: Notice your breathing

If you are alive, you breathe all the time, but how often do you notice it? For the next 30 seconds, pay deliberate attention to your breathing. Do not try to change it in any way. Notice whether you are breathing through your mouth or nose. What does the sensation feel like in your nose or mouth? Can you notice the air in your lungs? Are you breathing into your chest or belly? What thoughts go through your mind?

Do not try to breathe differently. Just notice what is happening as you breathe for the next 30 seconds. Now close your eyes and notice what happens as you breathe.

Mindfulness means being more aware and noticing what is happening. When you are mindful, you are using your 'second self' or 'observer self', that part of you which observes what you are doing. Spend a moment or two listening to the sounds in your environment. By paying attention, you can probably hear things you were not aware of before. But you are also aware now of the process of listening. Part of the mind experiences; part of the mind notices the experiencing.

Key idea: The meaning of mindfulness

Mindfulness has been defined as the awareness that emerges when you pay attention in a particular way, namely:

✳ on purpose
✳ in the present moment
✳ non-judgementally
✳ to things as they are.
    (Williams et al., 2007)

It means using your 'observer self' to notice yourself as well as your senses to notice the environment.

> **Remember this:** Mindfulness is not the same as savouring
>
> Mindfulness is similar, in some ways, to savouring, which was described in Chapter 2 as a strategy for increasing pleasure by paying attention to our experiences. We savour by lingering on the pleasant parts of our experience. In mindfulness, we pay attention to all of the experience. For example, suppose that you are enjoying a picnic with your children. You are immersed in conversation and paying attention to every detail of how your young children are enjoying themselves. Just then an older child accidentally kicks a football towards you. Your savouring will be interrupted. You may well feel an initial irritation, or even the start of a fight/flight reaction. Mindfulness means having the choice of how to respond to that stimulus. You can choose, if you wish, to admonish the child angrily, therefore ruining the atmosphere. Or you can choose to kick the football back with a friendly smile.

Mindfulness is a component of several third-wave CBT therapies, including acceptance and commitment therapy (ACT), mindfulness-based cognitive therapy (MBCT) and compassion-focused therapy (CFT). These therapies were designed primarily to help overcome psychological problems such as stress, anxiety and depression; however, there is good reason to think they can also help with well-being and so they should be part of the positive psychology toolkit. In this section we will discuss the first two of these therapies; we will discuss CFT in the next chapter.

Acceptance and commitment therapy (ACT)

ACT (pronounced as one word, 'act') is a therapy created initially by Steven Hayes and colleagues in the 1980s. It is one of the fastest-growing therapies and has an expanding evidence base, though it would be fair to say that the evidence for it or the other third-wave CBTs is not nearly as extensive as for traditional CBT. ACT involves six core processes (Harris, 2009), namely:

▶ Contact with the present moment – being aware of the here and now, the opposite of being on autopilot.

- ▶ Defusion – noticing your thoughts rather than being caught up in them. 'Thoughts are not facts' and, 'thoughts are just mental events' are two examples of ways to defuse thoughts.

- ▶ Acceptance – instead of avoiding or struggling against negative emotions, the idea is to accept them as part of the human experience.

- ▶ Self-as-context – you use the observing self, which notices you doing the thinking, as opposed to the self which experiences things directly. This perspective recognizes that we are not our thoughts, our moods or our feelings.

- ▶ Values – knowing what matters to you in life.

- ▶ Committed action – courageously and proactively doing what is needed to satisfy your values.

The last two are familiar: knowing what matters was covered in values clarification in Chapter 3, and committed action can be helped by the step-by-step planning to move in your valued direction which we looked at in Chapter 5. The other four principles are mindfulness-based ideas which can help further by putting values into action.

Imagine Mandy knows that her valued direction is to change careers. To do this she has to prioritize updating her CV and applying for new jobs. According to what you have learned so far, she should set a SMART+ goal, work out the required steps and overcome any obstacles. But suppose that some of the key roadblocks are emotional. Mandy spends a lot of time worrying, dwelling on past failures in interviews, and is plagued by negative thoughts such as, 'I am secure where I am; I shouldn't leave' and, 'I won't get the job I am after anyway'. Of course, reading case studies illustrating successful career changes (like Ken's in Chapter 6) and using CBT could help Mandy. But ACT offers an alternative approach. She uses her observing self to notice her thinking, and she notices that she is worrying and ruminating. Mandy needs to become more in contact with the present moment. She can defuse her thoughts about failure, 'there's the old failure story', and she can recognize that it is just a thought, not a fact. She knows that leaving her current post takes her out of her comfort zone, but that is all right, because she can accept that negative emotions are part of being alive. She thinks about her valued direction and realizes that staying in her current job will not take her there. Having freed herself from the emotional barriers, she is now in a good position to take committed action.

> **Key idea:** ACT is an evidence-based third-wave CBT therapy
>
> ACT combines mindfulness with values clarification to help people overcome emotional obstacles to well-being. Its popularity is growing and, although it has been used mainly for clinical populations, there is every reason to think it could help the general public to lead more fulfilling lives.

Meditation

You can practise mindfulness on a daily basis, for example by mindfully washing up, or eating mindfully. There is, however, another time-honoured way to become more mindful. It's called meditation.

There are, in fact, a number of different types of meditation. The two we will look at here are mindfulness meditation and loving kindness. Meditation may help you feel relaxed, but that is not really the point of it. Meditation is best thought of as mind training, helping you to become more aware and to concentrate better.

MINDFULNESS MEDITATION

Though based on ancient Buddhist spiritual practices, modern mindfulness meditation strips away its religious and metaphysical assumptions. Its aim is to provide an evidence-based treatment that can benefit everyone. Two group-based programmes have proved particularly popular: MBSR and MBCT. Mindfulness-based stress reduction (MBSR) was developed in the 1970s by Jon Kabat-Zinn in the USA. It combines stress reduction with mindfulness meditation. MBSR has been shown to be effective in treating physical and psychological symptoms of a range of problems including chronic pain, fibromyalgia, cancer, depression and anxiety. It has treated well over ten thousand patients.

Mindfulness-based cognitive therapy (MBCT) is a more recent, partly British, development based on MBSR. MBCT incorporates some elements of CBT, such as activity scheduling, although the emphasis is on being curious about negative thoughts rather than challenging them. Evidence at present suggests its specific added value is in helping prevent a relapse of depression in people who have been depressed more than twice.

The 'Try it now' exercise earlier about noticing your breathing is an example of a very short mindfulness meditation. When learning mindfulness, you will be instructed to practise meditation for up to an hour a day. A typical programme will include the body scan, mindfulness of breathing, mindfulness of sounds and walking meditations. You can find free downloadable examples of some of these and further resources at the author's website http://www.timlebon.com/meditation.html.

MINDFULNESS AND OUR EVOLVED BRAINS

Earlier we saw how our brains have evolved to contain different systems: an old brain that reacts automatically, quickly and emotionally and a new brain that reacts more deliberately, slowly and logically. One of the benefits of mindfulness is that it helps train both brain systems. Our observer self learns to become more aware of our 'monkey mind' jumping about from one thought to the next like a monkey jumping between trees. We learn to notice when it gets anxious and angry (old brain) or ruminates and worries (new brain). A non-judgemental attitude and here-and-now focus mitigate against further spiralling into negative thinking. The more we learn to notice these largely automatic processes, the more we are able to respond wisely.

Meditation also literally changes the physical structure of your brain. People who meditate grow bigger brains. Brain scan research at Harvard and Massachusetts Institute of Technology (MIT) has demonstrated that experienced meditators have developed increased thickness in the brain systems concerned with attention and sensory input.

A good analogy is going to the gym; just as lifting weights, for instance, develops muscles, so meditation builds the brain's potential for happiness, compassion and emotional intelligence.

BENEFITS OF MEDITATION

Numerous research studies have shown the benefits of meditation, which include happiness, less stress, less susceptibility to depression and better physical health.

Healthy workers who underwent an eight-week MBSR programme developed a stronger immune response to a flu vaccine as well as increases in left pre-frontal cortex activity (associated with happiness) compared with a control group. Another six-week meditation workshop led to more positive emotions and more savouring, better relationships and reduced illness.

A study of medical students found that those who meditated reported greater spiritual experiences, more empathy, less anxiety and less depression than the control group.

Remember this: Meditation requires commitment and regular practice

There are many studies that show that mediation is beneficial but, unlike many of the techniques described in this book, the benefits may not be immediate. It is a skill that needs to be practised regularly for weeks if not longer for the benefits to be reaped.

LOVING KINDNESS MEDITATION (METTA)

In loving kindness meditation you attempt to cultivate loving towards all sentient beings. (Metta is a Buddhist term for meditation aimed at developing unconditional love for all beings.) Usually you begin by wishing happiness on yourself, then on those close to you, then other friends and people you know, and finally to all sentient beings. One version[82] has you recite the following slowly to yourself:

> May I be free from enmity, affliction and anxiety, and live happily.
>
> May those I love be free from enmity, affliction and anxiety, and live happily.
>
> May all beings be free from enmity, affliction and anxiety, and live happily.

There is evidence that, for many people, regularly carrying out similar meditations over a few weeks increases positive emotions and, as predicted by Fredrickson's broaden-and-build theory, their personal resources and well-being (Fredrickson, 2009).

You can find free recordings of loving kindness meditations at http://www.positivityresonance.com/meditations.html and detailed instructions at http://www.wikihow.com/Practice-Loving-Kindness-Meditation-(Metta)

Case study: Mathieu Ricard – the happiest person alive?

Mathieu Ricard is the son of two French intellectuals, the philosopher Jean-Francois Revel and the painter Yahne le Toumelin. He had a happy childhood and as a young man mingled with leading artists and thinkers. But the high-flying intellectuals his parents mixed with weren't any happier or better than other people. 'I often had the uneasy feeling that life was slipping through my fingers – as if I was only using a fraction of my potential'. Having been inspired by films about Tibetan monks, he decided to travel to India to find out more. He continued his education and gained top honours in his PhD in molecular biology. At the age of 26 Ricard emigrated to Nepal to become a Buddhist monk.

Ricard became translator for the Dalai Lama and became known to a wider audience when, in 1999, he co-wrote a book with his father: *The Monk and the Philosopher: A Father and Son Discuss the Meaning of Life*.

But it wasn't until a few years later, in 2003, that Ricard became really famous when, in *Destructive Emotions*, Daniel Goleman wrote about Lama Oser, a monk of Western origin who had meditated for over 10,000 hours. Oser was tested by neuroscientist Richard Davidson on MRI scanners that could detect the amount of positive and negative emotion in the brain. When he was meditating on compassion, Lama Oser went off the scale. A few years later, Lama Oser was revealed to be none other than Mathieu Ricard.

The press labelled him 'the happiest man in the world', a title he laughs off. He is the happiest person tested so far on MRI scans, but as he admits, that's a tiny fraction of the population.

As impressive as his MRI scan results was Ricard's ability to stifle the startle response. When we hear a loud noise, the 'old brain' responds instinctively in a number of ways – we may flinch, back away and our heartbeat may quicken. When meditating, Ricard was subject to a very loud and sudden noise, as loud as a pistol firing in your ear. Ricard reduced the startle response enough for it to be unobservable.

Whether or not Ricard is the happiest person on earth, he is a striking example of someone who practises what he preaches. He has done more than his 10,000 hours of practice to become an expert, he gives away proceeds from his books to worthy charities, he still meditates regularly. I once attended one of his workshops, and was struck not so much by what he said – after all, I knew that from his books – but by his aura. There was something about him – warmth, openness and humour – that made me think his path was a worthy one. Some pretty hard-nosed journalists who have met him agree (for example, see http://www.independent.co.uk/news/people/profiles/matthieu-ricard-meet-mr-happy-436652.html)

You can read his ideas in the book *Happiness* and see him speak at http://www.ted.com/talks/matthieu_ricard_on_the_habits_of_happiness.html

Focus points

❋ Emotional intelligence means bringing intelligence to your emotions. Daniel Goleman suggested five abilities that make up emotional intelligence.

❋ Our brains have evolved to keep us safe, but may not be well adapted to 21st-century life. We have a tendency to be oversensitive to danger.

❋ There is much evidence that meditation, such as loving kindness meditation, has many health and psychological benefits.

❋ Mindfulness means paying attention on purpose, in the present moment, without judgement.

❋ ACT and MBCT are two evidence-based CBT therapies that include elements of mindfulness.

? Diagnostic test answers

1 Being aware of your emotions.
   Managing difficult emotions.
   Using emotions to motivate yourself.
   Recognizing emotions in others.
   Managing emotions in others.

2 c) bringing intelligence to our emotions.

3 b) marshmallows.

4 To react quickly to potentially fatal dangers.

5 You could have included any five from CBT, active and constructive responding, knowing someone's strengths, increasing your flow experiences, motivating someone else by facilitating their flow experiences, understanding someone else's strengths and weaknesses and using this knowledge to improve their performance, step-by-step planning, optimism, using Gottman's tips on relationships, such as trying to find compromise and using calming and relaxation methods.

6 Mindfulness is paying attention on purpose, in the present moment, non-judgementally.

7 Both are increased awareness; savouring is specifically about pleasure and positive experiences whereas mindfulness is attending to whatever is present.

8 Contacting the present moment, defusion, acceptance, self-as-context, values and committed action.

9 Better health, reduced symptoms of some physical conditions, relapse management of depression, stress management, more happiness

10 Mindfulness and loving kindness meditation

Next steps

In many chapters in this book it has been suggested that positive psychology may be missing something if it does not consider wisdom, particularly practical wisdom. In the next chapter we finally explore what can be said about this elusive concept. Wisdom includes compassion, which is part of emotional intelligence and is also closely connected with loving kindness, which we have just looked at.

11
Wisdom

In this chapter you will learn:

- ► *about wisdom*
- ► *about psychological theories of wisdom*
- ► *about the wisdom in positive psychology*
- ► *about the need for practical wisdom*
- ► *about the potential contribution of philosophy.*

Diagnostic test

1 What is the difference between wisdom and knowledge?

2 Name three psychologists who have produced theories of wisdom.

3 Name three findings from positive psychology that could be considered to be part of wisdom.

4 How many of the seven statements below do you think a wise person would agree with?

   a When I'm upset with someone, I usually try to put myself in his or her shoes' for a while.
   b I either get very angry or depressed if things go wrong.
   c I often do not understand people's behaviour.
   d Ignorance is bliss.
   e It's not really my problem if others are in trouble and need help.
   f There is only one right way to do anything.
   g Simply knowing the answer rather than understanding the reasons for the answer to a problem is fine with me.

5 A 15-year-old girl wants to get married straight away. What should she consider and do? Jot down your advice for her.

6 Do people get wiser as they get older?

7 Name four attributes you would associate with compassion in compassion-focused therapy (CFT).

8 You and your partner have just booked into a hotel room on a warm night. Your partner wants the window open but you are concerned about the noise if the window is open. What would you do?

9 Name a philosopher you would associate with the term 'practical wisdom'.

10 According to Barry Schwartz and Kenneth Sharpe, what is wrong with Seligman and Peterson's strength theory'?

What is wisdom?

The Chambers dictionary defines wisdom as:

> The ability to make sensible judgements and decisions, especially on the basis of one's knowledge and experience; prudence and common sense.

However, when most people think about wisdom they conclude that there is more to it than this definition suggests.

Try it now: Think about the qualities of a wise person

Spend a few moments thinking about a wise person. It could be a famous person, someone you know, or even a fictitious character. Then reflect for a few moments on why you have chosen that person. What qualities do they have that make you say that they are wise? Write down your choice of person and the qualities they embody.

Who did you choose? Famous people often selected include Nelson Mandela, Jesus, Gandhi, King Solomon, the Dalai Lama, Socrates and Oprah Winfrey. Fictional yet wise characters who often come up are Dumbledore, Gandalf and Yoda.

Key idea: Most people have a fairly clear understanding of what wise people are like

The qualities people typically associate with wise people include:
* understanding the human situation
* being able to reflect thoughtfully about important issues
* acting benevolently, compassionately and with good judgement.

In other words, as well as having practical common sense, wise people are good people who understand life and people.

Psychological theories of wisdom

THE BERLIN GROUP'S THEORY OF WISDOM

The most concerted effort to produce a psychology of wisdom has been carried out by Paul Baltes and his colleagues based at

Berlin University. Their research has concluded that wisdom demands competence in five areas, namely:

- ▶ knowing about the human situation, including human nature

- ▶ being able to make decisions well

- ▶ knowing about stages of life and human development

- ▶ appreciating that people have diverging life goals and that values are, in a sense, relative

- ▶ understanding the uncertainties of life

In the Berlin Group's view, wisdom involves knowledge, but relevant knowledge, about the human condition rather than the sort of knowledge that is tested on TV quiz shows. The group also states that wisdom has a practical element, about knowing how to proceed in life as well as knowing what is the right thing to do.[83]

The Berlin Group has provided a creative way of trying to measure wisdom. Positive psychologists tend to use self-rating scales (like the VIA strengths questionnaire). However, wise people tend towards humility, so a wisdom self-rating scale is likely to give inaccurate results. To get round this problem, the group has devised hypothetical dilemmas. They then rate people's responses to see how wise they are. Here is the example that you first encountered in the diagnostic test at the start of this chapter.

Try it now: A short wisdom test

A 15-year-old girl wants to get married straight away. What should she consider and do? Jot down your advice for her.

How would your answer compare with the Berlin Group's? Being guided by their five criteria, a wise person might say:

▶ Knowing about the human situation, including human nature

It might be human nature for the girl to ignore your advice, so you might have to frame it carefully. For example, you might start by empathizing with her and then ask her to list the pros and cons of getting married now.

▶ Being able to make decisions well

You would first aim to understand the situation well. Why does she want to get married now? Does she have a life-limiting illness, for example? Is she pregnant? What does she fear will happen if she does not get married? What does she think will happen if she does get married? What does the law say about her getting married now? You might suggest that she considers all the things that matter now, things that will matter in several years' time and all the parties affected. You would help her to make a decision that satisfied as much of what is important as possible.

▶ Knowing about stages of life and human development

A wise person would be aware that the girl might think very differently about her decision in a few years' time. You might tell her about Sternberg's triangular theory of love and ask her which type of love it is, and how she sees the relationship changing in the next few years. You would also want her to consider other things she might miss out on if she gets married, such as her education and career.

▶ Appreciating that people have diverging life goals and that values are, in a sense, relative

The dilemma does not explicitly say which era the girl is living in or which culture she is from. It would be very different if she lived in, say, 15th-century Verona from 21st-century Britain. Even if she lives in the present day, you would want to check the value system of her culture or subculture to make sure you were not imposing your values.

▶ Understanding the uncertainties of life

You and the girl should realize that nothing is certain. If she is marrying for love, then it is not certain that this will last. The uncertainty of the future mitigates against drastic measures that preclude other future options. On the face of it, this would count against marriage.

Did you take these five criteria into account? Baltes would have counted you as wise only if you had done so. Some people would respond in a very dogmatic, black-and-white way. For example, they might say, 'Fifteen-year-old girls are too young to marry, it's against the law, and she needs to be talked out of taking such a step.' For the Berlin Group, wisdom involves taking a very different, more circumspect and thoughtful perspective.

ARDELT'S THREE DIMENSIONS OF WISDOM

Monika Ardelt has made two main contributions to the psychology of wisdom. Ardelt acknowledges that self-reports to determine wisdom are problematic, but has nonetheless devised what is probably the most sophisticated questionnaire to measure wisdom, the 39-question 'three-dimensional wisdom scale' (3D-WS). The seven statements in question 4 of the diagnostic test at the start of this chapter represent some of the questions in the 3D-WS (Ardelt, 2003).

You can take the complete test by visiting http://www.nytimes.com/packages/flash/multimedia/20070430_WISDOM/?mkt=magazinelink3.

Ardelt agrees with the Berlin Group that wisdom combines knowing about life (the cognitive dimension) and being able to reflect on life (the reflective dimension). However, she thinks that the Berlin Group's theory underplays the emotional aspects of wisdom, which she calls the affective dimension. Ardelt emphasizes that wise people feel compassion for others and are generally able to overcome emotional obstacles to thinking and acting wisely.

Taking Ardelt's theory of wisdom into account, compassion-focused therapy (CFT), a third-wave CBT approach, should be considered one of the few evidence-based approaches that may enhance wisdom.

COMPASSION-FOCUSED THERAPY (CFT)

CFT has been developed by Paul Gilbert and colleagues largely in the UK, building CBT 'with a heart'. It has been used extensively with people who suffer from shame, helping them build more self-compassion. While there is limited evidence that it can increase the well-being of non-clinical populations, it is included in this section because it illuminates the connection between compassion and wisdom and also provides some practical exercises to increase compassion and wisdom.

CFT draws on the old brain/new brain distinction we encountered in the last chapter. It adds to this the idea that the brain contains at least three emotional systems, one concerned with pleasure and achievement (the drive system), one with protection against danger (the protective system) and a third with soothing and contentment (the soothing system). It conceptualizes psychological problems as arising through an imbalance of these three systems, especially a deficiency in the soothing system.

A key element of CFT is a 'not your fault' focus. We are born with brains that make it tricky for us to be happy; the 'old brain' is geared to make us overprotective and, through no fault of our own, the soothing system may be underdeveloped. What is within our power is to build the soothing system. We can do this in a number of ways, including:

▶ considering the true nature of compassion

▶ learning calm soothing breathing and safe place imagery[84]

▶ building an image of a perfectly compassionate being

▶ meditating on how the compassionate being would respond to difficult problems and how it would relate to us.

▶ The true nature of compassion

Think of a compassionate person. Who did you think of? Jesus? Martin Luther King? Nelson Mandela? Florence Nightingale?

Whoever you thought of, the chances are that they were kind, for this is often the first quality we think of when we think of compassionate people. But were all those people kind in a sentimental way? Or were they also people of action, who were tough when they needed to be and had the courage to bring about change in the world? Were they not also wise in that they understood the human condition and what was required to improve it?

According to CFT, compassion has the following four elements:

▶ wisdom

▶ strength

- ▶ warmth
- ▶ responsibility.

Remember this: The true nature of compassion

Compassion is not just about being warm and kind. It is not sentimental.

A helpful CFT exercise is to develop an image of a perfectly compassionate being. Your compassionate ideal could be a real historical figure or an imaginary being. It does not even have to be human, but it does have to embody wisdom, strength, warmth and responsibility and any other attributes that you think are important for compassion.

Once you have developed an image of your compassionate being, you can try the following meditation.

Try it now: A conversation with your fully compassionate being[85]

Close your eyes. Spend a few moments getting fully relaxed, by slowing down your breathing and, if you wish, visiting your safe place. Bring to mind your fully compassionate being. Imagine it being with you. Notice where it is in relation to you, its posture, facial expression and tone of voice. Notice how close it is to you and whether it embraces you.

Ask it a question, or about a problem or dilemma that is troubling you. Listen to its answer, and respond openly, expressing any anxious, angry or sad feelings. Listen to what your fully compassionate being says back to you. Continue the conversation until you feel the problem has been resolved in your mind and all your concerns are addressed.

STERNBERG'S BALANCE THEORY OF WISDOM

Robert Sternberg (1998) has proposed a third psychological theory of wisdom. He proposes that wisdom is all about balance. Wise people can balance:

- ▶ their own interests and those of others
- ▶ long-term and short-term interests
- ▶ whether to adapt, shape or select environments.

Renewed Items 13/02/2017 12:17
XXXXXX7700

Item Title	Due Date
atal impact	06/03/2017
ommunity	06/03/2017
ear nothing	
he Heist	06/03/2017
ead man's time	06/03/2017
psychology	
tmatic growth	
chieve your potential	06/03/2017
hrough positive psychology	

For example, recall the following question posed in the diagnostic test at the beginning of the chapter. Imagine that you and your partner have just booked into a hotel room on a warm night. Your partner wants the window open but you are concerned about the noise if the window is open. What would you do? A wise person would not just consider their own interests, they would also take their partner's into account. Moreover, they would not just consider the implications of how the problem is resolved for the night, but for the whole holiday and indeed as a precedent for future joint decision making. The wise person would also consider whether it was better to put up with the heat (adapting), get a fan or open the window and get earplugs (shaping the environment) or go to a new hotel (select a new environment).

OTHER QUALITIES OF A WISE PERSON

Notwithstanding all their positive qualities, it is important to remember that the wise person is human. A wise person may be unlucky and so fail at a particular task. A wise person may sometimes lack self-control and do something morally wrong. However, the wise person will recognize their frailty, and use their wisdom to overcome it as often and as best as they can. This is well illustrated in this classic tale from Homer's *Odyssey*.

Case study: Wisdom in ancient Greece – Odysseus and the Sirens

As told by the poet Homer, Odysseus (Ulysses in Latin) provides a good example of wisdom in action.

On his way home after the Trojan War, Odysseus was travelling through seas controlled by the Sirens. These were sea nymphs who lured sailors to a certain death with their beautiful singing. Odysseus had a dilemma, because he wanted to hear their singing, not just because it was beautiful but also because it was said to make the listener wiser. But he obviously didn't want to suffer the fate of other sailors. He asked the goddess Circe for advice. She advised him to ask his crew to tie him to the ship's mast tightly and refuse his subsequent orders to sail towards the Sirens or untie him. The sailors should stuff wax in their ears so they couldn't hear the song.

Odysseus did as instructed. When they approached the Sirens, Odysseus begged the sailors to untie him and to sail closer towards the Sirens. True to their orders, the sailors bound him tighter and ignored his order. The ship passed through the seas safely.

Key idea: Three theories and a definition of wisdom

Three theories of wisdom have been considered. The Berlin Group's definition has five criteria, including a practical element and knowledge of the human condition. Ardelt emphasizes the emotional as well as the cognitive and reflective dimensions of wisdom. Sternberg's theory sees balance as the defining quality of the wise person; balancing long- and short-term interests and individual interests and the general good.

My own definition of wisdom, which I believe sums up what is best in the three theories, is as follows:

> 'Wisdom is the possession of knowledge about what matters and deep understanding about the universe, the human condition and human nature, combined with good judgement, and the disposition to try to put this knowledge into action.'

Do you get wiser as you get older?

It has to be admitted that the psychology of wisdom is still in its relative infancy. Psychologists have several theories of wisdom (it would be better if there was only one) and ways to measure wisdom (even if it is agreed that self-reports are not necessarily reliable). Yet they have made relatively little progress so far on the causes of wisdom, let alone designing deliberate interventions to make people wiser. One question that has prompted research is whether people get wiser as they get older. Since experience is one element of wisdom, one would expect that wisdom might increase with age. Does research back up this idea? The short answer is – not really. Studies show increased wisdom up until early mid-life, after which cognitive performance often deteriorates and wisdom, if anything, seems to be reduced, at least as measured by psychological tests. Paul Baltes concluded that, 'The current evidence is not that the majority of older adults, in areas such as professional expertise and wisdom, demonstrate superior performances when compared with the young.' (Baltes, P. and Baltes, M. (eds), 1993)

> **Remember this:** The positive psychology of wisdom has far to go
>
> Attempts to develop a positive psychology of wisdom have in truth not got very far. There is no one agreed definition of wisdom, and self-reports, the usual method of measurement, are not very reliable. The finding that is most often reported in the press, that wisdom grows with age, has not been consistently found to be true. In terms of practical interventions, compassion-focused therapy (CFT) offers one of the most promising approaches.

The wisdom in positive psychology

To what extent can studying positive psychology make you wiser? Although it is a young science, it is arguable that positive psychology has already made a significant contribution to humanity's understanding of flourishing and well-being. These include facts such as:

▶ Happier people enjoy better health and are more altruistic and creative.

▶ Experts have usually put in the equivalent of ten years of deliberate practice before achieving the highest standards.

▶ Much of meaning and purpose comes from work, intimacy, spirituality and transcendence.

▶ Optimists have better health, specifically a lower risk of heart attacks.

▶ People are more likely to experience flow in their jobs than in their leisure time.

▶ There are simple exercises one can carry out, such as 'Three good things' and using a strength in a new way, which increase happiness in the short and long term.

In addition, positive psychology offers the opportunity to develop the self-knowledge and self-awareness that is part of wisdom. For example, if you have carried out the exercises in this book then you will be wiser about yourself in that you can now answer the questions in the 'Try it now' below.

Try it now: Practical wisdom and personal knowledge from positive psychology

You can take stock of the personal knowledge and practical wisdom you have gained from this book by noting down your answers to the following questions.

✳ What activities have I identified where I can find flow?
✳ What have I identified as my top 'signature' strengths?
✳ What have I identified as things that will probably make me feel happier if I do them?
✳ What important values have I identified?
✳ What can I do to find meaning and purpose in my life?
✳ What can I do to improve my relationships (intimate, work and friends)?
✳ What can I do to help me achieve my goals and accomplish more?
✳ What can I do to help me deal with difficult emotions and be more resilient?

The need for practical wisdom

Wisdom is by no means totally neglected by positive psychology. Many positive psychology books have short sections on wisdom. As we have seen, positive psychologists have begun to develop theories of wisdom. Wisdom is one of the 24 strengths in the VIA strengths catalogue.

However, Barry Schwartz and Kenneth Sharpe (2011) have argued that Aristotle's ideas about practical wisdom suggest serious shortcomings in the role assigned for wisdom in positive psychology. Practical wisdom is the capacity to know the right thing to do in specific situations, to be skilled at carrying out the right action, and to want to do it. It is the virtue of wise decision making, of Odysseus when dealing with the Sirens and of King Solomon in the Bible.

For Aristotle, practical wisdom is not one virtue among many, it is necessary and foundational; it is a master virtue. It is the virtue that allows us to decide what a particular situation calls for. It is practical wisdom that tells you how to balance the five parts of PERMA in your life. It is practical wisdom that tells you when to be an optimist and when a defensive pessimist. It is practical wisdom that tells you when to use a strength and when to manage a weakness. It is practical wisdom that distinguishes moral goals (like an act of kindness) from immoral ones (like robbing a bank or committing a terrorist act). In other words, without practical wisdom all of the tools of positive psychology can be misused.

Another key idea for Aristotle is his theory of the golden mean. Too much or too little of a strength is problematic. For example, if we have too much bravery we are rash, but if we have too little we are cowardly. Just how much bravery we need depends on the situation. This depends on context, and we need practical wisdom to make the right decision. Aristotle would not have been impressed by any suggestions that we should always have a 3:1 or any other ratio. As Aristotle said, 'The person who is angry at the right things and towards the right people, and also in the right way, at the right time and for the right length of time, is praised.' (Aristotle, *Nicomachean Ethics*, 1999 translation)

When it is set alongside Aristotle's ideas about practical wisdom, some of positive psychology's recommendations appear simplistic. For example, identifying your strengths and using them as much as possible may result in inappropriate use of a strength. Engaging in more flow activities may put a relationship or other key values in jeopardy. Making a plan towards a personal goal may not be so good if the goal is robbing a bank. Responding to what your partner perceives to be good news in an active constructive way may be unhelpful if what she or he perceives to be good news is actually bad news. Having a subjectively meaningful and purposeful life is not good for society if you happen to be a terrorist.

Remember this: Positive psychology has been criticized for underestimating the importance of practical wisdom

Drawing on Aristotle's theories of practical wisdom and the golden mean, Barry Schwartz and Kenneth Sharpe have criticized positive psychology for being philosophically naïve. Their argument is that context and judgement are key, and that taking the 'more is better' approach (as with strengths) or looking for a universal ratio (as with the positivity ratio) is misguided.

The approach taken in this book has been to suggest a wiser positive psychology, which has more emphasis on values and more sensitivity to context. For example, it recommends that you do the following:

▶ Decide on your important values through values clarification and reflect on these wisely, for example balancing short- and long-term interests.

▶ Achieve a wise and realistic optimism by combining optimistic thinking for agency thinking with defensive pessimism for pathways thinking.

▶ Work to overcome negative emotions as well as enhancing positive experiences.

▶ Use your strengths to help move in your valued direction and at the same time manage your weaknesses and be aware of the possibility of overusing strengths.

▶ Use flow activities to achieve meaningful things rather than just during trivial activities.

Key idea: This book has attempted to bring practical wisdom into positive psychology

Throughout this book we have been sensitive to the idea that practical wisdom is important, and this is reflected in both criticisms of simplistic positive psychology ideas and suggesting improvements.

The potential contribution of philosophy

'Science gives us knowledge, but only philosophy can give us wisdom.' (Will Durant)

In this book we have tried to present a version of positive psychology which takes ideas about practical wisdom more seriously. There remains one problem which has been sidestepped – how do you teach people to understand what matters, that is, to know what is morally good? Traditionally religion has had this role, but in a pluralistic and largely secular society we need viable alternatives.

Author Jules Evans suggests that philosophy should have a pivotal role. 'You can measure the extent to which a person feels their life is meaningful, but who's to say if it's a good or bad meaning? You can measure the extent to which they feel they're serving a "higher cause", but who's to say if it's a worthwhile higher cause or not. We need practical philosophy to develop our discernment, our practical wisdom, so we can choose between good and bad meanings to devote ourselves to.'[86]

One way forward is to integrate philosophy more into positive psychology.

Philosophical and psychological ideas can be combined to provide frameworks to help people live well, for example by developing enlightened values, making wise decisions and taking committed action towards their goals.

In this book we have already described several interventions which could be considered to be combing philosophy and psychology in an integrated framework, for example in Chapter 3 on values. Similarly, ACT could be considered to be a combination of philosophical ideas (for example about values and how to clarify them) and psychology (for example techniques for how to defuse difficult thoughts).

An integrative framework that can help with wise decision making and which has some empirical evidence to support[87] it is the following five-step procedure (LeBon and Arnaud, 2012). The five steps are as follows:

1 What exactly is the situation and the decision to be made? What do you feel about the situation and the need to make a decision?

2 What matters? What are the outcomes that you would like to attain?

3 What options do you have?

4 Which option best satisfies what matters?

5 What needs to happen to put this option into practice? What is the first step? What might go wrong?

It should readily be seen that this framework provides a step-by-step approach to putting Aristotle's ideas about practical wisdom into action.

A different way forward is to teach practical and ethical philosophy alongside positive psychology. While it is beyond the scope of this book to develop these ideas in detail, we will briefly describe two possible approaches.

▶ Teaching philosophical theories about well-being and ethics, and helping people learn how to think wisely

Philosophers have come up with a variety of theories that can help people understand and resolve ethical questions more effectively. For example, philosophers have variously argued that the right action is the one that produces the best results (utilitarianism), the importance of following rules about what is right (deontological theories) and the need to inculcate virtues (virtue ethics). People could be taught about these theories not so much as competing theories, but as each providing valuable ideas about what matters in a situation. In addition, students can be taught how to reason about ethics, for example by considering hypothetical thought experiments like the experience machine or vignettes like the 15-year-old girl who wants to get married. They would learn the importance of providing good reasons to back up their thoughts and of considering possible complexities in such cases. They would learn to reason more wisely about values and dilemmas.

The 'philosophy with children' movement provides one such framework for helping children think more reflectively, often using a method called the 'community of enquiry'. British practitioner Peter Worley has developed these ideas further into a more rigorously philosophical framework. Research suggests that this method helps with children's intellectual development. Further research is required as to whether it helps with their moral development and their wisdom. The author, Tim LeBon, has also taught 'practical philosophy' classes where the students develop their own ideas about well-being on a weekly basis at the same time as learning about philosophical ideas about well-being.

▶ Philosophy-based interventions

Although much recent philosophy is highly theoretical, for the ancients philosophy was very practical. In the West, Stoics and Epicureans were leading lights among philosophers who proposed practical ideas. In the East, Buddhist philosophy influenced spiritual practice, including meditation and mindfulness. As we have seen, research has shown that both mindfulness and loving kindness meditation have significant and lasting benefits. However, relatively little work has been done to test out whether practical ideas from Western philosophies are beneficial. Stoicism forms the basis of CBT, so there is reason to think it may be beneficial. However, the creators of CBT did not have a very thorough knowledge of Stoicism and may have ignored many useful ideas contained within it. Among some key Stoic ideas are the following:

▶ There are some things in life we have control over and some things over which we do not really have control. We should focus our energies on the things we can control. This is a similar idea to the 'Serenity Prayer' which we first encountered in Chapter 9.

▶ One of the things we can control is our intentions. We should approach life like an archer who does all within their power to hit the bull's-eye. Having done that, the wind may blow the arrow off target, and we should accept that. Our intentions are like the archer's aim. The outcome of our acts is like hitting the target. It is our intentions rather than the outcome which we should focus on.

▶ You can also control your emotions. Emotions depend on judgements about what will happen and whether it is good or bad. Change the judgements and you will change the emotions.

▶ We should treat things which we cannot control – such as how other people respond to us – as 'nice to haves'. We should aim not to get too upset if these things do not come our way.

▶ We should live in harmony with nature. We are connected with all other beings, but we should not think that we are at the centre. We should treat others as brothers and sisters, as part of the commonwealth of beings.

A project organised by the University of Exeter involving a group of academics and therapists, including the author of this book, began in 2012 to try to find out if it was possible to provide an empirical base for Stoic ideas.

Participants were recruited mainly via the internet and given Stoic readings and daily exercises to carry out for a week. Their well-being and flourishing were measured before and after taking part in the experiment. Many participants showed significant improvement. The experiment was repeated in 2013 with a much larger set of participants and the positive results were confirmed.

Although encouraging, caution needs to be exercised when interpreting this result. There was no control group and it is possible that the improvement could have been partly a placebo effect. Another way to test whether Stoicism has a positive impact is to see if there is a positive association between Stoic attitudes and behaviours and well-being. This was tested in 2013 by developing the Stoic Attitudes and Behaviours Scale. Over 2000 people took the SABS scale as well as the SWB and SPANE (positive and negative emotions) scales you were encouraged to take in Chapter 1 of this book. We found that there was indeed a significant association between Stoicism and all the well-being measures.

Try it now: The Stoic Attitudes and Behaviours Scale

Take the Stoic Attitudes and Behaviours Scale by visiting http://blogs. exeter.ac.uk/stoicismtoday/. Calculate your score. A score above 40 is higher than average.

The research suggested that three Stoic attitudes and behaviours were particularly strongly associated with well-being, namely:

▶ Making an effort to pay continual attention to the nature of your judgements and actions (mindfulness).

▶ When an upsetting thought enters your mind, reminding yourself it is just an impression in your mind and not the thing it claims to represent.

▶ Considering yourself to be a part of the human race, in the same way that a limb is a part of the human body.

Another finding, which supports the idea that Stoicism could be part of positive psychology, is that Stoic attitudes and behaviours were more associated with positive emotions than the absence of negative emotions. Against the stereotype of the stiff upper lip, practising Stoicism turns out to be particularly associated with joy and contentment. For more information, including recordings of Stoic meditations to download, see http://blogs.exeter.ac.uk/stoicismtoday/.

Key idea: The potential of practical philosophy

As well as integrating philosophical ideas into positive psychology, there is a case for practical philosophy working alongside it. Philosophy with children and philosophy-based wisdom interventions provide two examples.

Focus points

✻ While the positive psychology of wisdom is in its infancy, three main theories of wisdom in positive psychology are associated with the Berlin Group, Ardelt and Sternberg.

✻ Compassion-focused therapy can help us be more compassionate and, therefore, more wise.

✻ There is much wisdom in positive psychology, including theoretical wisdom and more personal practical wisdom.

✻ It has been argued that Aristotle's practical wisdom is foundational and a master virtue. Schwartz and Sharpe have cogently argued that positive psychology needs to do more to take practical wisdom into account.

✻ This book has attempted to integrate practical wisdom into its account of positive psychology. It has done this by integrating philosophical ideas and also by advocating a balanced approach to well-being. It has been suggested that there is a role for practical philosophy in helping people learn how to be practically wise.

Diagnostic test answers

1 Wisdom is 'knowing how' as well as 'knowing that'. Wisdom is also knowledge about the human condition and human nature rather than knowledge that could win prizes on TV quiz shows.

2 Baltes and the Berlin Group, Ardelt and Sternberg

3 There is a long list in the section on 'The wisdom in positive psychology'. In fact, you could count most of the 'Key ideas' from this book.

4 Only a) When I'm upset at someone, I usually try to 'put myself in his or her shoes' for a while.

5 The text contains a detailed answer, incorporating the Berlin Groups five criteria for wisdom.

6 There is not much evidence to back up this popular belief.

7 Wisdom, strength, warmth and responsibility.

8 The text suggests that a good answer would incorporate elements
   of Sternberg's balance theory of wisdom.

9 Aristotle.

10 It lacks practical wisdom, being too simplistic in suggesting that
   you just use more of a strength regardless of context.

Next steps

**In the final chapter we will look at how positive
psychology is carried out with individuals, in
schools and in business. We will also draw some
final conclusions about the status of positive
psychology.**

12

Positive psychology in practice

In this chapter you will learn about:

► *positive psychology self-help, coaching and psychotherapy*
► *positive psychology in education*
► *positive psychology in business and organizations.*

In this final chapter we will see how positive psychology can be used with individuals, children and in groups.

Diagnostic test

1 Who came up with an early happiness programme involving 14 fundamentals?

2 What is the name of the Australian school which has pioneered embedding positive psychology into the school curriculum?

3 With which American organization has Seligman recently developed an extensive resilience programme?

4 Name three third-wave CBT approaches that could be considered a positive psychology approach.

5 Is prioritizing happiness a good or bad idea?

6 Which major company is well known for allowing its workers to have one day a week working on their own projects?

7 Is there any evidence that guided self-help works better than reading a self-help book on your own?

8 What is the name of Michael Frisch's approach that combines CBT and positive psychology?

9 Is Seligman's positive psychotherapy aimed more at helping people with depression or anxiety?

10 How long did the positive effects of the UK adaption of the Penn resiliency programme last in a pilot trial?

Positive psychology self-help

Many of the techniques and much of the research of positive psychology has been aimed at individuals. There are many ways that individuals can potentially benefit from positive psychology. For example, they can read a book like this one and try out the exercises to see if they work. In fact, now is an excellent time to retake the tests and compare your happiness and other ratings.

Try it now: How happy are you now?

Retake both the SWLS and SPANE tests in Chapter 1. How do your scores compare with your baseline scores? To what do you attribute this change? Recall that the happiness pie chart puts 40 per cent of happiness down to voluntary activities and only 10 per cent down to circumstances. Remember also that this is only an average!

How much change do you put down to the exercises you have carried out as a result of reading this book? Which ones do you think have been most effective? You might find the list of interventions in 'Appendix B: The positive psychology toolkit' helpful.

Sonja Lyubomirsky (2007) recommends a 'trial and error' approach to positive psychology exercises. She advocates trying them all and seeing which ones work best for you. Now would be a great time to review the exercises and decide which ones you would like to continue on a regular basis.

You might like to make it your goal to become an expert in doing your favourite positive psychology exercises. Even half an hour's regular practice is likely to reap benefits. Here is one man's story of how he incorporates positive psychology into his daily routine.

Case study: Pawel's daily positive psychology workout

It's a good idea to try and find a time and environment where you can regularly – preferably every day – carry out your favourite positive psychology exercises. One way to do this is illustrated by Pawel, who has a regular personal development time he calls his 'hour of power'.[88]

Pawel gets up early each morning and walks or runs in the nearby park. Sometimes he will vary this by practising yoga or going to the gym for about 30 minutes. He then meditates for about 20–30 minutes, practising vipassana meditation, a Buddhist meditation aimed at gaining insight into the workings of the mind. He rounds off the hour of power by thinking about and visualizing states and emotions he wants to experience during the day to come, mainly love, gratefulness, passion and compassion.

He has discovered that yoga and other exercises make him more active and positive, especially when done in the morning. Meditation improves his concentration and mindfulness. Thinking of all the positive states for the day helps him remember what is important in his life and feel more confident.

You'll notice that Pawel combines a range of activities which help improve body and mind. It's also probably helpful that it's part of his daily routine. Just as many people go to the gym, and we all do regular routine activities like cleaning our teeth, you might like to start doing a regular positive psychology workout.

Remember this: Regular practice is essential

In this book you have learnt a large number of skills which can help you achieve your potential and be happier. Like with other skills, such as learning a musical instrument or a language, practice is essential. Indeed, the theory we learnt in Chapter 10 suggests you need 10,000 hours of practice to become an expert in these techniques! A good way of doing this is to include practising positive psychology skills into your daily routine.

Positive psychology coaching and psychotherapy

Although reading self-help books and practising exercises on your own can be helpful, research has shown that more benefit is to be gained from guided self-help. This means having someone help you understand the theory and practice and regularly set you home practice. People usually seek life coaches, psychotherapists and counsellors to guide them in this way.

It is not known how many coaches and therapists are informed by positive psychology. It is certainly fair to say that compared with other paradigms, like CBT and psychoanalysis, positive psychology coaching and psychotherapy are in their infancy. A number of books have been written to guide coaches and therapists, notably Michael Frisch's massive *Quality of Life Therapy* which contains an enormous number of techniques and exercises and integrates ideas from CBT and positive psychology. Rashid and Seligman have created a protocol for what they call 'positive psychotherapy', which is aimed mainly at helping overcome depression. You can read an overview of the 14-session therapy in Seligman's book *Flourish*. However, at the time of writing, a promised treatment manual has yet to be published. For further information see www.ppc.sas.upenn.edu/positivepsychotherapyarticle.pdf and http://www.authentichappiness.sas.upenn.edu/newsletter.aspx?id=1553.

Rashid and Seligman's package of interventions is by no means the only one possible. Way back in the 1970s and 1980s, happiness pioneer Michael Fordyce ran successful workshops which taught students his '14 fundamentals of happiness'. The students reported increased happiness immediately after the sessions and after several months' follow-up.

It is instructive to review Fordyce's 14 fundamentals:

1 Be more active and keep busy.

2 Spend more time socializing.

3 Be productive at meaningful work.

4 Get better organized and plan things out.

5 Stop worrying.

6 Lower your expectations and aspirations.

7 Develop positive, optimistic thinking.

8 Get present-oriented.

9 Work on a healthy personality.

10 Develop an outgoing social personality.

11 Be yourself.

12 Eliminate negative feelings and problems.

13 Close relationships are number 1.

14 VALHAP – the secret fundamental (this means valuing happiness).

It seems that in fact quite a lot was known about how to be happy back in 1977! One key finding from Fordyce's early work is hidden in the secret fundamental, number 14. Despite sceptics' suggestions that valuing happiness is counter-productive, Fordyce found that prioritizing happiness pays dividends.

Remember this: Prioritizing happiness is a good idea

Fordyce's pioneering work and subsequent studies show that, contrary to popular belief, prioritizing happiness is not counterproductive. The trick is not to worry about happiness but to learn and practise the skills that lead to happiness and to do things that make you happy.

Positive CBT

In this book we have argued for integrating CBT into positive psychology. Some psychologists have attempted to do the opposite: integrating positive psychology into CBT. Banninck's *Practising Positive CBT* combines CBT, positive psychology and solution-focused therapy. The author proposes a version of CBT that focuses on strengths and solutions rather than weaknesses and problems. Whether positive CBT builds an evidence base to match traditional CBT remains to be seen. What is less debatable is that traditional CBT can be usefully informed by positive psychology. Here are some ideas that I personally find useful in conducting a style of CBT informed by positive psychology.

1 Ask clients about their strengths in the first session. If they cannot think of any, ask them what those who appreciate them most would say, or what they are most proud of in their life.

2 Clients undergoing transitions (for example, after illness or accident or in mid-life) may have lost sight of their values. They may have lost hope because their previous ways of fulfilling their values have become blocked. With these clients, it is often useful to help them clarify their values and use step-by-step planning to help move towards satisfying them.

3 When doing behavioural activation and activity scheduling, be aware of the range of positive emotions that clients may experience. There is more to positive emotion than just pleasure. Consider mentioning flow ('when you are feeling really absorbed in what you are doing') and asking them to think about how they can get more flow in their lives.

4 Although a CBT therapist often has to be challenging and needs to ask the client to do what they would rather not do (such as face a fear), aim to make therapy warm and friendly. Positive emotions and positive relationships are valuable.

5 Towards the end of therapy, CBT therapists aim to produce a blueprint, which includes a summary of what clients have learned and how they can use this once they finish therapy. Drawing on positive psychology, you can include a positive five-part model showing positive attributes, as shown.

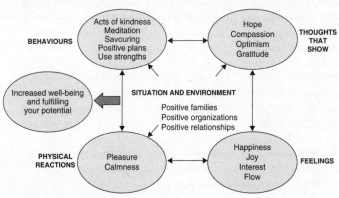

A positive five-part model

Finally, we have already seen how many third-wave CBT approaches could be considered part of positive psychology. These include MBCT, CFT and ACT. A noteworthy collection of articles is Kashdan and Ciarrochi (eds) 2013 *Mindfulness, Acceptance and Positive Psychology*.

Key idea: Positive psychology and CBT could be a powerful combination

We began this book by comparing positive psychology with an adolescent who has distanced themselves a little too far from their elder relatives. We have argued for a more inclusive approach, and for this reason have advocated including CBT in positive psychology. Conversely, there is scope for CBT to be informed by positive psychology. We have pointed out a number of ways CBT in which could potentially be enhanced by incorporating ideas and a warmer style from positive psychology. This applies to traditional CBT as well as the third-wave CBT approaches.

Positive psychology in education

Educators from Aristotle to Daniel Goleman have argued that the early years are a key window of opportunity. Children learn quickly and easily form habits. For this reason, positive psychology in education is a very good idea; implementing it, especially in the UK state system, may prove more challenging.

In *Flourish*, Seligman gives a glowing account of Geelong Grammar School in Australia, a top boarding school which has wholeheartedly entered into the spirit of positive psychology. As well as teaching positive psychology classes, Geelong has attempted to embed positive education into the whole curriculum. For example, English teachers look for character strengths in Shakespeare plays and sports coaches ask players to remember the good things they have accomplished in games.

In the UK, independent school Wellington College in Berkshire has been at the forefront of implementing positive psychology in the classroom. Wellington has a different model from Geelong, with positive psychology being implemented mainly in well-being lessons as opposed to being embedded in the whole school.

Case study: Wellington College

Under the leadership of its Master Anthony Seldon and its senior well-being teacher Ian Morris, Wellington College has been teaching well-being lessons since 2006. Well-being courses have six strands:

1 Physical health – this module focuses on the importance of diet and exercise. In addition students learn (and may even repeat!) the marshmallow test teaching them about executive control.

2 Positive relationships – as well as dealing with friendships and other positive relationships, this strand looks at conflict resolution, an important topic for adolescents.

3 Perspective – this strand is mainly about building resilience, including ideas about mindsets, mindfulness, optimism and CBT. Pupils aren't just taught about them, they are taught how to do them, for example, they are taught how to meditate.

4 Engagement – this strand covers flow, strengths and positive emotions.

5 The world – this introduces a moral aspect to the education, helping pupils think about sustainability and their relationship with the environment.

6 Meaning and purpose – drawing on Frankl, this strand helps pupils explore personal meanings and helps them start to think about their sense of direction in life.

Since well-being lessons started, academic grades have improved from 69 per cent to 93 per cent A/B grades. Although there are no ways of knowing whether this effect is in any way due to the well-being lessons, both Seldon and Morris are confident that the lessons have had a long-term positive impact on pupils.

Perhaps the most well-known attempt to implement positive psychology ideas in education is the Penn resiliency programme (PRP). This is a group-based intervention usually delivered in twelve 90-minute lessons. The curriculum includes learning how to foster optimism, strengths, social skills and achievement. There is considerable empirical support for the programme. In the USA it has been shown to reduce and prevent depression (for at least two years) and it also reduces conduct problems and increases optimism and well-being. In the UK, a pilot programme attempted to implement the PRP in nine state schools. However, the results of the pilot have proved somewhat disappointing.[89] While there was a short-term improvement in depression, school attendance and academic performance, this disappeared soon after the end of the academic year. There was no significant impact a year after the lessons had finished. What had gone wrong? A number of problems were identified: in many schools there was insufficient backing from senior management; auxiliary staff were sometimes used to teach lessons; some schools used the lessons to try to solve problem behaviour, although the lessons were intended to be universal and to tackle emotional difficulties and not problem behaviour; some lessons were scheduled irregularly and class sizes were often above the 15 recommended. There was also a feeling that the material was too didactic; perhaps UK children would respond better to a more participatory learning experience.

Remember this: Management 'buy-in' is essential

When working within organizations, it is important to have sufficient 'buy-in' to implement the programmes effectively. The disappointing experience of resilience lessons in UK state schools may not be so much down to the materials themselves (which worked better in the USA) but to not prioritizing the programme sufficiently within the schools.

Unfortunately, this means that the prospects for more positive psychology in UK state schools are not good. Perhaps a forward-looking government will ring-fence more funds to try out another positive psychology programme more fully. In the meantime, there is no reason why inculcating the habits of positive psychology should not be a part of good, positive parenting.

Positive psychology in the workplace

Since positive psychology aims to increase effectiveness as well as well-being, there is clearly much scope for it to be helpful in the workplace. Some of its most helpful applications include:

▶ Using strengths – helping people to understand and use more of their strengths at work. This can be done by using the inventories and by individual mentoring to help people put their strengths into practice.

▶ Enabling flow by designing working environments that facilitate it – the absence of noise and distractions is important, as is setting the right level of challenge.

▶ Intrinsic motivation – allowing staff to get involved in projects which they find interesting and worthwhile for their own sake is conducive to flow, well-being and higher productivity. Participatory working practices, such as Google's allowing their workforce to devote 20 per cent of their time to their own projects, can enhance intrinsic motivation.

▶ Teaching people about optimism, meditation, resilience, emotional intelligence and other ideas from positive psychology – there is a lot of scope for training days to include material from this book.

▶ Making the workplace a happier place – while this might sound very idealistic, research shows that positive emotion increases health, creativity and achievement. So a happy workforce makes good business. Encouraging team events, socializing after work and having a friendly 'open-door' policy are all possible ways of implementing this.

Key idea: Positive psychology in the workplace

There is much scope for applying the ideas in this book in the workplace. This is a good example of a win–win solution. From the company's point of view, positive psychology has the potential to improve staff retention rates, reduce sickness and increase productivity. It will also make the workplace more interesting and enjoyable for the workforce.

Case study: Positive psychology in the workplace

Shona Lockhart runs a small translation company and is also an enthusiastic student and practitioner of positive psychology. Here she describes how she has brought positive psychology into her workplace.

'Focusing on strengths has been crucial and a big insight for my staff. It is never easy to know how much people are taking on board, but when an employee recently applied for an internal promotion her whole application and CV focused on how she uses her strengths at work in different ways. I was so proud of her for applying the learning and she got the job.

'Responsibility is one of my strengths, which makes me feel responsible for the happiness of my employees. A big lesson for me (and one which I am still learning) is that I can only do so much and the responsibility for their happiness lies with them.

'I try to run monthly positive psychology-based meetings; although not everyone buys into the idea I think that it is having a positive effect on people at work. We begin every meeting by focusing on what has gone well and what we are proud of and that sets every session on a positive tone.

'The acts of kindness idea works pretty well, but I think we were already a kind and considerate team. We have extended the idea of acts of kindness to customers and have introduced the idea of customer hugs (small ideas such as remembering birthdays, sending small boxes of chocolates or sending thank you cards) or just staying as close to customers as possible, ideally over the phone rather than by email, as this gives everyone a sense of connection to others.

'We have a strict rule of requesting customer feedback after every single job, which is not just a good way of ensuring the client is happy but again reinforces personal connection. Frequently when we ask for feedback we get really positive testimonials and we share these round the office and praise the individual responsible. I think this gives everyone a great sense of pride and job satisfaction. We keep a file of nice things customers have said about us and it's a great place to look for inspiration when anyone is having a bad day.

'Above all I try to instil a sense of continual learning. No one is made to feel ashamed because they do not know something – everything can be learned and improved on. I always ask my employees to come to me with solutions rather than problems, which gives them the belief that they are capable of working out the majority of things for themselves.'

You can read more of Shona Lockhart's work at http://www. thehappinessexperiment.co.uk

Perhaps the largest-scale implementation of positive psychology is the involvement of Seligman in teaching resilience to the US Army. Alarmed by the high rates of suicide, mental illness and substance abuse, the US military called in Seligman to create a 'comprehensive soldier fitness programme'. Costing $125 million, the programme focuses on building resilience in five dimensions: physical, emotional, social, family and spiritual. The philosophy of the programme is that prevention is better than cure. The programme incorporates some of the ideas in this book, including teaching optimism, Gottman's relationships tips, the benefits of positive emotions and using strengths. Although the programme has its critics, in 2013 a report evaluated it positively, concluding that, 'it helps to reduce the odds of developing diagnosable mental health issues among soldiers'.[90]

Focus points

❋ Positive psychology is a very practical discipline, the findings of which can potentially help individuals as well as those in education and in the workplace.

❋ Perhaps its greatest influence at present is through self-help books. It is recommended that readers pick their favourite exercises and build them into their daily routine. A list of interventions from this book is to be found in 'Appendix B: The positive psychology toolkit'.

❋ Evidence shows that guided self-help works better than unguided reading. Coaches and psychotherapists have begun to be informed by ideas from positive psychology.

❋ Education presents a unique window of opportunity for young people to build positive psychology practice into good habits. While some independent schools have undertaken successful initiatives, the state sector is more constrained by curriculum rigidity and a lack of resources. Unfortunately, a pilot of the Penn resilience programme in the UK had disappointing results.

❋ The workplace is another obvious win–win in terms of both a happier and a more productive workforce. The most notable implementation of positive psychology in organizations is in the US Army, where, although it has its critics, it has also been heralded as a success.

Diagnostic tests answers

1 Michael Fordyce.

2 Geelong Grammar School.

3 The US Army.

4 MBCT, CFT and ACT.

5 It is a good idea.

6 Google.

7 Yes, guided self-help is more effective.

8 Quality of life therapy.

9 Depression.

10 Only for the academic year in which the pupils took the course.

Appendix A: The thoughts and behaviours log

▶ **Step 1: Write down a brief description of the specific situation you want to work on**

Think of a specific situation for which one or more of the following statements are true:

▶ I am feeling overwhelmed/distressed/depressed/other negative emotion – perhaps more than is warranted by what has happened.

▶ I am not behaving in a way that is conducive to the long-term well-being of myself and/or those I care about.

▶ I want to understand and change my current thinking and behaviour.

Write down the situation you would like to work on.

Hints

Just write down a sentence or two stating the situation. At this stage you do not need to go into much detail.

Pick a specific example, not a general description of an issue, e.g. 'My boss criticized me last Wednesday afternoon at 2p.m. over my report', rather than 'My boss is critical of me.'

▶ **Step 2: Become more aware of your thoughts and images**

Take yourself back to being in that situation. Imagine a thought bubble coming out of your head. What would be in that bubble? Are there any images or pictures as well as words? Write down your thoughts in quotation marks, e.g. 'I will not get the job.'

Hints

▶ If you have written down a question, turn it into a statement, e.g. 'Will I ever get a job?' becomes 'I don't think I will ever get a job'. This is because you want the thought to represent a statement that can be true or false – a question cannot be true or false.

▶ For the same reason, 'I want' statements should be turned into the statements that they imply, e.g. 'I want everything to be nice' translates into 'Everyone should be nice'.

▶ Step 3: What are the emotions and feelings that come up when you think like this?

First, write down the emotions and feelings, then rate how strongly you feel them. Rate them from 0 to 100, e.g. anxiety 60, sadness 40.

Hints

▶ Emotions and feelings tend to be expressed in one word, e.g. 'down', 'worried', 'stressed', 'hopeless' and 'guilty'.

▶ Place a number for the intensity even if this seems arbitrary as this will help you evaluate the effectiveness of this analysis later.

▶ Check that you can connect each emotion with a specific thought that leads you to feel this way. If there is not a thought/image that connects to the emotion, you need to go back a step and identify a new thought/image.

▶ Step 4: What does thinking and feeling like this in this situation tend to make you do? What are the short-term and also unintended longer-term consequences of these actions?

Write down your answers to these questions. Examples of actions and behaviour include: procrastinate, worry, ruminate, have a drink, browse the internet, go for a run, speak to a friend.

Hints

▶ Write down what you actually tend to do, not what you think you ought to do.

▶ Do not forget to add both the intended and unintended short- and long-term consequences. This can help you decide whether what you do is helpful or not.

▶ Step 5: What thinking traps might you be prone to in this situation?

For each thought, decide which thinking trap might apply.

If you think no traps apply, put 'None'.

Here is a list of thinking traps, their meaning and examples:

Thinking trap	Meaning	Example
1 Jumping to conclusions	Assuming that bad things have happened or will happen, without enough evidence. There are two types of jumping to conclusions:	
	i) Mind-reading – thinking you know what people are thinking when you don't	'She thinks I'm stupid.'
	ii) Fortune-telling – thinking you know what is going to happen when you don't	'They are going to turn me down.'
2 Extreme thinking	Thinking in an all-or-nothing way or overgeneralizing:	
	All-or-nothing thinking	'It's all your (or my) fault.'
	Overgeneralization	'I never have any self-control.'
3 Catastrophising	Overestimating how bad things will be if a feared event were to happen.	'It's a disaster!'
	This often involves underestimating your ability to cope with adversity or how other people may help you out.	'I'll be ruined!'
4 Unhelpful personal rules	Saying that things should or must happen when there is no real basis for this and it isn't very helpful to make this demand from the universe.	'I must do it perfectly.'
		'People should always be nice to me.'

▶ Step 6: What are more realistic or constructive thoughts and images?

For each thinking trap, use this table to work how to dispel it.

Thinking trap	How to dispel the thinking trap	Example
1 Jumping to conclusions	What is the evidence for my negative thought? What is another possibility? What are the odds?	'There is a possibility that she thinks I am stupid but I have no evidence for this view and it's just as likely that she thinks positively about me.'
2 Extreme thinking	What is a more balanced perspective? Is it true that this is always the case? How much responsibility can I fairly place on me or others? What would a sympathetic friend say?	'I'm 30 per cent to blame, but it was hard to foresee the bad traffic so I'll put 70 per cent down to bad luck.'
3 Catastrophising	What is the worst that can actually happen? How could I deal with that? What or who might help out? Have I dealt with similar before?	'I'd rather that didn't happen but if it did I'd cope.'
4 Unhelpful personal rules	What rule in the universe says this must happen?	'Perfection isn't attainable; I'll do my best.'
	Does it help me to have this rule?	

Now write down your more helpful and realistic thoughts.

▶ Step 7: Action plan

What can you do that follows from these more realistic and constructive thoughts?

What is your action plan?

Hints

- ▶ Ask yourself, 'What do I want to achieve in this situation? What can I do that will take me a step towards doing this?'

- ▶ Read back the more realistic and constructive thoughts. What do these suggest you do?

- ▶ Create a specific action plan: what to do, when to do it, what to do if there are obstacles, what can help you do it.

▶ Step 8: Results

Put yourself back in the original situation with the realistic thoughts (step 6) and the more helpful action plan (step 7).

What mood, emotions and feelings come up for you now? Rate them from 0 to 100 in intensity.

Hints

▶ Read back what you have written in steps 6 and 7 and notice what feelings come up for you.

▶ Do not just re-rate the negative emotions; put down new emotions as well.

Appendix B: The positive psychology toolkit

Tool	Purpose	Chapter
SWLS	Measure satisfaction with life	1
SPANE	Measure positive and negative emotions	1
Personal reset buttons	Be able to recover quickly from negative emotions	1
Activity scheduling	Become more aware of and schedule activities to get more positive emotions including enjoyment and achievement, overcome low mood	1
Three good things	Cultivate gratitude and a sense of control. Be able to plan more good things	2
Feeling grateful	Cultivate gratitude and reduce hedonic adaptation	2
Savouring	Increase enjoyment of pleasures	2
Values clarification	Become more aware of important life values	3
Best possible self	Be more optimistic and clarify and plan to put into practice your values	3
Strengths measures (VIA, CAPP and StrengthsFinder 2.0)	Know your strengths	4
Set a SMART+ goal	Helps achievement and planning	5
Step-by-step planning	Helps you achieve your goals and move in your valued direction	5
Seligman's 3Ps	Helps you me more optimistic and achieve more	5
Frankl meaning Venn diagram	Helps you identify potential ways of achieving meaning and purpose in your life	6
Meaning in life questionnaire	Measure the presence of meaning and search for meaning	6
Life orientations scale	Measure your meaning mindset	6
Random acts of kindness	Increase meaning and purpose in your life	6
Loving kindness meditation	Develop feelings of kindness	6
Flow audit and scheduling	Understand sources of flow and plan them	7

Further reading

Agassi, A. (2009) *Open: An Autobiography*, London: HarperCollins

Ardelt, M. (2003) 'Empirical assessment of a three-dimensional wisdom scale', *Research on Aging*, Vol 25(3), May 2003, 275–324. Available at http://www.clas.ufl.edu/users/ardelt/empirical%20assessment%20of%20the%203d-ws.pdf

Aristotle (1999) *Nicomachean Ethics*, translated by T. Irwin), Indianapolis: Hackett

Arnaud, D. (2010) *The Development and Testing of an Emotion-Enabled, Structured Decision-Making Procedure : A thesis submitted for the degree of Doctor of Philosophy* available at http://bura.brunel.ac.uk/bitstream/2438/4516/1/FulltextThesis.pdf

Aron, A. and Westbay, L. (1996) 'Dimensions of the prototype of love', *Journal of Personality and Social Psychology*, 70(3), 535–51

Baggini, J. and Macaro, A. (2012) *The Shrink and the Sage*, London: Icon Books

Baltes. P. (2004) *Wisdom as Orchestration of Mind and Virtue*, available only as a free pdf at http://library.mpib-berlin.mpg.de/ft/pb/PB_Wisdom_2004.pdf

Baltes, P. and Baltes, M. (eds) (1993) *Successful Aging: Perspectives from the Behavioral Sciences,* Cambridge: Cambridge University Press

Bannink, F. (2012) *Practicing Positive CBT: From Reducing Distress to Building Success,* Chichester: Wiley-Blackwell

Baumeister, R. (1991) *Meanings of Life,* New York: Guilford Press

Bellioti, R. (2004) *Happiness is Overrated,* Lanham, Maryland: Rowman and Littlefield

Ben-Shahar, T. (2007) *Happier,* New York: McGraw Hill

Biswas-Diener, R. and Dean, B. (2007) *Positive Psychology Coaching: Putting the Science of Happiness to Work for Your Clients,* Hoboken, NJ: Wiley

Bloom, B. (1985) *Developing Talent in Young People*, New York: Ballantine Books

Bolt, M. (2004) *Pursuing Human Strengths: A Positive Psychology Guide,* New York: Worth Publishers

Boniwell, I. (2012) *Positive Psychology in a Nutshell,* Berkshire: Open University Press

Brickman, P. and Cambell, D. T. (1971) 'Hedonic relativism and planning the good society', in M. H. Appley (ed.) *Adaptation-level theory*, New York: Academic Press

Brown, N. J. L., Sokal, A. D. and Friedman, H. L. (2013) 'The Complex Dynamics of Wishful Thinking: The Critical Positivity Ratio', *American Psychologist*

Bryant, F. and Veroff, J. (2008) *Savoring, A New Model of Positive Experience,* New Jersey: Laurence Erlbaum Associates

Buckingham, M. and Clifton, D. (2005) *Now, Discover your Strengths,* London: Pocket Books

Buddhaghosa and Ñāṇamoli, B. (trans.) (1999) *Visuddhimagga: The Path of Purification*, Seattle: Buddhist Publication Society

Butler, G. (1999) *Overcoming Social Anxiety and Shyness: A Self-help Guide Using Cognitive Behavioural Techniques,* London: Robinson

Butler, G. and Hope, A. (2007) *Manage Your Mind,* Oxford: OUP

Carlson, M., Charlin, V. and Miller, N. (1988) 'Positive mood and helping behavior: A test of six hypotheses', *Journal of Personality and Social Psychology*, 55, 211–29

Carnevale, P. J., Cohen, S., Doyle, W. J., Turner, R. B., Alper, C. M. and Skoner, D. P. (2003) 'Emotional style and susceptibility to the common cold', *Psychosomatic Medicine*, 65, 652–57.

Compton W. (2005) *Introduction to Positive Psychology*, Belmont, CA: Wadsworth

Covey, S. (1992) *The Seven Habits of Highly Effective People*, London: Simon and Schuster

Csikszentmihalyi, M. (1990) *Flow: The Psychology of Optimal Experience*, London: Rider

Csikszentmihalyi, M. (1996) *Creativity: Flow and the Psychology of Discovery and Invention*, New York: Harper Perennial

Csikszentmihalyi, M. (2004) *Good Business: Leadership, flow and the making of meaning*, New York: Viking Penguin

Csikszentmihalyi, M. and Robinson R. E. (1990) *The Art of Seeing: An Interpretation of the Aesthetic Encounter*, Los Angeles, California: Getty Publications

H.H. Dalai Lama and Cutler, H. (1998) *The Art of Happiness*, London: Hodder & Stoughton

Damasio, A. (2005) *Descartes' Error: Emotion, Reason, and the Human Brain*, London: Penguin

Danner, D. D., Snowdon, D. A. and Friesen, W. V. (2001) 'Positive emotions in early life and longevity: Findings from the nun study', *Journal of Personality and Social Psychology*, 80, 804–13.

de Botton, A. (2013) *Religion For Atheists,* London: Penguin

De Neve, J., Diener, E. Tay, L. and Xuereb, C. (2013) 'The Objective Benefits of Subjective Well-Being', to appear in J. Helliwell, R. Layard and J. Sachs (eds) *World Happiness Report*

Deci, E. L. and Ryan, R. M. (1985) *Intrinsic motivation and self-determination in human behaviour*, New York: Plenum

Diener, E. and Biswas-Diener, R. (2008) *Happiness: Unlocking the Mysteries of Psychological Wealth*, Oxford: Blackwell

Diener, E. and Seligman, M. E. P. (2002) 'Very happy people', *Psychological Science*, 13, 81–84.

Dweck, C. (2006) *Mindset: How You can fulfil your potential*, New York: Ballantine Books

Ebersole, P. (1998) 'Types and depth of written life meanings' in P. Wong and P. Fry (eds), *The human quest for meaning: A handbook of psychological research and clinical applications* (pp. 179–191), New Jersey: Laurence Erlbaum Associates, Publishers

Edwards, B. (2013) *Drawing on the Right Side of the Brain*, 4th edition, London: Souvenir Press

Ericsson, A. el al. (2007) *The Making of an Expert*, http://www.uvm.edu/~pdodds/files/papers/others/everything/ericsson2007a.pdf

Eid, M. and Larsen, R. (2008) *The Science of Subjective Well-Being,* New York: The Guilford Press

Emmons, R. A. (1999) *The psychology of ultimate concerns: Motivation and spirituality in personality*, New York: The Guilford Press

Emmons, R. (2013) *Gratitude Works! A 21-day Programme for Creating Emotional Prosperity,* San Francisco: Jossey-Bass

Erikson, E. H. (1963) *Childhood and society*, 2nd edition, New York: Norton.

Evans, J. (2012) *Philosophy for Life and other Dangerous Situations,* London: Rider

Fredrickson, B. L. (2009) *Positivity,* New York: Crown

Fredrickson, B. L. and Losada, M. (2005) 'Positive affect and the complex dynamics of human flourishing', *American Psychologist*, 60(7), 678–86

Fredrickson, B. L., Mancuso, R. A., Branigan, C., and Tugade, M. M. (2000). The undoing effect of positive emotions. *Motivation and Emotion*, 24, 237–258.

Frankl, V. (1946/1987) *Man's Search for Meaning* London: Hodder & Stoughton

Frankl, V. (1965) *The Doctor and the Soul*, New York: Alfred A. Knopf

Frisch, M. (2006) *Quality of Life Therapy,* New Jersey: Wiley

Fry, P. S. (1975) 'Affect and resistance to temptation', *Developmental Psychology*, 11, 466–72

Garratt, G. (2012) *Introducing Cognitive Behavioural Therapy (CBT) For Work: A Practical Guide,* London: Icon Books

Germer, C. and Segal, R. (2012) *Wisdom and Compassion in Psychotherapy,* New York: Guilford Press

Gilbert, P. et al. (2010) *Training Our Minds in, with and for Compassion: An Introduction to Concepts and Compassion-Focused Exercises*, available at http://www.compassionatemind.co.uk/downloads/training_materials/3.%20Clinical_patient_handout.pdf

Gilbert, P. (2010) *The Compassionate Mind,* London: Constable

Gilbert, P. (2010) *Compassion Focused Therapy*, London: Routledge

Goleman, D. (1996) *Emotional Intelligence: Why it can matter more than IQ*, London: Bloomsbury

Goleman, D. (2003) *Destructive Emotions,* London: Bloomsbury

Gottmann, J. and Silver, N. (1999) *The Seven Principles for Making Marriage Work*, London: Orion

Govindji, R. and Linley, P. A. (2007) 'Strengths use, self-concordance and well-being: Implications for strengths coaching and coaching psychologists', *International Coaching Psychology Review*, 2(2), 143–53

Grewal and Salovey (2006) *Benefits of Emotional Intelligence in A Life Worth Living: Contributions to Positive Psychology* (eds Csikszentmihalyi, M. and Csikszentmihalyi, I.)

Greenburger, D. and Padesky, C. (1995*) Mind over Mood,* New York: Guilford

Grenville-Cleave, B. (2012) *Positive Psychology: A Practical Guide*, London: Icon Books

Griffin, J. (1986) *Well-being: Its Meaning, Measurement and Moral Importance,* Oxford: OUP

Gunaratana. N (2002) *Mindfulness in Plain English,* Somerville MA: Wisdom Publications

Haidt, J. (2006) *The Happiness Hypothesis,* London: Arrow

Hall, S. (2010) *Wisdom: from philosophy to neuroscience,* New York: Alfred A. Knopf

Hammond, J., Keeney, R. and Raiffi, H. (1999) *Smart Choices,* Boston: Harvard Business School Press

Harris, R. (2009) *ACT Made Simpl ,* Oakland, California: New Harbinger Publications

Hefferon, K. and Boniwell, I. (2011) *Positive Psychology: Theory, Research and Applications*, Maidenhead: Open University Press

Ifcher, J. and Zarghamee, H., 'Positive Affect and Overconfidence: A Laboratory Investigation' (July 1, 2011). SCU Leavey School of Business Research Paper No. 11-02. Available at SSRN: http://ssrn.com/abstract=1740013 or http://dx.doi.org/10.2139/ssrn.1740013

Irvine, W. (2009) *A Guide to the Good Life,* New York: OUP

Jackson, S. and Csikszentmihalyi, M. (1999) *Flow in Sports*, Illinois: Human Kinetics Publishers

Joseph, S. (2013) *What Doesn't Kill Us: The New Psychology of Post-Traumatic Growth,* New York: Basic Books

Kahneman, D. (2011) *Thinking Fast and Slow,* London: Penguin

Kashdan, T. and Ciarrochi, J. (ed.) (2013*) Mindfulness, Acceptance and Positive Psychology*, California: Context Press

King, L. A. (2001) 'The health benefits of writing about life goals', *Pers Soc Psychol Bull* 27(7): 798–807

Kirschenbaum, H. (2013) *Values Clarification in Counselling and Psychotherapy*, Oxford: OUP

Langer, E. (1989) *Mindfulness,* Cambridge MA: Merloyd Lawrence

Layard, R. (2005) *Happiness, Lessons from a New Science*, London: Penguin

LeBon, T. (2001) *Wise Therapy*, London: Continuum

LeBon, T. and Arnaud, D. (2012) 'Existential Coaching and Major Life Decisions', in E. Van Deurzen and M. Hanaway (eds) *Existential Perspectives on Coaching* (pp. 47–59) Basingstoke: Palgrave-Macmillan

Leitzel, J. D. (2000) 'A confirmatory factor analytic investigation of the tripartite model of depression and anxiety in high school adolescents', dissertation, *Abstracts International*, 2000-95024-186 (Dissertation Number AA19976359)

Levine, M. (2000) *The Positive Psychology of Buddhism and Yoga*, New Jersey: Laurence Erlbaum Associates

Linley, A. (2009) *Average to A+: Realizing Strengths in Yourself and Others*, Coventry: CAPP Press

Linley, A. et al. (2010) *The Strengths Book*, Coventry: CAPP Press

Linley P. and Joseph, S. (2004) *Positive Psychology in Practice*, Chichester: Wiley

Linley, P. A., Nielsen, K. M., Wood, A. M., Gillett, R. and Biswas-Diener, R., (2010) 'Using signature strengths in pursuit of goals: Effects on goal progress, need satisfaction, and well-being, and implications for coaching psychologists', *International Coaching Psychology Review*, 5 (1), 8–17

Lunenburg, F. (2011) 'Goal Setting Theory of Motivation', *International Journal of Management, Business and Administration Volume 15 Number 1*

Lyubomirsky, S., Tkach, C. and Sheldon, K. M. (2005) 'Pursuing sustained happiness through random acts of kindness and counting one's blessings: Tests of two 6-week interventions', Unpublished manuscript, Department of Psychology, University of California, Riverside

Lyubomirsky, S. (2007) *The How of Happiness*, London: Sphere

Macaro, A. (2006) *Reason, Virtue and Psychotherapy*, Chichester: Wiley

Marsh, A., 'There's No Business Like FLOW Business' (2005) http://www.fastcompany.com/53363/theres-no-business-flow-business

Marsh, A., 'The Art of Work' (2005) http://www.fastcompany.com/53713/art-work

Minhas, G. (2010) 'Developing realised and unrealised strengths: Implications for engagement, self-esteem, life satisfaction and well-being', *Assessment and Development Matters,* 2, 12–16

Morris, I. (2011*) Teaching Happiness and Well-Being in School: Learning to Ride Elephant,* London: Continuum

Morrison, M., Tay, L. and Diener, E. (2012) 'Subjective well-being across the lifespan worldwide', paper submitted for publication, University of Western Ontario

Nakamura, J. and Csikszentmihalyi, M. (2009) *Flow theory and Research*, in S. Lopez and C.R. Snyder (eds), The *Oxford Handbook of Positive Psychology*, Oxford: OUP

Nelson, D. W. (2009) 'Feeling good and open-minded: The impact of positive affect on cross-cultural empathic responding*', Journal of Positive Psychology*, 4, 53–63.

Nettle, D. (2005) *Happiness*, Oxford: OUP

De Neve, J. and Oswald, A. (2012) 'Estimating the Influence of Life Satisfaction and Positive Affect on Later Income Using Sibling Fixed-Effects', CEP Discussion Papers dp1176, Centre for Economic Performance, LSE

Nezu, A. Nezu, C. and D'Zurilla, T. (2007) *Solving Life's Problems*, New York: Springer

Norem, J. (2001) *The Positive Power of Negative Thinking,* New York: Basic Books

Nolen-Hoeksema, S. (2000) 'The role of rumination in depressive disorders and mixed anxiety/depressive symptoms', *Journal of Abnormal Psychology*, 109, 504–11.

Oishi, S., Diener, E. and Lucas, R. (2007) 'The optimum level of well-being: Can people be too happy?', *Perspectives on Psychological Science*, 2, 346–60

Pennebaker, J.W. (2004) *Writing to Heal: A Guided Journal for Recovering from Trauma and Emotional Upheaval*, Oakland: New Harbinger Publications

Perry, S. (2001) *Writing in Flow*, Ohio: Writer's Digest Books

Peterson, C. (2006) *A Primer in Positive Psychology* Oxford: OUP

Peterson, C. and Seligman, M. (2004) *Character Strengths and Virtues: A Handbook and Classification,* Oxford: OUP

Popovic, N. (2005) *Personal Synthesis: A complete guide to personal knowledge,* London: PWBC

Pressman, S. D. and Cohen, S. (2012) 'Positive emotion word use and longevity in famous deceased psychologists,' *Health Psychology,* 31, 297–305

Rath, T. (2007) *StrengthsFinder 2.0,* New York: Gallup Press

Reivich, K, and Shatt??, A. (2002) *The Resilience Factor,* New York: Broadway Books

Revel, J-F., and Ricard, M., *The Monk and the Philosopher,* New York: Schocken Books

Ricard, M. (2003) *Happiness,* New York: Little, Brown and Co.

Robertson, D. (2012) *Build your Resilience,* London: Hodder

Robertson, D. (2013) *Stoicism and the Art of Happiness,* London: Hodder

Russell, B. (1930) *The Conquest of Happiness,* London: Unwin

Rust, T., Diessner, R. and Reade, L. (2009) 'Strengths only or strengths and relative weaknesses? A preliminary study', *Journal of Psychology,* 143(5), 465–76, http://dx.doi.org/10.3200/JRL.143.5.465-476

Sage, N., Sowden, M., Chorlton, E. and Edeleanu, A. (2008) *CBT for Chronic Illness and Palliative Care,* Chichester: Wiley

Mayer, J. D. and Salovey, P. (1995) 'Emotional intelligence and the construction and regulation of feelings', *Applied and Preventive Psychology,* 4, 197–208.

Salzberg, S. (1995) *Loving Kindness,* Boston: Shambala Publications

Schwartz, B. (2005) *The Paradox of Choice: Why Less is More,* New York: Harper Perrenial

Schwartz, B. and Sharpe, K. (2011) *Practical Wisdom: The Right Way to do the Right Thing*, New York: Riverhead Books

Seligman, M. (1998) *Learned Optimism: How to Change your Mind and Your Life*, New York: Free Press

Seligman, M. (2002) *Authentic Happiness*, London: Nicholas Brealey

Seligman, M. (2011) *Flourish*, London: Nicholas Brealey

Seligman, M.E.P., Steen, T.A., Park, N. and Peterson, C. (2005) 'Positive psychology progress: Empirical validation of interventions', *American Psychologist*, (60), 5, 410–21

Singer, P. (ed.) (1994) *Ethics: The Oxford Reader*, Oxford: OUP

Snyder. C (2006) *Approaching Hope*, published online at http://www.sgiquarterly.org/feature2006Jan-2.html

Snyder, C. and Lopez, S. (2011) *Oxford Handbook of Positive Psychology*, Oxford: OUP

Sobel, D. (1995) Interview: Mihaly Csikszentmihalyi, *Omni*, 17(4), 73

Steptoe, A. and Wardle, J. (2011) 'Positive affect measured using ecological momentary assessment and survival in older men and women', *PNAS: Proceedings of National Academy of Sciences*, 108(45), 18244-18248

Sternberg, R. (1988) *The Triangle of Love*, New York: Basic Books

Sternberg, R. (1998) 'A balance theory of wisdom', *Review of General Psychology*, Vol. 2(4), Dec 1998, 347–65

Sternberg, R. and Jordan, J. (2005) *A Handbook of Wisdom*, New York: Cambridge University Press

Stuart, R. (1980) *Helping Couples Change*, New York: Guilford Press

Syed, M. (2011) Bounce: *The Myth of Talent and the Power of Practice*, London: Fourth Estate

Veale, D. and Willson, R. (2007) *Manage Your Mood: How to use Behavioural Activation techniques to overcome depression,* London: Robinson

Walker, M. (2013) *Happy Pills for All,* Chichester: Wiley

Weiner, E. (2008) *The Geography of Bliss: One Grump's Search for the Happiest Places in the World,* Hachette

Williams, C. (2009) *Overcoming Depression and Low Mood: A Five Areas Approach,* London: CRC Press

Williams, M., Teasdale, J., Segal, Z. and Kabat-Zinn, J. (2007) *The Mindful Way Through Depression,* New York: The Guilford Press

Williams, M. and Penman, D. (2011) *Mindfulness: A practical guide to finding peace in a frantic world,* London: Piatkus

Wiseman, R. (2009) *59 Seconds,* London: McMillan

Wong, P. and Fry, P. (1998) *The Human Quest for Meaning,* New Jersey: Laurence Erlbaum Associates

Worley, P. (2010) *The If Machine ,* London: Continuum

Yalom, I. (1980) *Existential Psychotherapy,* New York: Basic Books

Yalom, I. (1989) *Love's Executioner,* London: Penguin

Yalom, I. (1999) *Momma and the Meaning of Life,* London: Piatkus

Recommended websites

http://www.timlebon.com *Author website, includes resources on relaxation and meditation*

http:/www.authentichappiness.org – *lots of questionnaires and resources, Seligman and University of Pennsylvania site*

http://www.positivityratio.com/ *Barbara Fredrickson site*

http://thehowofhappiness.com/ *Sonja Lyubomirsky site*

http://internal.psychology.illinois.edu/~ediener/ *Ed Diener site*

http://www.centreforconfidence.co.uk/pp/positive-psychology.php *Useful UK site*

http://www.cappeu.com/ *CAPP Strengths Site*

http://positivepsychologynews.com/ *Positive Psychology News*

http://lists.apa.org/cgi-bin/wa.exe?A0=FRIENDS-OF-PP *Very active Mailing List*

http://www.actionforhappiness.org/ *Movement for Positive social change*

http://thehappinessexperiment.co.uk/ *Site set up by Shona Lockhart, featured as a case study for positive psychology in the workplace*

http://www.drpaulwong.com/ *Good for meaning and purpose*

http://www.gottman.com *Good for positive relationships*

http://www.llttf.com *Living Life to the Full; free CBT resources*

http://www.viacharacter.org/ *Articles on VIA strengths*

http://www.wisdompage.com *Wisdom resources*

http://worlddatabaseofhappiness.eur.nl/ *Happiness data*

http://cedar.exeter.ac.uk/iapt/iaptworkbooksandresources/ *Well-informed and free CBT booklets on overcoming worry, overcoming depression, goal-setting, problem-solving and behavioural experiments*

http://www.getselfhelp.co.uk *Lots of free self-help resources*

http://www.cci.health.wa.gov.au/resources/consumers.cfm *Good, free CBT-based booklets*

http://www.randomactsofkindness.org/ *Kindness Foundation*

http://psyphz.psych.wisc.edu/ *Richard Davidson's Lab for Affective Neuroscience*

http://blogs.exeter.ac.uk/stoicismtoday/ *Exeter Stoicism Today site*

http://news.bbc.co.uk/1/hi/programmes/happiness_formula/default.stm *With clips from the show*

http://strengths.gallup.com/ *Gallup strengths site*

Endnotes

1 From Martin Seligman's inaugural address to the APA
http://www.ppc.sas.upenn.edu/aparep98.htm

2 'Psychology as usual' is the term used by Seligman and others
to refer to psychology before 'positive psychology'. Although
Seligman gives the impression that before 1998 psychology
was mainly concerned with treating psychiatric problems, in
fact only one branch of psychology, abnormal psychology, is
concerned with this.

3 See, for example, Baumeister (1991). Even if children don't
tend to make people happy, this doesn't mean you shouldn't
have children; there may well be other good reasons for
having children.

4 Clark, D. (2006) 'Social Anxiety and its Treatment',
published online at http://www.gresham.ac.uk/lectures-and-
events/social-anxiety-and-its-treatment

5 A placebo is a substance or intervention which has no active
ingredients. Since often just being given an intervention can
produce a temporary improvement, it is important to verify that
an intervention is working over and above a placebo effect.

6 Retrieved from http://www.merriam-webster.com/dictionary/
happiness 6/5/2013

7 To see the difference, imagine everything is going well in your
life but you are at the dentist's; your overall state may be
that of well-being, but this will probably not be a pleasurable
experience. Conversely, imagine yourself watching a funny
episode of your favourite sitcom. This may be pleasurable
but, if you have just lost your job and broken up with your
partner, your overall contentment will be low.

8 It could be argued that the absence of negative emotions
makes SWB broader than happiness, although it could
also be pointed out that if you experience a lot of negative
emotions, you aren't happy.

9 'Affect' is the term psychologists use to cover feeling, emotion and mood.

10 The SWLS was created by Ed Diener, Robert A. Emmons, Randy J. Larsen and Sharon Griffin as noted in the 1985 article in the *Journal of Personality Assessment*. See http:// internal.psychology.illinois.edu/~ediener/SWLS.html

11 The SPANE was created by Diener, E., Wirtz, D., Tov, W., Kim-Prieto, C., Choi. D., Oishi, S. and Biswas-Diener, R. in 'New measures of well-being: Flourishing and positive and negative feelings', *Social Indicators Research*, 39, 247–66, copyright Ed Diener and Robert Biswas-Diener. See http:// internal.psychology.illinois.edu/~ediener/SPANE.html.

12 Positive psychologists tend to define what is positive or negative in terms of how they feel, i.e. a positive emotion feels good, a negative emotion feels bad. As we will see, a positive emotion is not always one that is good to have, for example sadistic pleasure. Neither is a 'negative' emotion necessarily bad, e.g. appropriate sadness.

13 The list of emotions is based on Fredrickson's lists in *Positivity*.

14 This is not to say that human flourishing can be reduced to happiness alone.

15 This thought experiment is based on Mark Walker's 'Method of Difference'. See Walker, 2013.

16 The average age of the nuns was 24.

17 This is the opposite of the spiralling downwards of well-being that can occur with depression.

18 'Behavioral activation interventions for well-being: A meta-analysis', Mazzuchellin, T.G., Kane, R.T. and Rees, C.S. http://www.ncbi.nlm.nih.gov/pmc/articles/ PMC2882847/#R24

19 We will see in Chapter 9 that in fact these negative emotions do not always serve us so well in the 21st century.

20 Lykken, D. (1999) http://www.timeshighereducation. co.uk/149473 (article retrieved 1/9/2013)

21 The 5-HTT gene is thought to play a part. See http://www.telegraph.co.uk/health/healthnews/8494966/Happiness-gene-discovered.html (retrieved 1/9/2013)

22 See Walker, M. (2013) *Happy People Pills for All*. Of course, both genetic screening and genetic engineering raise a lot of ethical questions, which Walker's intriguing book explores.

23 Fleeson's experiment is reported at http://online.wsj.com/article/SB10001424127887324144304578621951399427408.html (retrieved 1/9/2013)

24 Diener, E. et al. (1985) 'Happiness of the Very Wealthy', *Social Indicators Research*

25 http://www.uni-marburg.de/fb21/motologie/mitarbeiter_seiten/ls/storks.pdf

26 Veenhoven, R. (2013) *Happiness in Nations*, World Database of Happiness, Erasmus University Rotterdam, The Netherlands at: http://worlddatabaseofhappiness.eur.nl/hap_nat/nat_fp.php?mode=1 and http://worlddatabaseofhappiness.eur.nl/hap_nat/nat_fp.php?mode=8

27 The term was first used by Brickman and Campbell (1971).

28 Adapted from Seligman's *Authentic Happiness*.

29 Adapted from a study reported by Leyland at the BABCP Conference, London (2013).

30 This gratitude meditation was written by the author.

31 In an email to the *Friends of Positive Psychology* ListServer.

32 Philosophy is the study of fundamental questions about human existence, ethics being the branch which studies right and wrong and the nature of well-being.

33 See http://www.rochester.edu/news/show.php?id=3377

34 See http://www.psychology.hku.hk/ftbcstudies/refbase/docs/emmons/2003/53_Emmons2003.pdf

35 To confuse matters further, in the psychological literature these theories are often labelled 'eudaimonic' theories of

well-being – *eudaimonia* being the Greek word used by Aristotle to indicate living well and flourishing. In the philosophical literature they are more often called 'objective list' theories because their proponents usually list a number of values and virtues that are said to be objectively valid.

36 Our version of the informed preference satisfaction theory included reflecting on wisdom, so it overcomes this objection. However, versions of the theory that did not include wisdom would be open to the same objection.

37 If you have already done the 'Three good things' exercise, you can also look for patterns in the events that pleased you. What strengths helped make them happen?

38 Unless they are a coach well-versed in positive psychology.

39 DSM stands for *Diagnostic and Statistical Manual of Mental Disorders*.

40 Linley, on the other hand, endorses a more Aristotelian view.

41 For ideas about how to use your VIA strengths, see http://www.actionforhappiness.org/media/52486/340_ways_to_use_character_strengths.pdf

42 The terms achievement and accomplishment are often used synonymously, although for some accomplishment tends to be connected with expertise, and achievement with reaching goals.

43 The title of Syed's very readable book *Bounce: The Myth of Talent and the Power of Practice* (2011) betrays which side of the Nature/Nurture debate he is on.

44 See MacLeod, A., Coates, E. et al. (2008) 'Increasing well-being through teaching goal-setting and planning skills: results of a brief intervention', *Journal of Happiness Studies* 9(2): 185–96

45 SMART[+] is a term not in general use; it has been invented to represent SMART goals that also meet the four extra criteria suggested by Locke.

46 Rand et al. (2011), *Journal of Research in Personality*

47 Magaletta and Oliver (1999), *Journal of Clinical Psychology*

48 These are adapted from Snyder, C. R. (2006).

49 Defensive pessimism was developed by Nancy Cantor in the 1980s. See also Norem (2001).

50 From Keller's essay on optimism, freely available at http://www.gutenberg.org/files/31622/31622-h/31622-h.htm

51 The benefits of optimism have been found to be significant but not quite so large in other industries, e.g. optimism confers an advantage of between 20 per cent and 40 per cent in the car industry and banking (Seligman, 1998).

52 Seligman focuses on whether someone's explanatory style is optimistic or pessimistic. This is related to, but not identical to, common usage of the terms, which is more to do with an expectation of whether good or bad things will happen.

53 You can find out where you are on the optimism/pessimism scale by taking the Attributional Style Questionnaire (ASQ) at http://www.authentichappiness.org/.

54 Seligman's strategies for challenging pessimism are closely related to CBT (cognitive behavioural therapy) and have been used to help make people less prone to depression as well as helping them achieve their goals. For more about CBT see Chapter 9.

55 There are certain strengths most associated with achievement. Perseverance comes top; other particularly helpful strengths include gratitude, fairness, hope and self-control – so if these are your strengths then you can also tell yourself you have strengths key to achievement.

56 Like many popular quotations, it's hard to be sure that Edison actually said this. But he certainly said something very similar. See http://quoteinvestigator.com/2012/07/31/edison-lot-results/

57 These findings are summarised in Richard Wiseman's *59 Seconds* and also at http://www.theguardian.com/science/2012/jun/30/self-help-positive-thinking

58 The philosopher Bernard Williams has dubbed this the 'Gauguin problem'. Paul Gauguin is praised for leaving his family to paint in Tahiti; would we have said the same if he had turned out to be a moderate painter? Williams suggests that we can't always be sure in advance whether such decisions are worthy; a lot depends on 'moral luck'.

59 See http://www.psychologytoday.com/blog/in-therapy/201303/yalom-therapy-and-meaning

60 These five questions form part of Steger's et al.'s 'Meaning in life questionnaire'. They are presented separately as the two components (the presence of and the search for meaning) should be scored separately and not added together.

61 Irvin Yalom (1989), *Love's Executioner*, p. 12.

62 Ebersole (1998), Emmons (1999), Wong (1998) are the three researchers in question.

63 Alain de Botton's *Religion for Atheists* addresses the question of how atheists can find some of religion's benefits without being religious.

64 Schwarz, C.E. and Sendor, M. (1999), 'Helping others help oneself: Response shift effects in peer support', *Social Science and Medicine*, 48, 1563–75.

65 Many centuries earlier, Michelangelo reportedly exhibited many of these characteristics of flow when painting the ceiling of the Sistine Chapel in the Vatican.

66 Not all of these characteristics accompany every flow experience. Flow is a continuum, ranging from none of these characteristics being present (no flow) to all of the characteristics being present to a high degree.

67 A mnemonic is a word or phrase to help you remember an important idea.

68 One possible mnemonic to help you remember the eight characteristics of flow is SCOTS CIG.

69 From 'A lot of love in the lovemaking: Avoiding chaos, relationshipwise' in *Seattle Weekly*, February 13–19, 2002.

70 Gable, S. L., Reis, H. T., Impett, E. A. and Asher, E. R. (2004), 'What do you do when things go right? The intrapersonal and interpersonal benefits of sharing positive events', *Journal of Personality and Social Psychology*, 87, 228–45.

71 The five-part model is associated with Dennis Greenburger and Christine Padesky in *Mind over Mood* (1995) and Chris Williams's five-area approach on the website Living Life to the Full (http://www.llttf.com and a number of books (e.g. Williams, C. 2009).

72 These are the C and B in CBT – cognitions are thoughts and beliefs, B stands for behaviour.

73 Thanks to Carolyn, Jeremy and Vanessa for the photo of Lucy, who is cuddly and lovable!

74 A sometimes stands for 'activating event' in the ABC model.

75 The original Serenity Prayer used in Alcoholics Anonymous says 'God grant me', but the religious element is not essential. In Chapter 11, we will also note similarities between the Serenity Prayer and Stoic ideas.

76 The technical term is 'problem orientation'.

77 There are also problem-specific cognitive behavioural therapy (CBT) treatments for a range of other anxiety disorders including panic, social anxiety, specific phobias, obsessive-compulsive disorder (OCD) and post-traumatic stress disorder (PTSD). These are not discussed for reasons of space – in general with anxiety disorders avoidance is the problem and exposure and behavioural experiments are helpful.

78 The worry tree or 'Worry Decision Tree' is adapted from Butler and Hope (2007).

79 How four-year-olds did in the marshmallow test was a better predictor of how they did aged 14 than how they did in SATs (standard assessment tests) tests aged 4.

80 Emotional intelligence was originally defined as 'the ability to perceive emotions, to access and generate emotions so

as to assist thought, to understand emotions and emotional knowledge, and to reflectively regulate emotions so as to promote emotional and intellectual growth' by Salovey and Mayor (1995). Goleman's definition is broader.

81 Suggested answers:

a CBT 2

b Active and constructive responding 5

c Knowing someone's strengths 5

d Increasing your flow experiences 3

e Motivating someone else by facilitating their flow experiences 5

f Understanding someone else's strengths and weaknesses and using this knowledge to improve their performance 5

g Step-by-step planning 3

h Optimism 3

i Using Gottman's tips on relationships, such as trying to find compromise 5

j Using calming and relaxation methods 2

82 Cited in Buddhaghosa and Ñānamoli (1999), p. 302,

83 They also use rather unfriendly jargon, which is why their definition of wisdom as 'an expert knowledge system in the fundamental pragmatics of life' is excluded from the main text.

84 See Chapter 9, http://www.timlebon.com/relax.html and http://www.compassionatemind.co.uk/downloads/training_materials/3.%20Clinical_patient_handout.pdf

85 The 'fully compassionate being' is similar but not identical to the 'perfect nurturer' suggested by Deborah Lee to help people deal with shame. Note that there is much more to CFT than is explained in this brief treatment. See http://www.compassionatemind.co.uk/downloads/training_materials/3.%20Clinical_patient_handout.pdf or any of Paul Gilbert's books on compassion and CFT for more details.

86 Personal communication, 2013

87 See David Arnaud's research at http://bura.brunel.ac.uk/bitstream/2438/4516/1/FulltextThesis.pdf

88 The 'hour of power' idea was originally devised by self-help author Tony Robbins.

89 See https://www.gov.uk/government/uploads/system/uploads/attachment_data/file/197313/DFE-RB097.pdf

90 See http://www.ppc.sas.upenn.edu/csftechreport4mrt.pdf

Index